ACRACKNOPH(

Book Three of The Sid Til
by
M. J. Jackm

ISBN: 978-0-9905655-6-7
Paperback version (2nd edition)
© 2012, 2014 by M. J. Jackman
The right of M. J. Jackman to be identified as the Author of the Work has been asserted by him in accordance with the Copyright, Designs and Patents Act 1988.

Published by LL-Publications 2014
www.ll-publications.com

Edited by Zetta Brown
Proofread by Janet S.
Book layout and typesetting by jimandzetta.com
Cover art and design © 2014 by Patrick JP Currier
(www.patrickjpcdesign.com)

Printed in the UK, and USA

Acracknophobia – Book Three of The Sid Tillsley Chronicles is a work of fiction. The names, characters, and incidents are entirely the work of the author's imagination. Any resemblance to actual persons, living or dead, or events, is entirely coincidental.

Other Books by M. J. Jackman

The Sid Tillsley Chronicles
The Great Right Hope
A Fistful of Rubbers
Acracknophobia

All are available from Amazon, BN.com,
and other online retailers!

and then you

dissed the plums

and I was sad

John

Great praise for

The Great Right Hope
Book One of The Sid Tillsley Chronicles

"*The Great Right Hope* is one of the best vampire stories I have read since *Buffy the Vampire Slayer*. *The Great Right Hope* was keenly devised with wittiness and excitement in a way that the reader can appreciatively observe the pleasure that Jackman has displayed while creating his awe-inspiring world."

—Amy Ramsey
Ramsey's Reviews

"I never thought I could say I would be a fan of a character who is such a train wreck, but Sid is hilarious, entertaining and, strangely enough, charming. Maybe charming is too strong a word..."

—Bitten by Books
www.bittenbybooks.com

"Sid's alcohol and tobacco consumption should have killed him along with his frustration at gays, women and humour, yet his OTT persona seems endearing and believable because we've met parts of him in our own lives...Why should such a misogynistic, homophobic moron be lovable too? That's writerly skill for you. It is certainly the most unusual vampire book I've read and the most hilarious. Read it at your peril."

—Geoff Nelder
www.compulsivereader.com

A Few More Reviews for

A FISTFUL OF RUBBERS

Book Two of The Sid Tillsley Chronicles

"When blood thirsty vampires are a threat and are not your main concern, you know you have problems...Intriguing and offbeat, *A Fistful of Rubbers* is a strong recommendation."

—John Taylor
Taylor's Bookshelf/Midwest Book Review

"The action of Sid's right fist, supported by his Middlesbrough pals, and fuelled by Bolton Bitter beer, drives the story on its drunken, bruising and hilarious journey."

—Geoff Nelder
www.compulsivereader.com

"What I really liked about *A Fistful of Rubbers* is the interaction between Sid and the boys and the well-crafted dialogue. I really have not read anything quite like it. It is so refreshing to read a quirky and original vampire story that does not regurgitate the same old plotlines and characters that are so common in this genre. What we get instead is a fresh perspective and characters who are seared into your brain, whether you want them there or not."

—Bitten by Books
www.bittenbybooks.com

And finally, it ends with

ACRACKNOPHOBIA

"It's a mystery, a wonderment, how Jackman kept track of the twists and body count. Not even the most teeth-sharpened vampire aficionado will be able to guess how this one ends. I commend this book to all readers of both humour and vampire genres. Enjoy."

—*Geoff Nelder*
Cafe Doom

Acknowledgements

Well, guys, this is the last adventure for Sid Tillsley. Just want to say thanks for sticking with the big man. I hope you "got" the novels. I hope you understood the hidden meanings, messages, political agendas, and subtexts that will make this book a classic of the future destined for classrooms full of GCSE students. I hope you don't mind that I couldn't think of a decent finish and went with a wake-up-it's-all-a-dream ending.

Big shout out to the 'boro, not that I've ventured there for a night out in a few years. Thanks to the guys who test out the novels and make sure they ain't shite: Knotty, Maggot, Dave, Pat, Mallard, Berry, Dan to name but a few.

Cap doffed to Dr. Stiff who came up with the title for this novel.

Thanks to Peelo for all the support in making this trilogy happen. It took a lot of work to get here, and a lot of people think I'm fucking weird as a result. Thanks for believing in me. X

For me, time for something different... (call me old fashioned, but I want to write a book without dogging in it). Follow me on Twitter @Mark_Jackman if you're interested.

To the North

(even though I'm from the East).

Previously, on
the Sid Tillsley Chronicles...

IT HAS BEEN NEARLY THREE MONTHS since Brian Garforth buggered the Campire, Gunnar Ivansey, to death in The Miner's Arms' bogs. By committing this selfless act, Brian's semen, toxic to vampires, cleansed the world of one of history's most dangerous lamia. He did it for the good of the human race, but that didn't cut it with his best friend Sid Tillsley, the greatest vampire hunter of all time.

Sid witnessed "the *act*" performed by his best friend, and the beautiful partnership the drinking buddies shared was destroyed. For if there's one thing Sid, and other Northern men of purely heterosexual stone can't stand, it's *them lot*.

Peter Rathbone was transformed into a vampire after being bitten, something once thought impossible. Rathbone, a forty-something, greasy, horrible, vampire bastard living in Middlesbrough, found himself subjected to discrimination because of his race, which came to a head after a freak encounter with a group of randy pensioners in Kevin Ackroyd's allotment shed. His friends left him for dead, and the desecration of his vampire cape demanded revenge.

The last of the four drinkers, Arthur Peasley, hasn't had a good time of it, either. He lost his vampire missus Lucia during the birth of their son, and her father Borg Hemsman has taken the child, vowing to make Arthur pay for his forbidden love.

At least the joint vampire-human council the Coalition isn't bothering the lads, because according to all sources outside Middlesbrough, the lads are officially dead. Harry Dean was the commanding officer sent to destroy the Campire, Sid and his friends, and shut down The Miner's Arms, which the Campire had maliciously transformed into The First Swallow of Summer— Middlesbrough's first-ever gay bar. Instead, Harry saved the lives of the boys from the 'boro as he could see a time when they'd be needed.

Harry's compassion meant Sanderson did not die in vain. Sanderson was the best soldier the Coalition had. He'd fought to keep the lads alive, and he'd fought to find out who was leaking information about the Coalition's movements to its enemies. He never suspected the leak to be Caroline, the most powerful human representative on the Coalition. Caroline used Reece Chambers, the man who'd once guided Sid's hand in the vampire's world, to kill Sanderson. She'd acted out of interest for the human race, and her actions ensured the initiation of the Haemo project.

The Coalition believes Haemo, a drug that quells the vampire's need to feed, is the only hope of upholding the Agreement, the ancient pact ensuring peace between humans and vampires.

Reece Chambers' bounty for the assassination of Sanderson was access to the Haemo drug and its viral carrier. Through this, he discovered the key to the boys' power: Sid's ability to kill vampires with a punch; Brian's toxic-to-vampires semen; Arthur's sexual compatibility with the lamia; and Rathbone's annoying habit of not dying even when killed. The key is Bolton Bitter, and Reece is on the brink of discovering how its molecular building blocks have been inserted into the lads' DNA. Once he does, he will use it to transform his own genetic code into that of a warrior and become the hero he desires to be.

He is going to need every advantage, because the Agreement is crumbling before the Coalition's eyes. Vampires are becoming brash and uncaring of their feeding habits, fuelled by Gunnar Ivansey's martyrdom. Borg Hemsman, Lucia's father, is biding his time before he announces to the world that vampires walk the Earth and the Agreement is only a minor distraction in his mission to enslave mankind. And, he has a weapon—Arthur's son—a human-vampire hybrid completely and utterly unique.

The Coalition has mere days to hold on before Haemo is released onto the unsuspecting vampire nation whose killer instincts will be quenched when they breathe in the drug. If it fails and Borg Hemsman comes to power, life, as we know it, will end. And all of this has got to be done without the greatest vampire hunter of all time, Sid Tillsley.

He has other distractions...namely, womenfolk...

1

HE RAN A COMB through his hair and smiled like only the truly blessed could. Only hair this thick and this glossy could bring such total satisfaction. His hair—a 'do that defined mass and shine—brought jealousy to all onlookers who longed to run their fingers through it, wishing to God it were attached to their own lesser scalps.

He looked over his shades in the mirror and winked at himself with one baby blue. Others would call it vanity, and they'd be right. He loved himself for good reason. Why? Because his ice-white smile was devastating.

He wasn't just drop-dead gorgeous, he was completely and utterly unique and not snowflake-unique either. He would laugh in the metaphorical face of a million, no, a *gazillion* snowflakes. "Big deal," he'd say, "who gives a fuck about a frozen bit of shit water?" And, he would have the confidence to say it to the Creator himself. Why? Because his hair was awesome.

No one knows how the Creator of Life would react to such disrespect. But, one thing's for certain, this being's beauty had surpassed the Creator's wildest ambitions. The majesty of birth, the aurora borealis, the supernova at the end of a star's lifetime—all miracles of nature, yet all paled in comparison to the thing admiring itself in the mirror.

But what was he? How can one describe a complete anomaly, a mix of mortal and immortal, day and night, hunter and hunted? He was the only one of his kind...and he knew karate.

He adjusted the large white collars of his jumpsuit and gave himself double-thumbs up in the mirror. The leggings of the sparkling suit were a little on the tight side, but it sent out a signal, and the signal wasn't for the easily offended.

A queue had formed behind him. So engrossed was he in his reflection that he'd completely forgotten where he was. Awareness of his onlookers came about when a gentleman coughed. It was a cough induced by illness, not a polite cough to hurry him up. No one had tried to hurry the vain creature. Everyone who'd entered the toilets, who'd bothered to wash their hands, had fallen under his spell, mesmerised by this optic siren.

He turned to look at the men waiting patiently behind him. "Big," "burly," and "mighty ugly," were the words that flitted across his mind. He turned away from the tattoos and the leather, back to the mirror. Pushing his fingers through the jet-black hair, he ignored the awed gasps.

Another man, desperate to use the facilities, entered the toilets and sound flooded the cramped room. Desperate screams of the dying stirred the awe-inspired men out of their trances. They shook their heads free of the cobwebs before squabbling to get outside to see what caused such a panicked din.

Finally, he was left in peace, but unfortunately, it was time for him to go to work. He sighed. He was too pretty to get his hands dirty. He was made out of love, and even though he had the ability to bust a thousand heads with reverse punches and roundhouse kicks, it just wasn't his bag. His true purpose would one day come to light, or so he hoped.

He paused at the toilet door, a second of peace before the chaos. Psyching himself up, he threw open the door to a sea of madness. Waves of people streamed past, screaming, fighting, desperate to get out. Choosing his moment, he strode out towards the epicentre of the anarchy, but not so fast to break into a sweat.

The humans clambering past him in the narrow corridors reeked of terror like spooked gazelles. It was as if he moved in slow motion, walking casually through the screaming masses climbing over and trampling on one another. His presence split them like a rock in the tide, and it caused problems. When the chicks caught a glimpse of what headed their way, they couldn't help but stop and stare. He almost felt guilty when they disappeared underfoot, but he didn't let it bother him too much. They weren't that pretty.

He reached the double doors at the end of the corridor and stopped. He was about to enter the main hall. He adjusted the cuffs of his sequinned jumpsuit—and entered the building.

BORG HEMSMAN marvelled at the bloodletting. Blood poured down the many stairways of the auditorium, and not a chair in the tatty, repulsive, concrete eyesore was free from the spray of crimson. There was child-like wonder in the eyes of his brothers and sisters as they slaughtered the fleeing humans without a care. They were born again; they were free. By joining Borg, they'd thrown off the shackles of the Agreement and took their rightful place at the top of the food chain. Not for five hundred years had he been part of something so grand, so deliciously violent.

Five hundred years ago, his strength had waned with the birth of his beautiful daughter and the loss of his blood required for his wife to survive the childbirth. He was no longer able to rip trees out of the ground and punch holes through stone walls, but it was a small price to pay. Lucia had been his life.

It had filled his heart with pride when she'd taken a seat on the Lamian Consilium, but it brought him despair when she'd joined Michael Vitrago's abomination, the Coalition. Michael Vitrago, the Bloodlord, had taken the vampire down the unknown path of diplomacy, bureaucracy, and peace. Still, Borg had sat back and allowed Lucia to find her own way.

With the signing of the Agreement, he watched the vampire race fall ever further from grace, culminating in Vitrago's death and Lucia's disappearance.

And then, the worst day of his life; he'd found her dying in the bed of a *human*. That day was the beginning of the end of the farcical Agreement. Borg now wanted to bring things full circle and return to the times of violence, bloodshed, and death. He had one link to his daughter left, and he was going to use that link to spearhead the attack on mankind. He was going to show the world why humans are scared of the dark. His grandson would spit on his human heritage before enslaving the race.

Tonight was the first major offensive.

No one had attacked the very fabric of the Agreement before, not like this. Gunnar Ivansey had attacked the Coalition, but Borg was going to attack mankind itself, and news of tonight's massacre would spread far and wide.

Borg finished daydreaming and thrust out his hand at a fleeing human. He grabbed the scruff of its neck, repulsed by the greasy black hair within his grasp. Squeezing his fingers, his sharp nails broke the skin and entered the man's flesh. He probed and parted the muscle before reaching the spinal column. Taking hold, he revelled in the warmth of the muscles, and the feeling of complete control. He laughed, and couldn't stop as he watched his followers play with their food.

The old ways were returning.

THE CORRIDOR BROUGHT HIM out into the main concert hall just behind the stage. The smell of blood was overwhelming. He tried to ignore it and concentrated instead on a strand of hair that had broken free from his now-almost-perfect 'do. Repairing the damage was a quick, yet essential, operation.

An army of security guards should've barred his path to the stage, but now, they only presented a mild inconvenience. He stepped around their bodies, trying not to get any blood on his suede shoes. It was a tough task. The poor bastards had been ripped to shreds, and red clashed so garishly with blue.

A handful of stairs would take him onto a stage bathed in intense light from many spotlights. He climbed them with nervous excitement tickling his tummy. It was either that or gas. The spotlights and the accompanying heat brought the sweat he was trying to avoid but gave him a great view of the band who'd been so rudely interrupted. The four musicians lay on the floor, bleeding to death from some nasty wounds in some very nasty places. A bad way to go, but then, they weren't very talented.

Anyone looking out from this stage should've been greeted by the smiles of their adoring fans, but all he could see was a spectacle of violence. Vampires were wreaking havoc inside the concert hall housing this event. He'd caught the band playing earlier in the evening, and it was a horrendous din of wild guitars and screaming, longhaired hippies. The corner of his lip curled into a half sneer/half smile when he realised the screams of the dying band were an improvement over their set. "The Quest," he read from a banner lying on the stage, soaking up blood. The world wouldn't miss them, and the only people who would were being slaughtered right now.

About a third of the audience had made it out of the building to safety, and he felt a note of sadness at the unnecessary slaughter taking place. These kids were music lovers. It wasn't their fault they didn't know better. They weren't educated. They didn't deserve this.

He could see his grandpappy at the back of the hall. He was the only one with any grey hair. It was an old-fashioned 'do, slicked back over his head. He was slightly hunched and looked frail when stood next to the other vamps, but next to humans, he looked huge. He was having his way with a couple of luckless fans.

Over the last month, vamps had swarmed round his grandpappy like flies round shit, and they were all sick and depraved like the old man. Still, it was his grandpappy and the only link to his beautiful momma Lucia. He choked back a tear. He'd never met his momma, but how he missed her so.

His grandpappy had wanted him to lead this event. He wanted him to be "a figurehead to draw out the vampire race from hiding before taking their rightful place as rulers of the Earth." His grandpappy had wanted him to slaughter the band and kick off this public display of brutality. He pulled out a cheeseburger from his pocket, unwrapped it, and took a bite, savouring the greasy, cheesy goodness. Public displays of brutality just weren't his thang.

The old man would be pissed, but he could live with that. He was his own man or vampire or whatever he was. Born through impossible conception between a vampire and a human, and fully-grown from child to adult within a month, he was the only one of his kind. Shit, he deserved to be cut a little slack.

He walked to the front of the stage and nearly tripped over the microphone the lead singer had dropped. He picked it up. It felt right in his hand. It felt more right than anything had done in the long three months of life he'd endured. He wasn't put on this planet to kill. He was a gift sent from Heaven. He was sent here to entertain...and to bang hot chicks.

He tapped the microphone to make sure it was working and then drew it to his lips. A smile escaped before any sound. The humans were in for a treat. His voice was worth a thousand deaths.

"Well since—" He started with a couple of words, deep notes, reverberating, powerful. The notes added a moment of calm to the hell enveloping this Liverpool concert hall, but it was soon forgotten and chaos resumed.

"Well since my—" A little more for the crowd to get their teeth into and entice them from their panic to seek out the origin of the wondrous sound. Even the vampires postponed their sick games and looked to the stage where he stood, a shining white beacon, an angel from Heaven/Memphis.

It was time to give the audience, no, the whole goddamn world what it wanted.

He snapped his knee back and forth.

"Well since my baby left me!"

BORG TOOK HIS FOOT off a young teenager's throat. Her bulging eyes were balloons of fear. She looked up at him helplessly, and he longed to devour her. She was barely of breeding age and was the only victim of the evening who fulfilled his requirements for total satisfaction. There wasn't time for that, though. He watched disappointingly as she got to her feet and ran before something on stage caught her eye and slowed her escape. Borg wondered what captivated her, and slowly, he turned to face the stage. A sudden, sinking feeling hit his stomach that could only be caused by one thing.

"King," he muttered.

His face found his hands. With the loss of his daughter, the embarrassment on stage was, amazingly, the thing he loved most in the world. He'd given his daughter's son the grand name because that's what he'd envisaged the baby to become. He'd watched the boy grow at a supernatural rate until, a month after birth, he'd become an adult. Borg had feared King would become old way before his time, but the ageing had slowed when the boy turned into a man in his prime.

A man? Borg didn't know what to expect from a half-breed. King didn't need blood to survive, he'd no thirst for it, and he withstood daylight. The only reason Borg believed King possessed a single vampire gene was because of his undeniable beauty, even though he resembled his human father, Arthur Peasley. Still, King possessed the look and magnificence of the immortal. His eyes shone bright like his mother's, except his were a vivid blue, compared to his mother's green.

He was Borg's only link to his beloved daughter who died giving birth to him. She died because of that bastard Peasley. He'd treated her no better than a dog when she was an immortal queen living amongst lepers. Sadly, there was no chance of vengeance since the Coalition wiped out Peasley and his no-good friends.

Still, it wasn't King's fault he was his father's son. Borg would never forsake him, even though he was a bitter disappointment. Borg had hoped King would be a physical specimen, embracing the strengths of both species, a weapon to destroy any foe. However, King hadn't shown the slightest interest in fighting. He was inactive and lazy, and Borg was concerned that his grandson was putting on a little weight.

This was the start of a phased attack on the Agreement. It had to be done slowly. The final *coup de grâce* could only happen when Borg's following was large enough. The plan had been for King to take the stage and announce to the Coalition his presence. Unfortunately, King—once again—had failed to show he was capable of violence or even physical exertion. All he'd managed to do was sing.

The entire auditorium watched his grandson. The pubescent girl he'd toyed with had forgotten her near-death experience and stopped in her tracks to watch the performance. Even the vampires watched, and Borg had to admit that King's voice was the finest he'd heard in all his centuries.

The sound of gunfire in the distance didn't faze the crowd enchanted by King's song. The police, most likely backed up by the Coalition, were here. It was the cue to leave. This was not the time to take on Coalition forces. Borg couldn't afford casualties at this stage. Every vampire that followed him had a voice, and right now, it was the strongest weapon he had. They needed more followers, so when the ultimate attack was initiated, nothing could stop them.

Until then, Borg would carry out his plan to the letter. This attack was purely psychological, a thorn in the Coalition's side. It would take all their skills and resources to avoid it hitting the news. There would be hundreds of cameras here to capture snippets of the carnage, and this would be all over the Internet in a matter of hours. The Coalition's resources would be stretched, and vampires across the country, and around the world, would hear of the uprising and join him. He had more surprises in store for the useless Bwogi and his team of bureaucrats. This was just the beginning.

The gunfire grew ten times louder as bullets were fired inside the main building. This snapped the crowd out of their King-induced trance. Panic consumed the humans once more, and they fled the fang of the vampire and the sound of machine-gun fire.

None of the troops entering the hall wore police uniforms, meaning they were all Coalition. Borg thought he'd been given a long time to play. Police would've meant a more difficult clean up. They'd let their own race die in order to make their lives easier. And they called the vampire a monster.

"We are leaving, my lamia!" he cried before making his escape through the double doors King had entered. King was nowhere to be seen. When the men with guns had appeared, he'd fled.

Useless and cowardly. Borg cursed his own blood.

KING HATED THE GUNFIRE. He wasn't scared of guns, hell no. He loved shooting, but what he didn't like was sons of bitches shooting at him. He sat waiting in the limo for his grandpappy, who was bound to kick off. He had a cheeseburger on the go. The main reasons he'd left was because he'd run out.

No, there was no point getting involved in a hoedown. Sure, he was an expert in karate; he was that damned good, he could bring a roundhouse kick to a gunfight, but he was here to entertain not lay the smack down, and that's what he did. He'd given them a snippet of his powers. He just hoped the world was ready for the rest of them.

2

*"Good evening. This is the Ten O'clock News. In Liverpool,
nearly a hundred are feared dead after a shooting at a rock
concert. The Quest, a local band, was playing the second gig
of their tour of the Northwest in the Mersey Auditorium.
Eyewitness reports indicate a number of masked gunmen
entered the building and fired on the crowd and the stage.
Merseyside Police are due to release a statement later
today."*

—*Mersey News*

"'EH'UP, LADS. Me name is Sid, and I canna stand *them lot*."

"OK, Sid. While it's very good you've admitted you've got a problem,
you need to address it in a slightly different manner, OK?"

"Eh? What fooking problem?"

"Sid, you're here because you have a problem, are you not?"

"I've got a problem? Well what's your fookin' problem, pal?"

The monstrous skinhead pointed a mighty sausage at the young
councillor with the floppy hair. Dan Shire didn't realise how much danger
he was in. The word "problem" was not one to bandy around in the north
of England, especially if you weighed ten stone wet through.

Dan took it in his stride. He was a professional. He had been assigned
the impossible task of turning this group of violent, homophobic
sociopaths into cuddly, rainbow-flag wavers. It would be tough, but he
was the man for the job. He surveyed the group of five. It was as if
everyone were related. Skinheads, beer bellies, red faces, missing teeth,
tattoos, football shirts, and anger were the fashion of the hour in the
Smithson Estate where all these gentlemen resided. The biggest of the
group was known as Sid Steely, and he was the one Dan had the most
trouble with.

"Now, now, Sid, I'm here to help." Dan looked at the other four men
sat shoulder-to-shoulder in a circle inside his small, cramped office. "I'm
here to help all of you, and you're all here to help each other. Through
these sessions, you have the chance to turn yourselves into more rounded
human beings capable of socialising under any circumstances."

"What the fook are you on about?" asked Sid.

Sid dressed differently from the others, almost smart, although his
clothes didn't fit him very well. Sid wasn't the brightest penny in the pile,
so Dan simplified things. "Sid, I can help you."

"Help with what?" asked Sid, looking bemused and scratching his fat, bald head.

"I am going to help you all let go of the anger and hatred welling up inside you."

"I wasn't fooking angry until you started chewin' on about me having a fooking problem. Maybe you're the problem, pal." Sid's beady eyes narrowed.

The four other skinheads murmured agreement.

Dan put the cup of tea he held on the table in the middle of the circle and raised his hands in a calming manner. "Maybe *problem* was a bad word. Let me put it another way: Do you think there's anything wrong with your attitudes? Do you think your discrimination against gay men and women is socially acceptable?"

"I don't know what 'socially acceptable' means, but what I do know is *them lot* caused my best friend to b...b...bu...have relations with a m...man."

"Really?" asked Dan, leaning forwards in his chair. "Your friend was forced to have intercourse with another man?"

Sid's hands clamped over his ears. "Shurrup, mon, using them filthy words!"

All the skinheads looked uncomfortable. "Intercourse" was a word to make everyone except biology teachers feel uneasy.

"Sid, this is important. If we can find the root cause of your hatred, we will be one step closer to ridding you of your homophobic tendencies. What happened to your friend?"

Sid crossed his arms a little tighter. "I told you, didn't I?"

"Do you hate gay men because your friend had a homosexual encounter?" The H-word brought more reverberations that were uncomfortable to the homophobes' ears. Bums shifted restlessly in chairs.

"Listen here, Brian Garforth was one of the finest swordsmen in the Northeast. He's been through thousands of birds, I ain't shittin' ya." Sid leaned forwards, as if he didn't want his words to pass the circle's boundary, an invisible barrier to the outside gay world. "One of *them lot* cornered him in the bogs, and within five minutes...buggary was afoot."

Dan ignored the hushed, fearful whispers travelling around the circle. "Do you hate Brian, Sid?"

"All I'm saying is that if Brian can catch it, any fooker can. And I'll tell ya this, I ain't risking it."

"You can't catch gay, Sid!" said Dan.

"Brian Garforth did."

Dan Shire rubbed his freshly shaved face. He made an effort to look well presented at these sessions, professional even. He wondered why he bothered. He was still young, only thirty, and the droves of homophobes, racists, fascists, Nazis, and idiots he encountered hadn't broken his spirit yet. Unfortunately, there was no standard operating procedure for dealing with abnormalities like Sid Steely.

The other skinheads looked nervous after Sid's revelation of contagious homosexuality. They were stupid enough to believe it.

"Right, time-out," called Dan. "Sid, you're mistaken. You can't catch it. It's *not* a disease. Sid, your friend must've been harbouring homosexual tendencies long before his encounter."

"I haven't got a fooking clue what you just said." Sid looked to the others for help, and luckily, a less-tattooed skinhead, the thinker of the group, translated.

"Garforth's always been a bummer."

Sid's long face told Dan he was suffering. Sid's best friend had lived a lie for years, and Sid hadn't suspected a thing. Now, Sid felt betrayed.

Dan knew it must hurt, but this was a breakthrough in the treatment. A turning point.

Sid cocked his head. "So, you're saying he's always been a—what was it?—bummer? Fook me. It's fooking everywhere these days."

"Don't say 'bummer,' Sid," said Dan firmly. "And no, homosexuality is nothing new. Homosexuality was documented as early as 2400 B.C.—"

"That's bollocks," said Sid. "Boy George invented it."

Dan continued, ignoring the ridiculous statement. "The first recorded depiction of homosexuality was recorded in Egypt, 4400 years ago. Khnumhotep and Niankhkhnum were both male servants of the Egyptian king Niuserre and were buried—as a couple—in the same tomb, the walls of which were decorated to indicate that they were intimate."

All shuddered at the word "intimate." Any words that someone's mother might use for discussing sex were uncomfortable on the ear, and it had nothing to do with sexual orientation.

"So Egyptians are gay?" asked Sid.

Dan winced. "Look, you can't come out with sweeping statements like that."

"I don't bloody know," said Sid, looking exasperated. "How do I know they haven't been bred that way," said Sid innocently.

"How on earth can you breed someone to..." Dan didn't let his temper get the better of him. It was best for his own safety if he didn't. "All I'm trying to say is that homosexuality is not new. In fact, it's rife in the animal kingdom. Monkeys, rats, even penguins have exhibited homosexual behaviour."

"Penguins!" Sid's eyes widened. He looked down at his cup of tea and spied the empty chocolate biscuit wrapper on the saucer. "Fooking 'ell!"

"It's part of life, Sid. There's nothing to be scared or threatened by. Societies' acceptance of homosexuality has cycled from generation to generation. You must admit, people are more open about it now than twenty years ago, for example."

"Not entirely sure what you said, lad, but there are loads more of *them lot* around, these days."

"We have to get to the root of why you feel the way you do. We need to discover why you're scared and threatened, and then, we can move on, integrating you into society."

Sid didn't interject, which was a positive for Dan, so he continued. "We need to look back and find the defining moment that sent you on this path." Dan reached down to get a notepad from his bag.

"Probably when Garforth bummed him," said a gruff voice.

Dan put the pad on his lap, looked up, and wondered why one of the group was sliding down his seat towards the coffee table.

"What's wrong with Nigel?"

None of the group dared mention the unbelievably quick straight left that had darted out like a homophobic cobra. None of these skinheads had heard of Sid Steely. All, however, had heard of Sid Tillsley and knew that the man sitting in front of them was the very same. Rumours about Sid being at these meetings said he was going soft. These rumours were unlikely to spread further.

"Nigel said he was tired and wanted to go to sleep," said Sid innocently.

Dan looked doubtful. Nigel slid completely off his chair, cracking his head on the table before finding the floor. His eyes were still wide open. Luckily, he was breathing. "Shall we call for help?"

"Nah, he's reet. He'll wake up in about twenty minutes. It was only a little jab, like."

Dan's jaw dropped open. "You *hit* him?"

"Only a little. Carry on, you were doin' reet," said Sid, ushering Dan along with a wave of his hand.

"'Carry on?'" repeated Dan, unsure of the best approach. The rest of the skinheads nodded frantically, moving their chairs away from Sid. Dan had seen violence in these sessions many times before but never so swift, silent, and, for want of a better word, civilised.

"Aye, he'll be reet. He was just playing silly buggers, that's all."

The vacant stare of the group's unconscious member made Dan uncomfortable. "So...as I was saying, we need to discover the defining moment that turned you homophobic."

"That's obvious, mon," Sid answered.

"Go on."

"I was born up North."

"Go on."

"I've finished."

Dan paused, clicking his teeth together. "Being Northern doesn't automatically make you homophobic," he said slowly.

Sid looked to one of his fellow skinheads and raised his eyebrows before fixing Dan a patronising stare. "I think you'll find it does."

"Of course it doesn't."

Sid shook his head. "No gays born up North, pal. Fact."

"What about your friend, Brian?"

"As I said, Brian was turned."

Dan closed his eyes. He was back to square one, again. "Well, I'm from Leeds."

"So?" Sid shrugged.

"And I'm gay."

Dan wondered if he'd played his ace too early and if his ace was really an ace at all. The three other conscious skinheads took it in their stride. They were here because the courts made it part of the rehabilitation for their hate crimes. Most of the people booked into this programme weren't really homophobic, not deep down. Most of their attacks were based on finding scapegoats or trying to fit in. Dan had the odd tough nut to crack. In Sid Steely, he'd found his toughest.

Every muscle in the man's body was in spasm, and his knuckles were bright white from gripping the arms of his chair. The blood had drained from his normally red face, and the pupils in his beady eyes were dilated. His mouth hung wide open in shock, with his nicotine-stained teeth on show. Sweat dripped from his great bald head, down his face and neck, to soak the top of his shirt.

Dan was unaware of Sid's journey towards liberal thinking. Before the Campire had turned Sid's world upside down, even the thought of such an act would've shut down the blood supply to Sid's brain and closed his ringpiece tighter than the Death Star's blast doors. Brian Garforth and Arthur Peasley had tried to condition the big man against the Pink Side, but, sadly, it wasn't enough. Sid was unable to defeat Gunnar Ivansey, the Campire. Witnessing Brian's selfless, alternative act had proven too much.

"Are you OK, Sid?"

Sid came to with a start, making him pull both arms of the chair off. Blood slowly returned to his face, but he continued to pour with sweat. His fellow rehabilitees watched silently with morbid curiosity.

Sid hadn't been completely shut down by *Pink Alert*. Dan didn't know that he'd witnessed a miracle; he simply hoped Sid didn't beat him to death with the arms of the chair. Dan was used to dealing with anger and violence but not genuine fear, and that was what Sid suffered from.

"You...are...one...of...*them lot*?" he said robotically.

"Yes."

Sid paused, deliberating internally. "Oh."

"Are you OK with that, Sid?" asked Dan carefully.

"And you're from...Up North?"

"Yes."

"Are you sure?"

"Yes."

"And penguins are gay?"

"They can be."

More internal deliberation. "I like penguins."

"So do I. Guess we have something in common." Dan looked at his watch. "Right, that's time for this week. I must say, we've all made excellent progress, and next time, I think we'll be in a position to really get to the bottom of your fears and anger." He looked at the unconscious skinhead on the floor. "Sid, can you help Nigel?"

With a speed beyond his size and physical condition, Sid picked up Nigel in one arm and bolted out the door before the rest of the men trudged out after him.

Dan laughed to himself. Some people were simply beyond help. "Won't be seeing him again," he said, closing the door to the audible thump of Nigel being dumped and left for dead so Sid could run faster.

3

The official death toll arising from the mass shooting in Merseyside is ninety-eight. We spoke to an eyewitness who was in the crowd when the massacre started.

"It was terrible. I've never heard so much screaming in me life. Everyone was so desperate to get out, trying not to get trampled. We could hear the bullets whizzing over our heads. They were maniacs. I don't think I'll ever sleep proper again."

—Channel 5 News

HARRY DEAN MOPPED HIS AMPLE BROW. This sort of work tired both the body and the soul. It didn't help that he was out of shape. He pushed back what little greying hair he had and replaced his flat cap. Two nights ago when the Coalition had called him to sort out the massacre at the concert in Liverpool, he'd thought things couldn't get any nastier. He was very wrong.

"Please...I...I...," said the slight, middle-aged man, sobbing uncontrollably in front of Harry. He looked like he'd taken a dip in a pool of blood, completely soaked from top to toe. Even the most experienced of psychiatrists wouldn't be able to bring this man back from the brink of insanity, and Harry didn't think a pat on the back was going to help. Consolation wasn't Harry's strong point.

"I...I...didn't do it. I swear I didn't do it."

Harry would've believed him, even if he lived in a world where vampires were nothing more than fantasy. And oh, what he'd give to live there. "I know, sir. Just try to calm down."

"How could anyone do this?" he screamed, clawing at his face, digging his nails into cheeks, trying to take away the pain inside by inflicting it on his own flesh. Harry didn't try to stop him.

The poor bastard was slumped on his knees, his trousers saturated in the blood that covered the floor of the small village hall. Every movement caused a small wave to traverse the floor tiles, spreading it ever farther.

The man howled again and spread more blood over his face as he tore at his hair; at least this blood was his own. He would give every last drop of it to turn back time and save these scouts, just children, from the horror, the slaughter.

Harry couldn't tell how many young lives ended here, nor was there any way of determining the exact causes of death. Corpses hadn't been left, just body parts.

Harry got down to business. "Come, sir, let's get you out of here. We need all the information so we can hunt down the bastards who did this."

The man nodded, but Harry had to lift him up from the floor to get him to follow. Harry ignored the blood transferred to his clothing. His ill-fitting suit was filthy anyway. Harry couldn't remember the last time he'd taken a shower, let alone washed his clothes.

The blood was impossible to avoid. It covered every flat surface, sprayed on every wall, and dripped from the ceiling. Harry was hard as they came, but even he didn't want to think what soft tissue he treaded on leaving the hall.

The call had come in a half an hour ago, and it was nothing but chance that placed Harry in the area. Even though the scale was much smaller, this had the potential to be just as dangerous as the concert attack. Attacking a scout troop? This was the sickest thing he'd seen in all his years.

"What time will their parents arrive?"

"Nine," said the man.

Fuck, thought Harry. It was 8.20 p.m. The most protective of parents would arrive early, meaning Harry and his team had to be out of here in twenty minutes, tops.

Harry eventually coaxed the man out from the horror in the hall and into a tiny kitchen near the entrance to the hut. This was the only place spared any violence and free from blood. "You're the scout leader?"

"Yes."

"Were there any other adults helping you out?"

"No. Just me and the...and the..."

"How many kids were in there?"

The scout leader was shaking. "Twelve."

"How many did this?"

"I...I...don't..." He trailed off, slumping onto a stool in the corner of the room.

"How many, damn it?" shouted Harry, desperate for answers. He advanced threateningly, grabbing the man by the scruff of the neck. "Or was it you?"

"What!" he screamed, wild eyed. "*Me*? Those animals did this! There was nothing...nothing I could do!"

Harry didn't like playing this game, but he had no choice. Covering this up was going to prove nigh on impossible. The call was already in the emergency services system and two coppers were on the scene. There was no plausible way of ending this...except one.

"How fucking many?"

"Three. There were three of them."

"What did they look—" Harry stopped short. He turned his back on the scout leader and rubbed the back of his neck. What was the point? There was no time. "Wait here." He left the distraught scout leader sobbing desperately.

More lives would be ruined because of the actions Harry was about to take. He went outside. The night air took away his breath and he pulled his coat tight around him. He reached into his pocket for his hip flask and took a big slug of vodka, his only means of escape.

Luckily, the hut was situated on a playing field a few hundred yards from any other residences, so it hadn't attracted any attention, yet. When the children's parents arrived, it would be a different story.

"Peterson, where are you?" he called through his radio.

Peterson was now his right-hand man. Each man's life was in the other's hands now. They were the only two people on the Coalition who knew Sid Tillsley and company were alive and well and living in Middlesbrough.

"With the police officers, sir. How long have we got?"

"No time at all. I'll be there in a second."

Harry made his way around the back of the hut to where Peterson was keeping the two coppers occupied. Harry judged them in a heartbeat.

"You know who we are, don't you?" he said.

"'Course we don't. Who does? We know we have to do what you say." The WPC was tiny but fiery and confident. There was a determination in her eyes. She was young and pretty and likely fighting sexism as well as criminals.

"Good enough. I trust you haven't made contact with HQ?"

"We got the orders. What happened in there?" she asked.

Harry ignored her and spoke to her partner. "What does your hunch say?"

The other officer was a big man, well built, and looked like he'd seen his fair share of violence. He shrugged his shoulders. Not the brightest and not that interested. Harry made his decision. "Both of you come with me."

He noticed the WPC's eyes narrow for a microsecond. She was suspicious. Good, it might just work. He entered the building once more. The fresh air had cleared his nostrils and the stench of blood and death assaulted them. He turned to the officers to note their reactions. The WPC couldn't hide the repulsed look on her face.

If you aren't useful, you can always disappear later, he thought. Harry was impressed that her partner didn't show any sign of unease. Even when they walked through the sea of blood to get a close-up, he didn't bat an eyelid. Still, he wasn't sharp like his colleague. He wouldn't want to be part of the Coalition. He wouldn't be able to pull off the bullshit.

"Peterson, take WPC...?"

She responded when Harry looked at her. "Jenkins."

"Take WPC Jenkins through to see the scout leader and get him to give her a full account of what happened. PC—what's your name?"

"Roberts."

"PC Roberts will help me assess the murder scene."

Harry waited until Peterson had taken Jenkins through to see the scout leader and shut the door. Then, Harry ushered Roberts towards a body on the floor. It was mostly torso, yet part of the neck and the lower jaw remained. When PC Roberts bent down for a closer look, Harry moved in behind. Grabbing Roberts' hair, Harry tore back Roberts' head and slit his throat with his old army knife, hacking and sawing until he reached the spinal column. The officer was strong as a bull and fought to the end, trying to scream but could only gargle his own blood.

Harry looked at his watch and grimaced. He called through on the radio to the agents patrolling the hut's perimeter. "Cremley, guard the front door. Everyone else inside, ASAP."

It took only a second to reconvene. Three agents were more than enough. "Collins, go get the petrol," said Harry to a young, female agent. "The rest of you throw what you can pick up of the bodies into the centre of the room. We need to make a pyre."

They didn't say anything, just got to work. They were hard, but they, like Harry, harboured deep psychological trauma. The sight of this small scout hut alone would break the hardest heart.

Harry opened the door to the kitchen to see how WPC Jenkins had taken the news of all that had befallen. She stood, wiping her eyes, trying to regain her composure. The scout leader hadn't stopped crying. Harry wasn't about to offer a tissue.

"Come with me, Jenkins."

She followed, and was subjected to the sight of the agents throwing the remains of the bodies together. She didn't say a word. Harry guessed her intuition told her something wasn't right.

"Well?" he asked her.

"I can't see how anyone could do such a thing, sir. I've never heard of anything like it. Never." Her voice wobbled, but she was doing well.

"Jenkins, you've exactly one minute to make a choice that'll affect the rest of your life. I can tell you the truth about what did this, but then, you will have to work for us. There'll be no going back. You'll work for the Coalition." She was pretty, real pretty. She looked much like his wife Annie had done when they'd first met.

Jenkins looked vacantly past Harry to where the agents were knee deep in gore. "And if I refuse?"

"You don't find out. You file a report. You go home. You get eyed up by every horny sergeant on the force until you lose those looks of yours and are finally taken seriously."

"And Roberts?"

Harry stepped in front of her line of vision in case she saw him lying dead under the bodies. "I'm asking you."

She looked him in the eye. "What did this, sir?"

"Vampires."

Her brow furrowed. "Vampires, sir?"

Harry had no time for this. "Do you think I'm laughing and fucking joking when a whole scout troop has been mutilated and their parents are on their way to pick them up? You think I'm playing games?"

She looked uneasy. It was only natural. "I...I..."

"I'll explain everything later, but we have to cover this up before the parents arrive. Vampires are real, kid, and they've been doing this shit since we swung down from the trees. If you join us, you can help hunt the bastards that did this."

She looked at him brightly, defiantly. He could tell she believed him, and she didn't want to show any weakness. "What do I have to do?"

He smiled, but only for a second, "Welcome aboard, Agent Jenkins. You are to be the witness of all this, and unfortunately, we have to pin it all on the scout leader."

Harry noticed her lip twitch. She was close to interrupting, but she didn't. Still, she had to be told. "Don't even think about it," he warned, waving a finger in her face. "It's what we have to do to cover this shit up."

"I...understand," she said, but she still looked back towards the kitchen where Peterson was comforting the scout leader.

"We need this to go smoothly. There can be no loose ends."

The WPC looked back at Harry quickly. "PC Roberts, will he be invited to join the—"

Harry cut her off. "There's only one position, Jenkins."

"He'll be alright though, won't he? We're togeth—"

"FUCK!" Harry screamed driving the knife he'd used to saw Roberts' neck in half under Jenkins' jaw. The force of the strike raised her up onto tiptoes. Her eyes rolled up into her head and blood spewed forth from her mouth and over Harry's arm.

"What are you doing?" screamed the scout leader, who ran out of the kitchen to see what the commotion was.

"Get your hands up!" yelled Peterson, following him out, pointing his pistol at the terrified man.

Harry knew the young lad had a bright future in the Coalition, but his soul was forfeit. Those good looks would fade, his stylish brown hair would turn to grey and disappear. He'd age quickly and die before his time. It was part of the job.

"What's happening?" The scout leader watched the agents unceremoniously throw the children's body parts into a pile, then to Harry, cleaning his knife of the WPC's blood, and then back to Peterson who'd turned from saint to sinner.

Harry bit his lip until it bled. He was forced to do acts that would guarantee his place in Hell. "Collins, I want no evidence left here." He said to the agent who'd fetched the petrol canister. She got to work dousing every wall, the floor, and every body.

"What's happening?" the scout leader repeated.

Harry wished there was another way. He walked past Peterson and the sobbing scout leader and locked the front door of the scout hut before speaking into his radio to the agent outside. "Cremley, kick the door in."

A second later Cremley's foot came crashing through. "Sir?" he queried.

Harry explained. "When the police come, they'll find a burning building. It will look like the massacre took place inside, and the cops who kicked in the locked door met the end of a maniac's knife who then set a blazing inferno for all to see."

Cremley nodded and took it all in his stride. "Shall I continue to guard the outside?"

"Yep, we must be gone ASAP."

Harry closed his eyes. The first thing that flashed across his mind was his wife, walking out of the front door, leaving him for good because he was too distant and not a loving partner. He'd tried. He'd tried so hard to be better, but how could a man utter sweet nothings to a loved one after a day like this? He regrouped before pulling his gun and marching on the scout leader.

"Get on top of the bodies," Harry snarled, his pudgy face didn't soften the effect.

"W...what?"

"I said get on top of the bodies."

"What...what are you doing?"

"GET ON TOP OF THE BODIES, NOW!" Harry screamed, advancing towards the hapless man, the gun's safety coming off.

"But...but..." he sobbed, backing away from Harry Dean's terrifying figure. The scout leader slipped on the blood, and hit the ground hard.

"Get the fuck up! GET THE FUCK UP!" Harry kicked him in the leg to grab his attention, not to wound him, and thought, *This man's so weak, so feeble. The scouts would've been able to overpower him.* He seemed a good man, one who'd probably never committed an act of violence in his life. Harry still hadn't asked him his name. He didn't want to know.

Collins held the petrol can, breathing hard, trying not to look Harry in the eye, but she knew the nature of his next task. She strode purposefully towards the scout leader, and, after taking a deep breath, doused him in the flammable liquid.

"Oh, God, no...Please, no. Not this! Anything but this!" he begged, spitting out petrol and rubbing it from his eyes.

"Clear out!" called Harry, and the agents left the scene.

The scout leader sat on his knees, his hands clasped in prayer. "You can't do this! The pain—you can't leave me here!"

Once the agents had left, Harry burst into tears. "I'm so sorry..."

"They'll think it was me! You can't...you can't! I have a wife...my son was one of the boys here! They'll think I did this! YOU CAN'T!" He jumped up and ran for the door, but it was all futile. Harry's left boot caught him full in the stomach, winding him and leaving him on the floor, his face down in the blood. Harry grabbed the scruff of the man's neck and dragged him over to the pile of bodies. "I'm so sorry."

"They'll think...I did it. My wife...you can't let my wife live the rest of her life thinking I'm a child killer...you can't." He tried to resist being dragged and Harry slipped in the blood, falling on top of the scout leader.

"Fuck you! FUCK YOU!" screamed Harry, angry at himself at what he was about to do. Harry got up awkwardly, slipping again, not able to control his numb limbs. He left the man at the base of the pyre, crying into his hands. He took out his lighter.

"At least make it quick. Please! I *beg* you!...I don't deserve this."

Harry considered it, but the wounds to the body would pose more questions for forensics, and this whole cover-up was a fuck-up at best.

"I'm so..." What was the point of saying anything?

Harry forced himself to watch the man writhe in agony. He drained his hip flask dry. The screams lasted until the scout leader breathed in enough flames to burn his vocal cords to a cinder. Tears streamed down Harry's cheeks and the flames grew closer, but Harry wanted to watch this through to the end. Hell was going to welcome Harry Dean with open arms.

4

Deputy Commissioner Jeff Waine from the Metropolitan Police announced today the number of missing persons has more than tripled in London in the last month, the greatest rise since the force was established. He reminded the public to take basic precautions in ensuring the safety of themselves and their loved ones.

—*Cockney Chat, ITV*

"MY NAME IS CHRIS, and I'm an alcoholic."

"Hi, Chris," said all but one.

"It's been over two weeks since my last drink, and I'm struggling." Chris sat with his elbows on his knees and his head in his hands, talking to the floor. "My wife...my wife left me six months ago."

"For fook's sake," came a deep, bored voice. "He told us this, last week."

"Please, Mr. Steely, don't interrupt." Paul Spencer was the qualified councillor with the mission of bringing these men back from addiction. He'd done the job for twenty years and had cracked the toughest of nuts, but unbeknownst to him, he'd never dealt with a former vampire hunter from Middlesbrough before.

Chris was only a young man, and he had a young family. He stared through bloodshot eyes at the man-mountain in front of him. He wouldn't have heard of Sid Steely before, but he would've heard of Sid Tillsley, and that man sat before him.

"She...she...was having an affair with some..." Chris broke down once more and wept into his hands.

"Take your time, Chris, we're here for you," said Paul.

Sid Steely rolled his eyes.

A fire ignited in Chris's eyes. "She was fucking some bastard at the hospital she works at."

"And, like last week, I told ya to get yourself out there shaggin' again." Sid thrust into the air from his chair for effect. "A few beers with the lads, a night on the pull, and you'll forget all about that rotten slag."

The councillor rightly sensed danger when Sid mentioned a night on the beer. He surveyed the six alcoholics in front of him, all completely different in every way except for the look in their eyes. He knew that look; he'd seen it in the mirror.

"That's not the answer and you all know it. That's why you're here.

Chris, you stood up and told us you're an alcoholic. Sid, Chris knows he has issues."

"'Course the poor lad has an issue. His slag wife—" Sid was momentarily put off by Chris's sobs, "—has been getting the shit banged out of her—" again, more sobs, "—by every fooker on the Smithson Estate. Even Brian Garforth did her, and he's a *them lot*!"

Chris curled up into a ball, shaking on the floor.

"Look what you've done now!" said Sid to the shocked councillor.

Paul pointed at himself. "What *I've* done?"

"Yeah! All he wants is a beer to drown his sorrows and you're making him feel reet bad about it."

"He's an alcoholic!"

"That is such a dirty word," said Sid, shaking his head.

"He came here on his own free will. I'm trying to help him."

"Fooking looks like it," said Sid, pointing at the depressed alcy. "Poor lad."

Paul sat forwards in his seat and pointed at Sid. "You were the one who sent him over the edge telling him that his missus was having the shit banged out of her!"

Chris howled.

"Come on, lad." Sid reached forwards and slapped Chris on the back, momentarily silencing his cries by winding him. "All this talk of drinking is making me thirsty, and you need a beer. We can make it down the boozer for opening time."

Sid got up. The other alcoholics looked uncertain.

"Sid, for the love of god, sit back down!" said Paul.

"Howay, mon, let's talk about it down the boozer."

"You're an alcoholic. We can't *go* 'down the boozer.'"

"Boring fooker," said Sid, crossing his arms defensively before sitting back down.

"Why are you here if you don't think you have an alcohol addiction?"

Sid shrugged and said sulkily, "Dunno."

"You have to admit you have an alcohol addiction."

"I love a beer, me," agreed Sid.

"You need to admit you're an alcoholic."

"I ain't a fooking alcy."

"Yet, you rely on alcohol."

"A man needs to get leathered on top notch Bolton Bitter every now and then. Not that I can drink top notch Bolton Bitter anymore, mind."

"You not drinking down The Miner's anymore, Sid?" asked one of the Smithson Estate locals.

"Fooking *them lot* bar now, like. I canna be drinking in there with *them lot*, you know."

"You're joking. A gay bar?" said another reforming drunk.

"Changed its name and everything. Called The First Swallow of

Summer now," said another attendee of Alcoholics Anonymous.

Sid gave the man a ferocious look, and Paul stepped in to bring the session back on track.

"Sid, you have an addiction. At the moment, you can't set foot in a pub because you won't be able to avoid temptation."

"What you talking about now?"

"If you set foot in a pub, you will drink alcohol."

Sid looked utterly bemused. "Why else would I go to the boozer if it ain't for a fooking pint?"

The councillor bit his tongue before taking a deep breath and continuing. "You're an addict?"

"No, I ain't."

"Do you want a drink every day?"

"Doesn't everyone?" said Sid, looking around at the other alcoholics for support who nodded their agreement.

"No they don't!" shouted Paul, trying to erase the thought. "Sid, do you drink every day?"

"Not properly."

"Men should have no more than three to four units of alcohol a day," Paul lectured.

"What the fook does that mean?"

"You should have no more than two pints of bitter, each day."

"Fook off. What twat came up with that number? Some Southern pansy, I reckon. Fook me, 'tis all right for bairns, but not for men. Not for *real* Northern men."

"So I suppose, if you wanted, you could stop drinking whenever you wanted, right?"

"Don't be daft, son. Why would I want to do that?"

"Then you're an alcoholic, aren't you?"

Sid's face darkened. "Are you fooking deaf? I told you I weren't."

"You've been coming here for a month now," said the frustrated councillor. "You're currently booked into every course that this centre has to offer. You were kicked out of the 'Stop Smoking' group for setting fire to your chair with the cigarette you hid behind your back. You were kicked out of the 'Anger Management' group because you angered the counsellor so much he ended up punching a pregnant woman in the next session."

"He was a reet twat, he was."

"And I don't have to mention what happened during your English GCSE exam, do I?"

Sid had the decency to look embarrassed. "Yeah... Ha! That was a little bit naughty, I admit. But come on, lad, I ain't doing too badly, am I, like?"

"'Ain't doing too badly!'" shrieked Paul. "We've got absolutely bloody nowhere. You're a *drunk*. I don't know why the fuck you come here!"

Sid shut up and refused to make eye contact.

"Well?" demanded Paul.

Finally, he relented. "The missus makes me come here. She makes me go to loads of these fooking classes."

Stunned silence.

Paul regained a little composure after letting the F-bomb go in his frustration. "Really?" He couldn't imagine anyone making this stubborn bastard do anything.

"Aye. Why else would I be wearing this shit jacket, these shit trousers, and these fooking uncomfortable shit shoes?"

"It's good you're here, Sid, but that isn't necessarily the right reason for coming. You have to want to help yourself. Why does she think you have an alcohol problem?"

Sid waved a hand dismissively in Paul's general direction. "You know what women are like, always trying to change ya."

"Alcoholism is a serious affliction. Are you violent when you're drunk?"

Sid scratched his chin. "When you say 'violent,' how violent do you mean?"

"Do you become aggressive? Do you raise your voice? Are you physical?"

"Physical?"

"Would you push someone, maybe even strike them?"

"I've been known to throw a swift jab, now and then."

Paul looked around at everyone in the room who were all nodding their heads so hard, they were in danger of falling off.

"Ever been violent towards a woman, Sid?"

Sid blew out heavily. "After working all them nights in the 'boro on the doors, after all the stilettos in the back of me head, the knees to the knackers, the scratching and the biting, I can safely say I wasn't as violent as I should've been."

"Is your partner scared you'll hit her?" asked Dan, deadly serious.

"No fooking way. I'd never lay a hand on her. She just wants to change me, like all women do. They all try and change their blokes. My mate Arthur was shaggin' some vampire bird, and she was just as bad."

Paul let the vampire comment pass as drunken delusion. "Sometimes they're doing what's best for us."

"It ain't just the drinking, though, it's everything. The kebabs, the curries, the fish 'n' chips, they've all gotta go. Look!" Sid pulled up his Marks and Spencer's jumper to reveal a monstrous, hairy belly. "I'm wasting away, mon. She's got me going to these and some anti-*them lot*-bashing counselling sessions. I've never bashed a *them lot* who didn't have the wandering hands, although I did throw one out of a first-floor window, once. I feel bad about that one, like."

Paul closed his eyes; this guy was a train wreck. "Were you drunk when you did that?"

"Aye, but only 'cos I was about to shag his ma'am, and I was hoping drinking would give me the staying power of a racehorse."

"Were you with your wife at the time?"

"This was way before her, and anyroad, I ain't married. As I said, the missus just wants to change me because she's a woman."

"Why is she with you?"

"Eh?"

"Well, it seems that she's trying to change absolutely everything about you."

Sid scratched his chins. "Guess she sees me as a bit of a rogue. Birds love the bad boys."

"I guess there're bad boys and there're violent drunks."

"Drunk?"

Paul nodded. "You have one of the worst cases of alcohol dependence I have ever seen, heard, or read about."

"Well, you're the worst fooking—whatever it is you do—I've ever heard of! All I want is a pint, and you've been on your high horse ever since I got here! You've ruined poor Chris's day, going on about his slag wife, and now, you've ruined my day by trying to make me feel reet bad!"

"You don't even want me to help you, do you?"

"All you're doing is making me want to go down the boozer for a beer."

Paul had had enough. He jumped to his feet and pointed to the door. "Well, you might as well piss off down the pub, then, the lot of you!"

"That sounds like a plan to me, like!" said Sid, brightening up.

The alcoholics looked around at each other, not really knowing what to do.

"Go on," said Paul. "Fuck off!"

"HOWAY THE LADS!"

The battle cry got them. With the exception of the inconsolable Chris, they all scurried outside, free as pissed-up birds.

Sid followed after them, picking Chris up with a scoop of his mighty arm.

Paul looked on in horror. This was worse than last week when Sid had brought his own booze.

SID RAN FOR FREEDOM. The pub called. He hadn't had a proper session in almost two months, and a pint of draft was going to be nectar.

He charged out of the council building, with Chris sobbing underarm, but he came to a complete halt when something barred his way. Chris's sobs were replaced with sound of wind being driven from his lungs as he fell the considerable distance from under Sid's perpetually sweating armpit and onto the pavement. There was only one thing that could stop Sid Tillsley drinking beer.

"Oh, erm...hello, love."

5

Vampire mania has swept the nation. The feature film, based on a best-selling vampire novel, is tipped by bookies to break all UK box office records on its opening weekend. We spoke to moviegoers leaving Newcastle's premiere to see if they enjoyed the fangtastic bloodbuster.

"Ooooh, me an me girlfriends love it! He's lovely is the lad starring as the goody. Ah love it when he goes aal gold an tha' in the sun. It's canny hoo he loves tha lass he's gannin oot wi', tho' it's a bit weird when he watches hor sleep, leik. If our Darren did tha', I'd assume he wez up te ne canny good wi' tha' spitting snake of his."
— *Some shite on Channel 4*

THE FIRST SWALLOW OF SUMMER was an unusual pub, to say the least. The decor was ultra-stylish and ultra-modern, making it stand out in the rundown neighbourhood of the Smithson Estate. On the other hand, the vast number of bullet holes that riddled the walls, poorly covered with Polyfilla, gave it a degree of rough-as-arseholes, council-estate chic.

The First Swallow of Summer, formerly known as The Miner's Arms, a name that inspired terror in all God-fearing folk who lived outside the boundaries of the most violent council estate in the Northeast. Those born inside did not fear it but respected it as a place where only hardened men and even harder women could enjoy a beverage.

Everything changes.

The First Swallow of Summer was now feared by every member of the Smithson Estate for The Swallow was the estate's first and only gay bar, and the north of England was not a place that warmed to men looking pretty in pink.

Brian Garforth was Middlesbrough's foremost homosexual. No one knew exactly how his chance encounter with Gunnar Ivansey, the Campire, was leaked, but Brian would bet a penny to a pound that the horrible, greasy, little bastard Rathbone was behind it, and he was bang on.

Peter Rathbone had stopped drinking in The Swallow. He hadn't forgiven the boys for leaving him in the shit with the Allotmenteers. He got his fix of Bolton Bitter that he needed for survival elsewhere.

On this day of medium-to-heavy boozing, Brian was drinking with his good friend Arthur Peasley. These boys weren't bothered it was a gay bar.

They were men of the twenty-first century after all, and the beer in this gay bar was better than any other bar, gay, straight, bi, or curious.

"You had any of the gays in here, yet, Kev?" asked Arthur.

Kevin Ackroyd cleaned a glass behind the chrome-and-plastic bar. Once it had been beautiful aged oak, but that had gone with the refurbishment funded by the Campire.

"Well…" Kev twiddled his ginger 'tache, awkwardly, while turning his gaze to Brian. "I guess it depends on what you mean by gay."

Brian's gnarly knuckles turned white around his pint glass. "You fooking know I ain't gay, mon."

"Yeah, man," backed up Arthur, "Brian saved my life from that freaky piece of shit Campire. None of that would've happened if you hadn't turned this place into this…this…I still don't know what the fuck this place is meant to be!"

"It's fooking class, is what it is," said a proud barman.

"Fooking shite, mon!" spat Brian.

Kev's brow furrowed. "I thought your lot loved this sort of thing."

Brian slammed his fist on the bar. "For the last fooking time, I ain't gay! You got it?"

"Then why did you…you know…do the dirty?" Kev nodded his head towards the men's toilet.

Brian knew exactly what he was talking about. He'd gone through this too many times. He took a deep breath. "I saved Arthur."

"By bumming a vampire?"

"I saved Arthur's life, mon!"

"By bumming a vampire?"

"It was the only way I could stop him."

"Couldn't you have, like, punched him or something?"

"He was too strong, and Arthur was in trouble. I had to act."

"By bumming a vampire?

Brian tugged awkwardly at his black, greasy hair. "It wasn't like that."

"He saved my life, man," said Arthur, coming to the rescue.

"By bumming a vampire?"

Brian boiled. "Will you fooking stop saying that!"

Kev held his hands up. "Alreet, no need to get uptight, I'm just saying."

Brian stood, both hands on the bar, exhausted at the mental beating he'd taken. "Well don't. I ain't fooking gay."

"Whatever you say. Live how you wanna live, sister."

"You're calling me gay, but that outfit you're wearing is scandalous. I thought you'd get rid of it after the vampires left."

Kev admired himself in the mirrors on the other side of the pub. His bald head gleamed from the various downlights that were sporadically, yet stylishly, pointing down from the ceiling. The Campire had kitted Kev out in a whole new wardrobe. The tuxedo Kev currently wore was his favourite. A man wearing pink was comfortable with his sexuality. It clashed a bit with his ginger 'tache, and some of the buttons on his shirt had popped off, but he still looked mint, and definitely not camp. "This is class. You're the one wearing the gay uniform."

Brian was prepared to defend his red woollen suit, black Italian shirt and tie to the death. "How the fook can you call this gay?"

"Didn't you bum a vampire in it?"

"Two more beers," snapped Brian, changing the subject. "And make sure they ain't under the fooking line." He turned his back to the bar.

Kevin got to work pouring two perfect pints of Bolton Bitter. He'd had a brand new beer engine installed after the last one was wrecked in the fight between the vampires and the blokes from the vampire-council thing.

"So, Arthur," said Kevin, "in answer to your question, we've had no *other* gays in here. I was hoping you'd be a bit of a draw for them, actually."

"Me?"

"Aye. The lasses love your Hollywood look, mate. They can't get enough of a tall, dark, handsome man with a set of killer baby blues. That six-pack of yours is pretty rare in Middlesbrough boozers too. I was hoping the gay community would be into the same sort of stuff."

Arthur shrugged.

"Shame," continued Kev. "Got a job lot of Babycham in cheap. I'll have to do a bit of advertising, like."

"And no fooker will show up. Just like normal," said a still-seething Brian Garforth.

The lads bickered, but they'd done that for the last thirty years. Things would have been completely back to normal if it weren't for the lack of one Sid Tillsley. Sure, the place looked different, with the neon replacing the old, dusty lampshades; wooden floors instead of sticky carpets; chrome instead of wood; and paint instead of vomit, but it was the same boozer at heart. The same clientele still frequented the establishment. It was Sid who was missing, and it wasn't the same without him, meaning Kev's takings were shit.

"Any sign of Sid on your travels?" he asked.

"What do you mean 'on my travels?'" asked a sensitive Brian.

"Easy, now. Fook's sake, it was just a figure of speech. Though you lot love your little holidays, don't ya?"

"What the fook is that supposed to mean? I saved a life. You shag fooking sex dolls!"

"But they're *female* dolls, like," said Kev with a smug nod of his head.

"You have sex with pieces of plastic, wood, fake human hair, glue, and metal."

"Aye, but no cocks, Brian. There're no cocks."

"Piss off!" Brian snatched his beer from the greedy, goading landlord and turned his back on the bar yet again.

Kev's grin split his fat, red face. His beloved sex dolls were a bone of contention, and his allotment shed had been defiled in a way far worse than any public school boy had ever volunteered for. He knew the old bastards up the allotments had done it, but he had a suspicion Garforth was behind the whole ordeal. That's why he goaded him some more. "'Ere, I thought you lot were into your grooming. That bald batch is growing."

"Fook off, you bald, fat—"

"You two pack it in," said Arthur. "Kev, man, you can't afford to lose any more customers. You've already lost Sid and Rathbone."

"I forgot about Rathbone. What happened to him?" asked Kev.

"Who gives a shit about Rathbone?" said Brian.

"You guys have always given him a hard time," said Arthur.

"He's a horrible, greasy, little bastard who fooking dropped me in it," said Brian.

"Aye," agreed Kev. "I don't know what the little fooker is up to, but fook him if he ain't gonna drink me beer."

Arthur was on to a loser. "OK then, Sid, you've lost Sid. You can't afford to lose any more of us."

Kev hated to admit it, but Arthur was right. "You heard 'owt from the big fella?"

Arthur shook his head. "Not looking good, I'm afraid. Apparently, he's lost three stone in the last two months."

"That's terrible," said Kev.

"I know, man. He's in the best shape of his life, or so I heard. He's almost off the booze and fags and, worst of all..."

"Worst of all?" argued Kev. "There can't be 'owt worse than being cut off from my Bolton Bitter, can there?"

"Even if he was drinking, he wouldn't come in here," said Brian. "He thinks it's a gay bar."

Kev looked pointedly at Brian. "I couldn't possibly start to fathom where he got the idea from?"

"I fooking saved Arthur's life."

"By bumming a vampire?"

Arthur broke in. "This is getting right on my fanny! The two of you, just quit it!" Arthur then cooled his tone. "Strangest thing of all is that Sid's working."

"Well, he always did a bit, like," said Kev.

"And paying taxes?" said Arthur.

"Fook me," said Kev, shaking his head. "Only a bastard woman could do such a thing to a man." All the men took a minute to mourn the loss of their good friend before Kev continued. "Has anyone met her?"

"I haven't seen Sid for two months," said Brian. "He always manages to avoid me."

"He's always had a knack for avoiding you lot."

Arthur got the conversation flowing before the enraged swordsman could kick off. "I hear she's a real battleaxe. Rules him with an iron fist."

"Really? What the fook's he playing at? You'd think it was at least someone nice stopping him supping my ale," said a rueful, out-of-pocket barman.

"Aye," said Brian. "Arthur, how did you find out about her?"

"I did a plumbing job round the corner from her house. Turns out I was putting a shower in for a fella who knows Sid. Well...Sid'd knocked him out, before."

"What did he say?"

"He's shacked up with some crazy cat woman, apparently. Got loads of the furry bastards running around. She sounds like a nightmare. Apparently, Sid sat on one of the little critters, and the whole street heard the beating she tried to give him."

"Tried, eh? Take it he put her in her place," said Brian.

"No, he's never been one to raise his hand to a lady," said Arthur. "She tried to beat him, but he's never been too good at acknowledging pain, has he? Still, he took it. He didn't do anything."

"So why the fook's he with her?" asked Kev.

"The shaggin'. It's gotta be the shaggin'," said Brian, the prophet of doom. "It's been two years since he did it. The poor fooker has been traipsing round car parks, waving his old man at windshields and all for nowt. He's been on the fooking Internet looking for it. He got arrested for attempted murder because of it. Poor bastard. No wonder he ain't letting go. He's getting it and doesn't want it to stop."

"If she's got him paying taxes, cleaning up cat shit, and not letting him enjoy a good beer afterwards, then he's got to be getting something damned good out of it," said Arthur.

"Hang on..." Brian couldn't believe his ears. The smartest man on the Smithson Estate put two and two together. "Crazy cat woman? Sid getting a job? He ain't going out with that mental Sheila Fishman bird, is he?"

"Who's Sheila Fishman?" asked Kev.

"That horror who tried to get him done for benefit fraud 'bout eight months back. She and that vampire wanker tried to catch him working with surveillance cameras."

"Hadn't thought of that, man," said Arthur, shuddering at the thought of the hideous, mental woman who had graced The Miner's Arms on Ladies' Night many moons ago. "But it can't be. From what I've heard, this chick is an absolute doll!"

This raised the eyebrows of Kev and Brian and initiated the same response from both: "Bollocks."

"She's a stunner, apparently. I was told she's young-ish, blonde, got a nice figure with monster hooters. Yep, everything a Northern man could want in a woman, and she dresses tartily too."

"That's definitely not Sheila Fishman. She was minging." Brian shuddered at the memory. "Ah, mon, he never quite gets it right. She sounds great 'cos she's got great jugs, but he can't live his life like that, not our Sid. He needs us. He needs the boozer and the Bolton."

"He'd still be here if you hadn't bummed that vampire."

"Shut up!" Brian shot a glare at Kev. "Anyroad, what the fook is she doing with our boy? He's never been one to attract the finer ladies of the 'boro, has he?"

"That's a good point," said Arthur. "A little harsh, but it's sorta fair."

"Something's not right," said Brian, thoughtfully. "There's something going on."

"Women's intuition?" asked Kev.

"Look, you fat cun—"

"Cool it, the both of you. This ain't getting Sid back. We've gotta do something. We can't lose a good man, and you're right, Brian. Something's fishy."

"Enough is enough." Brian downed his pint. "Let's get him back."

"Hell yeah!" said Arthur. "With Sid's big right hand, maybe we have a chance of tracking down my son."

"You had any luck?" asked Brian.

"Nah, I'm still grieving," said the father, putting down the wonderful liquid which made everything all right. "I don't know where to start, but I'm gonna need the big man if we're gonna have to infiltrate some major vampire lockdown shit."

"After a couple more pints, mate," said Brian looking nervous. "I ain't spoken to him since...you know. I'm not sure if he'll even speak to me. This ain't gonna be fun."

Kev put his hand on the Bolton tap. "I'm always here for you, Brian."

"Fook off."

"We'll find my son," said Arthur, "and then, I've got a roundhouse kick waiting for Lucia's papa. Those vampire sons of bitches will have been feeding him lies that I treated his mother like dirt. He needs to hear the truth."

Brian fingered the Cumapult. "I've got a rubber jonny with his name on it."

Kev giggled.

6

Michael Walsh had led the scout group for a number of years, and the local community of the sleepy Lancashire village has been left in shock. Neighbours have been keen to defend his wife Susan, who lost her only son in the terrible ordeal that led to eleven other child fatalities as well as those of two local police officers. Investigations continue.

—Lancashire Life

CAROLINE STRODE into the Great Hall of the Coalition headquarters. Silence filled the cavernous room. The councillors were running on fumes, even the vampires. She smoothed her skirts and took a seat at the round table where the Coalition councillors sat, nine humans and eleven vampires. She was the last to arrive; she knew they'd wait for her. She ran the show.

There had once been twelve of each, but the numbers had dwindled since the Firmamentum and the arrival of Sparle and Tillsley. Betrayal, murder, and deceit had led to the loss of numbers. Sanderson was gone; Vitrago was gone; Lucia was gone. Caroline wondered how many more would fall before the end.

For someone so short and slight, she commanded a dominant presence sat bolt upright in her chair, measuring her fellow councillors as she scanned the room. Her dark skin helped hide the bags under her eyes, an unavoidable side effect of sleep deprivation. Her short, cropped hairstyle was low-maintenance. She had no time in her life for vanity.

She spared the councillors any niceties, not that she'd ever been one to use them. "Is Garendon in the lab?" she asked, noticing his empty seat.

"Yes, he is, unfortunately," said Augustus, who lounged in his chair with his leg resting over the arm. He sat like he was watching a football match at home, but his taut jaw muscles told the truth; the vampire was struggling.

Caroline, bit the inside of her cheek, not letting her anxiety reach her face. She knew what Augustus thought of the Haemo project. The long, fair hair, dazzling eyes, and effortlessly stylish dress sense were the perfect camouflage for the killer that lay beneath. "No problems with Haemo, I hope?" she asked.

Augustus's leg started to twitch.

"No, not at all," said Charles. "The Haemo project is the only thing that's going well in the whole bloody country."

"Good." Everything was going as Caroline had planned, although she'd hoped that Charles, the fat, pompous toad, would've had a heart attack by now. His red face suggested it was imminent.

Garendon had performed miracles ensuring Haemo was an effective airborne drug. He was brilliant. If the vampire population knew that one of their own had created Haemo, Garendon would be hunted down and made an example of. Caroline didn't think it'd ever crossed his mind that he was going to drive his own race into the shadows. He tackled the assignment the same way a talented high school student would their science project. She was going to be a hero for what he'd accomplished.

"We're just trying our best to hold on. Haemo can't come quick enough," said Rempstone. He was the youngest member of the Coalition, although the fresh face was now lined with stress. He had been perfectly groomed on his first day, but now, he sported three-day-old stubble.

"Is that so," said Caroline. "Isn't it your job to ensure that we do hold out? You're in charge of this country's security. Even after the release of Haemo, it will be in the country's best interest if vampirism remains secret. Your predecessor Sanderson, until his unfortunate change of heart, ensured the Agreement was rock solid."

"No disrespect, Caroline, but I was drafted into this role when things had already passed a critical point," Rempstone said through gritted teeth. "We were doomed before I even set foot in this room. And, please, don't compare me to a man who killed several of our agents."

Rempstone would do anything to climb the corporate ladder. He was too pretty for his role, which under normal circumstances required a soldier, not a blue-eyed boy with conditioned blonde hair and perfect teeth. The young agent was a bureaucrat through and through, and that made him extremely malleable.

Mentioning Sanderson galled her. His death was one thing she regretted and it still played on her conscience, but it would all be worth it once total peace and something a hundred-fold stronger than the Agreement was established. "We are talking about the safety of the country, not your yearly pay review. Get on top of it."

"I am doing my best," he said, throwing up his hands.

"Are we any closer to finding Sanderson?" asked Augustus.

Caroline remained silent. Reece Chambers had ensured that Sanderson's body would never be found.

Rempstone shook his head. "No. If he doesn't want to be found, he won't be. He's too good. And, we can't afford to put any agents on it, we're so stretched."

"It's the right thing to do," said Augustus. "He can still cause trouble, but without access to the Coalition's information systems, he won't be a big threat like a rogue vampire."

Augustus had changed his tune considerably over the last couple of months. Caroline had watched him like a hawk since the initiation of Haemo. He hated it, as any feeding vampire would. But with Borg's uprising, Augustus had to consider his position carefully, and following Haemo would give him the best chance of survival and a boost in political power. Caroline knew he'd always follow the stronger party, no matter what.

All the vampires sitting on the Coalition backed Haemo's launch, she was sure of it. It was just a shame there was no physical might behind any of them. They'd travelled too far down the road to turn back. The vampire nation wouldn't forgive any of them. If Borg found out about Haemo, no amount of backtracking or double-crossing would stop him leaving any vampire involved nailed to a post and waiting for dawn.

"We're relying on the police too much. Awkward questions are being asked," added Rempstone.

"What about the army? I assume you're maximising your resources," asked Caroline.

"Yes," said Rempstone, "but the vampires are attacking locations sporadically. We haven't got enough soldiers to cover the UK, and we need the police. We're tested further each day; the attacks are becoming bolder and the destruction more disturbing. Not to mention that vampires are flooding in from Europe, and there is nothing we can do to stop them. They are flocking to Borg."

"We need to find him fast," said Caroline. "How is Harry Dean holding up?"

"Probably drunk, somewhere," said Charles.

"He's still the best we've got," she replied. Charles was a man Caroline could rely on for coming up with nothing useful. He wasn't bright, but he was extremely well connected and only seemed to get kicks out of putting others down. He was a natural-born critic, but he wanted the Haemo project to succeed, and Caroline had a fair idea that it was for no other reason than to see the look on the vampire councillors' faces.

"Dean is doing just fine," said Rempstone curtly.

"How about we ask him ourselves?" said Caroline.

"As you wish," said Rempstone, turning up his nose.

Caroline tried not to smirk. The little shit was hurting from the last time Dean had stood in this room and gone over his head to ensure more resources.

Rempstone walked to the console that rose from the floor in the Great Hall and pressed the appropriate buttons. After a few seconds, ringing came from the room's speakers.

"Yep," said a gruff voice.

"Dean, it's Rempstone."

"What d'you want? I'm busy."

"I'm phoning from the Coalition meeting. You're on speaker phone,"

Rempstone added before Dean could start shooting his mouth about what he thought of him.

"That doesn't make me any less busy. What d'you want?"

"How are you coping, Harry?" asked Charles.

"Ups and downs, Charles. On the plus side, I'm on the M56 and miraculously getting fifty to the gallon, but on the down side, I recently killed two police officers and burned an innocent man alive so that his wife and family will think he's a child killer."

The silence was frosty, even Charles didn't have a snotty remark.

"What happened?" asked Augustus. "Was it Borg Hemsman?"

"A few vampires ripped a scout troop to shreds and left the scout leader alive. The vamps called the police themselves. This was a tester. If we hadn't been on the scene so fast, there would've been twenty-or-so parents phoning the papers and their politicians with the story. It's Hemsman's style, not just in the brutality, but also in the calculated nature of the attack. Fuck me, it's one incident of many. It's happening all over the country. You got any closer to tracking him down?"

"No," said Bwogi. "We were hoping you had. The vampire community draws ever further from our influence. The ones who talk to us know nothing of Borg's movements."

It was the first thing that Bwogi had said in a long time. Once he'd tried to take charge of this group, but that was only because he felt guilty for putting the vampire elder Ricard to death. Things would have panned out differently if Ricard was still alive. Caroline never would have gotten away with the manipulation of this council. She'd played it so Bwogi would suggest the initiation of Haemo, and now, its launch was the only hope he held onto. He was weak. The only thing he and Caroline had in common was their African heritage.

"Borg's testing us," said Harry. "He's gathering more soldiers, and when he thinks he's strong enough, he'll come down on the Agreement and this country like a nuclear fucking missile. We're running out of time. He's growing bolder. That attack on the gig was insane."

"Yes," said Rempstone. "We've done our best to limit the damage he caused. Fortunately the band, The Quest, was not a big draw."

"Why do you reckon Borg attacked them?" asked Bwogi.

"Possibly because they have a large Internet following," said Rempstone. "Mobile phone videos have appeared on YouTube. Luckily, no vampire activity has been filmed, although the Internet is rife with rumours of it. Blaming it on a group of rampant teenage school kids vowing a suicide pact somehow worked. We had to put bullets in everyone and everything."

"We've had to call in some big favours with Number 10," said Charles.

"Amazingly," said Rempstone, "the Internet has been hit with more videos of Borg's mystery singing accomplice than the actual attack itself."

"Have you seen the video, Harry?" asked Caroline.

"No, ma'am. Been too busy to catch up with TV."

She ignored the sarcasm. He reminded her of Sanderson, and she liked him for it, but he was more levelheaded than Sanderson and less likely to fly off the handle. If only he could stay off the booze. Yet, he sounded coherent. She hoped he could hold it together until Haemo was released. "Are you near a computer, Dean?"

"Aye, got my laptop sitting next to me. Hang on."

Meanwhile, Rempstone sent through the video via satellite. "Coming through now. Not bad footage for a camera phone."

The shaky video footage played out, giving Harry insight to what happened during the Liverpool attack. A figure dressed in white walked onto the stage.

"Who the hell is that?" asked Harry.

"That's Borg Hemsman's accomplice," said Charles.

"If anyone else had sent this, I'd have said they were taking the piss. Borg's *accomplice*?" he asked. "You sure?"

"He wasn't killed, or attacked, so he had to be part of his entourage," said Rempstone.

"You think he's a vampire?"

"I've never seen a fat vampire before," remarked Augustus humourlessly.

"Borg ain't the kind of guy who'd entertain a human, though, is he?" replied Harry.

"True, but I can't believe that thing is one of us," said Augustus.

"Harry," said Caroline. "I want you to work exclusively on tracking down Borg Hemsman. You must find him, and maybe his friend here will jog people's memories."

"I'm on it, ma'am," said Harry. "But, if I may?"

"Go on."

"I can't see how we're gonna get through this."

"Don't worry, Harry. Stay vigilant. We have something up our sleeve," she said and indicated to Rempstone to cut the line.

"At least Haemo is still a secret," she said. "Although, it would be nice to give the troops some hope. Things are bad right now."

"It's only going to get worse," Bwogi moaned. "And what if Haemo doesn't have the influence we think it will?" his voice wavered.

"Haemo will ensure your survival," she said. "If the vampires' world reaches the public, we will already have the cure to the disease."

"Disease?" questioned Augustus. "You can't seriously take that route."

"Will mankind have it any other way?" asked Charles.

"Maybe if they knew of all the gifts we'd bestowed on them throughout the ages, they wouldn't be so quick to judge. Can we not discuss a different approach?" said Augustus.

"As usual, what we tell the public and what we actually do will be two completely different things," said Caroline. "Selling it as a curable disease and limiting the number of leaked cases to the public will make the whole situation manageable. That will be our role if the Agreement is broken. We have a week until Haemo is pumped into the atmosphere. If the vampire comes into the spotlight before that, we'll have a much bigger uprising to deal with, possibly mass media coverage. I hope to God that Harry tracks down Borg."

HARRY PUT HIS LAPTOP TO ONE SIDE. He was glad of the brief break from fieldwork. His life had progressively worsened since he'd taken over from Sanderson. Poor Sanderson. Harry would've heard from him by now if he were still alive.

He took a bottle of hard stuff out of his glove box, toasted his absent friend, and enjoyed a long, soothing pull. He hadn't touched a drop in ten years, but after the attack at the gig, he'd taken to carrying a hipflask. At the scout hut, he couldn't help himself. He'd bought a bottle of vodka from an off-license and only stopped drinking when he couldn't remember anything. Torching an innocent man meant it was going to be tough to stop the flow. He had to find Borg and stop him going public. That would lead to thousands of more deaths. Taking the scout leader's life was necessary for that reason alone. But Harry still felt like shit. He took another slug.

He hadn't expected to be revisiting Middlesbrough so soon, and he'd always expected to be visiting Sid Tillsley, not Arthur Peasley. Arthur's uncanny likeness to the fat man on stage couldn't be a coincidence, but Peasley did have one of those faces that was so familiar. Harry typed in the postcode for the Smithson Estate into the sat nav and floored the accelerator. Time to find out what the boys from Middlesbrough had been up to.

7

A memorial concert for The Quest and their fans will be held later in the year. Several big-name acts have been signed, and the concert will generate money to support the families grieving lost loved ones.

—Mersey News

KING KICKED BACK in front of the television, lounging in his pants and dressing gown. He loved watching TV in bed and glued himself to the box whenever possible. Yeah, hanging with vampires would be considered cool by most, but he wasn't most. He was one in a billion...seven billion to be precise. Not to mention that vampires didn't tend to watch much TV; they were boring sons of bitches.

King was devouring a whole plate of peanut butter banana bread when his grandpappy pushed open the double doors of his luxurious bedroom. King sighed when he saw the look on the face of the miserable old vampire.

Borg took a few deep breaths. "I have finally calmed down enough to talk to you. Do you care to tell me what happened the other night?"

"Mmmpprrhh?" mumbled King through a mouthful of peanut butter.

Borg tapped his foot irritably. "You were meant to attack the band, not sing to the fucking audience."

King raised a chubby eyebrow. He didn't often hear profanities from his grandpappy. "They were dead when I got there, man. I just thought I'd add a bit of sparkle to the night. Your boys had it all under control, didn't they?"

"They were dead when you got there because you were late! Too busy looking at yourself in the mirror again, I should imagine. You spend hours in front of it. I don't know what you see. You're getting fat." Borg pointed at some of King's podge sticking out of his dressing gown. "You're not a vampire. You're a disgrace."

"Fat? How dare you, man!" said King, pinching more than an inch. "What I did on that stage will sit in those poor bastard's memories a lot longer than your Halloween freak show."

Borg paced the floor while King got back to watching the television. "Your mother died for you. You could at least show her some respect. You spit on her grave with performances like the one at the concert."

"I put some good sounds down, baby."

"That's not what I meant!" screamed Borg before putting his fist through the television.

"I was watching that!"

Borg couldn't even look at him. "You are your father's son," he muttered.

King scowled at his grandpappy. "Don't compare me to him."

"Your mother gave her life to serve the vampire nation. She gave her life to our people. Your father, on the other hand, a pathetic *human*, treated your mother like a slave."

King covered his face with his hands. "I know."

"He kept her locked away in a detestable, flea-ridden flat, making her look after him as if she was beneath him."

"I know."

"If she'd come back to me, she'd still be alive. She could've raised you. You would've known her love, her tenderness, her—"

"I KNOW!" King got up and threw off his robe. He rummaged through his wardrobe until he found suitable attire.

A vampire ran into the room after hearing the commotion. "Is everything OK, sir?"

"Yes, Viralli. King, here, is just proving to me that he is no better than our food."

"Sir?" said Viralli using a fell tone that King recognised.

King eyed the colossal vampire up and down. Viralli looked like he'd been born on a battlefield. He wasn't pretty like the other vamps, and his shaved head didn't help his appearance. The stare he gave King said he'd gladly cut his head off without blinking, but this didn't perturb the hybrid. "Try it, bloodsucker. Just try it and you'll be on the wrong end of some karate before you know it."

"You've never even studied karate!" said Borg.

"I was watching Chuck Norris on the TV before you put your fist through it," said King, pulling on some jeans and a shirt.

"Where do you think you're going?"

"Out into town."

"You can't go off on your own. Viralli will go with you."

"That boring piece of shit will scare away all the chicks."

Viralli didn't say anything, but the unimpressed grimace said enough.

"Anyway," King continued, "Grandpappy, you give me all this shit about not following your master plan and not respecting my momma, but you've done sweet F.A. to track down that no-good papa of mine. Those boring stiffs at the Coalition may be feeding you a pile of crap. He may not be dead."

"The most important thing in your mother's life was the survival of the vampire nation," Borg said. "She believed the Coalition and the Agreement were what we needed. When you came along, she stood down. She gave it all up for you. I'm going to keep you safe and hopefully find out what good you can possibly do for the vampire race when we will rightfully rule this world once more." His face darkened, and he clenched his fist tight. "*Then*, if your father is alive, we will hunt him down."

"And until you do, you ain't getting the use of these bad boys." King unleashed some punches into the air; accuracy and power were low.

"Do you even care about your vampire brothers and sisters?"

"Hey, man, I'm an only child, and I mean that in more ways than one. How would you like it if there was no one else on the earth like you? That's lonely, man. Damn lonely."

"We're here for you," said Borg, reaching for King's shoulder. "You're not alone. You can stand at my side, and we can rule this world together. You can be a king of the vampires and a god to the humans."

"Hey, man, you saw what happened when I sung to them. They were captivated by my every note. I had them begging for more. The world will worship what I do best."

Borg quickly retracted his comforting hand. "And what is that, exactly?"

"Entertainment, man. I was put on this world to entertain."

"Your mother didn't die for you to sing to humans," Borg spat, his anger reaching new levels.

"My momma died for me." King hammered a chubby fist to his heart. "For *me!*"

"Humans are gone in the blink of an eye. Forget them. Wouldn't you prefer to live the life of an immortal?"

"If they're all as miserable as that ugly son of a bitch, there," said King, pointing at Viralli, "then I ain't so sure. Look at him, thinking he's so fucking tough and cool."

Viralli stared straight ahead, staying out of the family bickering.

"Viralli is an excellent soldier and a credit to the vampire race," said Borg.

"And look at the hate in his eyes. Do you think he'd accept me as a ruler? If you do, then you're more deluded than I thought. If I weren't your grandson, you'd have me put to the sword, man. You know it's true."

Borg shook his head. "You are different, but you represent a new age. You will represent the breaking of the Agreement, the beginning of a new epoch. The disaster Michael Vitrago caused will be considered a minor blip in our species' otherwise unblemished history."

"Yeah, well until then, I'm going out for some food."

"You've just eaten all this junk food." Borg pointed accusingly at the bed.

"I'm increasing my power to weight ratio." King fired off a round kick that only managed to reach knee height. "And then, I'm hitting the town."

"Viralli, go with him and make sure he doesn't get into trouble."

Both King and Viralli's shoulders dropped in bitter disappointment.

8

This has been the sixth murder in Dover in the last week. Police believe it's due to a wave of illegal immigrants who have forced their way into the country. At this time, Kent Police say they're unaware of any reason why this surge in illegal immigration is taking place, but they have doubled their presence at the docks.

—Southeast Today

SID HAD ALWAYS LOVED DRIVING. The Nissan Bluebird Turbo, Sunderland's finest, was, sadly, no longer his. The car had been seized and turned into a metal cube by Cleveland Police Force after Sid was arrested for soliciting in public toilets. He didn't know what "soliciting" meant, but, if he did, he would have definitely denied it.

It was the old Montego Estate that Sid really missed. Sure, it didn't have the pizzazz of the Nissan Bluebird Turbo, but Sid had developed a strong bond to that old motor car. It had a good run until he ran it over the edge of a cliff while pissed.

However, the big man was driving again and loving getting paid for something he enjoyed doing. At the age of forty-six, Sid Tillsley was in his first legitimate job, and it wasn't bad at all. He didn't have to watch his back for the Benefit Bastards, quite a dangerous manoeuvre while driving, and he picked up a regular weekly pay packet. The tax got him, but he could live with that. After all, it was what she wanted, and that was all that mattered. If he was going to make a decent woman out of her, then a respectable job was a prerequisite. Or, so he'd been told.

"NO...SLEEP...'TIL STOCKTON!" he sang.

Sid didn't know who the Beastie Boys were, but he was able to pick up the song lyrics and adapt them to fit quite relevantly to the task at hand. He was driving a bus to Stockton, a town just a few miles west of Middlesbrough, and it was best for all on board that he didn't fall asleep.

"Excuse me, young man, can you keep it down please?" came the croaky voice of an elderly lady at his shoulder.

"What's up with ya, flower?" he shouted over the music.

"My stop's coming up, and I'd be grateful if you can keep it down so you hear the bell when I ring it."

Sid turned in his seat to smile at the elderly lady whose eyes were glued to the road the careless driver veered across, causing the scattering of traffic. "'Course I will, pet. Just ring the bell when you're ready."

Sid turned back to the road and realised he was on the wrong side. He gave a little chuckle before making his way to the left side of the white lines. He gave the white-faced passengers a cheeky wink in apology for his little faux pas.

There was never a chance of a head-on collision. The general public got wind that there was a new kid in town after Sid somehow passed the interview to become a local bus driver. Every road user coming into close proximity of the Number Seven's regular route prepared for every eventuality.

He was officially dead, but everyone in the 'boro knew Sid, and no one was going to say anything as they all thought the vampires were posh wankers. Word had got round that the Coalition was full of Southern nancies, so they were definitely not telling them 'owt about the big man...plus, no one had their phone number.

After Sid landed the job, he could be seen around Middlesbrough learning his trade with a panic-stricken instructor hanging on for dear life while Sid tested out the vehicle's handling. How he passed would be a mystery, if it weren't for his right hand's reputation.

"DON'T...SHIT...'TIL STOCKTON."

Sid was back in song, and even though he was failing to entertain the packed bus with his crass version of the '90s' classic, they still hoped he'd abide by his new lyrics, even more so than the last. The bus didn't have a radio, so Sid was forced to bring an old stereo to work with him and taped it to the ceiling near the driver's seat. There hadn't been a single complaint (to his face).

"Excuse me, driver?...Driver?...DRIVER!" screamed the elderly lady. The rocking skinhead paid her no attention.

"Eh? What do you want?"

"You've gone past my stop," she said, waving her stick.

"Why didn't you ring the bell?"

"I did!"

"I didn't hear you."

"You were too busy singing!"

Sid shrugged his big shoulders. The uniform he wore was quite comical, but it did not amuse the old lady. He'd lost a load of weight since he'd cut down on boozing and the kebabs. But, he was still a fat bastard, and the shirt was skin tight. There was no way he was ever going to be able to button up the top collar, and his black tie was scruffily and hastily tied around it. But under the flab, it was obvious he packed the sort of muscle that most people associated with a rhino.

"How am I going to get home?" she said, increasing the frequency of her stick shaking.

"Can't I just drop you at the next stop?"

"We're half a mile away, it's raining, it's dark outside, I have arthritis in my hips and knees, and I'm ninety!"

"You old timers love telling us how old you are, don't ya? Bless ya, petal."

Before the old woman could bash Sid with her handbag, he came to her rescue.

"I'll swing her round for ya."

True to his word, Sid pulled hard on the right side of the wheel, skidding the bus dangerously on to the wrong side of the wet road. He slammed his foot on the accelerator and tried to make up the time by overtaking wherever possible before, once again, yanking hard on the right side of the wheel to come to a halt at the old lady's bus stop.

"There you go, pet," said the hero of the hour. He tried to turn in his seat, which was always a considerable task. "Eh? What're ya doing down there?" he said to the old lady, lying flat on her back, her legs in the air. "At your age!" he chuckled, before calling to the rest of the bus, "Can anyone who's getting off here give this game old bird a hand?"

Like rats from a sinking ship piloted by a pissed-up captain, the passengers piled off the bus, picking up the old lady on the way. Sid thought it was peculiar since most had purchased tickets to Stockton, another five miles away.

It wasn't long before he had a bus full of passengers to violate virgin ears with his musical talents. He pulled up just fifty yards from The First Swallow of Summer, and to the relief of the passengers, the musical tirade ended. Sid reminisced about the pub that used to be his life. He called it "The Swallow" now. Calling it "The Miner's" brought too many bittersweet memories. He reached into his top pocket, pulled out a cigarette, and popped it in his mouth. He'd bought it from the corner shop, like all regular punters did. He lit it and took a deep drag, remembering better times. It was only the twentieth of the day now he was a non-smoker.

The locals made their way off the bus, while the new passengers stopped by to pay. He let them all on, doing his best to get the change right. Sid had never been good at maths. No one was going to accuse him of short-changing them, and not even Sauron would risk underpaying.

"Hey, man!"

"Arthur!" Sid grinned, exposing every yellow tooth, pleased to see his old friend stepping onto the bus. "What are you doing here?"

Arthur gave the road a double point. "'boro centre, please, baby."

"Sure thing," said Sid, waving away the pound coin Arthur popped on the money tray.

"Cheers, buddy."

Sid shut the doors and drove away, completely forgetting that people were still waiting and completely unaware that an old man was stuck in the folding bus doors. Sid was taking his friend to 'boro centre, and there'd be no stops in between.

"How you been, Sid?" asked Arthur, grabbing on to the handrail by the driver's seat.

"Working hard, mon."

"I can see that," said Arthur, looking back at the disgruntled passengers. "Why don't you come down The Miner's and meet up for a beer? Everyone is missing you, man."

Sid took a second. "I don't think that's wise, mate. Missus don't really like me going out drinking. She's got me in Alcoholics Anonymous and I'm trying to knock boozing on the head."

"But you love beer, man."

Sid closed his eyes. This worried Arthur immensely as the bus nearly took out a string of pedestrians before the big man opened them again, redirecting the bus. "I need to commit to the missus. I canna keep living the lifestyle of a playboy, boozing, partying and the like."

"She tell you that?"

Sid nodded.

"When I was with Lucia, may she rest in peace, she was nagging me senseless, and you told me to get out and get down the boozer."

"But I canna." Sid gripped the steering wheel so hard, it started to bend.

"Why?"

"I...I just canna."

"That ain't a reason. Why can't you come down for a beer with us?" said Arthur cheeringly.

Sid indicated to turn left and ripped the paddle off the steering column. "'Cos I'm getting fooking married!"

"Awwww, FUCK!" Arthur screamed for all to hear. "Married? Sid, she's busting your balls, man! Alcoholics Anonymous? She's a control freak! Think of the advice you gave me," he begged.

"It's different. You've always been out shagging everything." Sid turned in his seat again to look down the bus. "How many of them you shagged?"

"Look at the goddamn road, man!" shouted Arthur, experiencing his second near-death encounter of the minute. Arthur surveyed the bus before pointing. "Only her, her, and...I *think* her."

The boyfriends of the three girls Arthur had pointed to all cursed and planned their break-ups.

"Exactly. You nail everything in sight. Me, two-year fooking drought and not for the want of trying."

"So you're with her for the sex, is that it?"

Sid weighed it up with the stroking of his chin. "It's part of the reason, like."

"You're getting your end away, now, but that will dry up. It did for me and it will for you. Come on, you can't be getting that much."

Sid didn't say anything and fidgeted in his seat. An uncomfortable moment passed before he blurted out, "No sex before marriage, mon."

"FUCK NO!" screamed Arthur, echoing profanity around the bus. "I thought that was illegal in Middlesbrough! What're you thinking?"

"In a week's time, I'm getting married, and I'm gonna get my end away, mate. I ain't gonna fook it up."

"A *week*!" Arthur shrieked. "Sid, you're making a dreadful mistake. You can't get married just so you can have sex, no matter how great her tits are. Can't you just hire a hooker?"

"You and...*your friend*...couldn't find me a lass when I was a vampire hunter, and look what happened to...*you know*."

"Brian saved my life. He did what he had to do. He's not stopped banging chicks since. He's straight as an arrow, man."

"He ain't fooking this up for me. I'm gonna get me end away, and I ain't catching *them lot*, so it's best I don't drink down The Swallow and just get married," said Sid, stubbornly.

"You're getting married so you don't catch gay?" asked Arthur incredulously.

"I ain't catching *them lot*!" shouted Sid before slamming on the brakes. He'd made Middlesbrough town centre in record time.

Arthur pinched the bridge of his nose and whispered under his breath, "This was a bad idea, man."

Sid opened the door, causing the old man jammed in the mechanism to fall out onto the concrete pavement. A few of the passengers got up and left, but most stayed on, hoping to catch their stops on the way back. More passengers got on...and so did a swordsman.

"Single to the Smithson Estate."

"You!"

9

Today, Middlesbrough General Hospital announced a massive reduction in the number of victims of violent crimes over the last two months. Dr Rashid, head of Accident and Emergency, said, "We've no idea why, but we are very pleased indeed. It's like everyone on the Smithson Estate has stopped getting punched."
—Eye on Middlesbrough

STRAIGHTENING HIS TIE, Gareth Wellington readied himself for the next consultation. This was going to be an uncomfortable fifteen minutes at best. At lunchtime, he'd drawn the short straw in the staff canteen, and it was now his responsibility to perform Peter Rathbone's work seeker's interview.

Rathbone was one of the top ten benefit fraudsters in Teesside, and getting one of the top ten into work, or nabbing them for fraud, would mean a considerable bonus come pay day. However, no amount of money was worth the fifteen minutes of uncomfortable, greasy silences that Gareth was about to endure.

At least with old Sid Tillsley, the worst that could happen was a broken jaw, but with Rathbone, there was never a threat of violence, only a threat of griminess. Gareth wasn't a clean freak. He'd leave the washing up in the sink, his clothes on the bedroom floor, or pop to the corner shop with only a swish of deodorant. But after being subjected to even a telephone call from the greasy, horrible, little bastard Rathbone, he would be forced to wash, shower, and scrub himself until he was sore, and not in a good way.

The door opened and in walked Peter Rathbone.

"You could've least had the decency to..." The word "knock" eluded Gareth due to side tracking of a comical nature. He burst into laughter.

Rathbone slammed the door behind him before taking a seat. "What the fook are you laughing at?"

"What are you wearing?" asked Gareth through the tears.

"What does it fooking look like?"

Gareth laughed until his cheeks hurt, while Rathbone crossed his arms with a look saying he wasn't impressed by the professional nature of an employee of the state whose wages were paid by the taxes he didn't contribute to.

"Are you dressed like that for a dare?" managed Gareth, regaining himself.

"What you talking about?" asked Rathbone, looking down at his get-up.

"Why are you wearing fancy dress?"

"What d'ya mean? This is my people's national dress." Peter adjusted his high-collared white shirt and bow tie and smoothed down his red velvet waistcoat.

"I thought you were from Middlesbrough?"

"You racist bastard!"

Gareth stopped laughing. Such accusations were serious business in the world of local government bureaucracy, and the walls were paper thin. "How is that racist?" he asked under hushed breath.

"You heard me," Rathbone stated at an amplified level. "I called you a racist bastard!"

"But you're white and from Middlesbrough."

"And I suppose that makes it OK, then, doesn't it?" said Rathbone with cutting sarcasm.

"But I'm white and from Middlesbrough."

"And that makes it all the more sickening." Rathbone spat on the floor in disgust.

Gareth regrouped after the horror of seeing the oyster that looked particularly slimy, green, and, more worryingly, alive, on the carpet. He had no idea what the horrible, greasy, little bastard was talking about. "Why are you wearing a cape?"

Rathbone raised his eyes. "Because I'm a vampire."

"I...see." Gareth bit his lip as a laugh almost escaped.

"Good. I want a job."

"W...what?" said Gareth, completely taken aback. The vampire comment was strange, so was the outfit, but this money-grabbing, lazy, waste of space wanting a job was really freaky.

"I want a job, ya deaf twat."

Gareth ignored the abuse. "That's very unexpected, I must say."

"Oh right, yeah. I suppose it fooking is, ain't it. Well, let me tell you, some of us want to work. You think we're all a bunch of lazy good-for-nothings, don't you?"

"Well, you've been collecting benefit for eighteen years." Gareth didn't need to look through his papers to know that. Everyone in the Jobcentre knew it.

"You racist bastard!"

The pencil Gareth held snapped in his hand. "How is that racist?"

"You're saying that my people are lazy good-for-nothings. You are tarring all of us with the same fooking brush."

"Ninety-seven per cent of the population of the Smithson Estate claim benefit of some description."

"But I told you I was a vampire, didn't I?"

"But..." Gareth was seriously confused, and once again, Rathbone attacked the man on the back foot.

"And, there again, more racism. More hate crimes my people have to endure." Rathbone spat, once more, on the floor.

"Will you please stop spitting on the floor?" asked Gareth desperately.

"You refuse to recognise my people's racial heritage."

"What?"

"You refuse to acknowledge me as a vampire, and then that face you made when I simply followed my people's tradition was despicable?"

"Face I made?'"

"Yes. When I spat on the floor. It's a vampire tradition."

Gareth watched the saliva soak into the carpet. "It's not a very nice one."

"You, sir, are a monster."

Everyone within two floors of Gareth's office would've heard Rathbone's ludicrous tirade. He emphasised every buzzword to get people listening and made sure he shouted all swear words and all allegations of misconduct. Even though it grated Gareth, the best way forward was to try and pander to the demands of the deluded madman.

"So you want a job? How about I find you a job, Mr. Rathbone?"

"Well that's what you're fooking here for." Rathbone settled back into his chair.

"Indeed. You're a qualified mechanic, aren't you?"

Rathbone nodded.

"Although I should imagine your skill set is out-of-date due to your...inactivity."

"Those days are behind me."

"Good. It shouldn't be too hard to get you into a local garage. We've had a surprising amount of work in that area recently."

"Aye, not surprising really. I haven't been doing 'owt on the side for a while, so there'll be a bit more legit work around."

Gareth took a moment. "Are you admitting—"

"Calm down." Rathbone pointed a pale bony digit in Gareth's direction. "I told you those days were behind me. Now, I'm looking for a job. Are ya gonna help me or not?"

Rathbone had ripped off the system for thousands a year, and it wasn't a secret. Gareth knew there wasn't any proof, and the paycheck at the end of the month would be worth it if he could get Rathbone into some sort of tax-paying job. He tapped away on the computer. "I'll look for some local garages."

"I told you, those days are behind me."

"You said you wanted a job."

"Aye, but I also said, ya deaf twat, that the mechanic days are behind me."

"I thought you meant your benefit-fraud days were behind you?"

"You racist bastard!"

"What!"

"Accusing me of benefit fraud!" yelled Rathbone through cupped hands.

Gareth stood up, knocking over his chair, leant across the desk, and whispered aggressively. "You just said you were working. How is that fucking racist?"

"How dare you talk to a customer like that? Using swearing words! In all my years, I've never heard such a thing," shouted Rathbone.

"Do you want a job or not?" Gareth snapped back.

"And here's me thinking it's *your* job to find me a job. You're not just racist, you're a wanker too."

Gareth chewed his bottom lip until he could taste blood. Then he chewed it some more. "What sort of thing are you looking for? Since you don't want to work in the trade where you possess your one and only qualification, we'll have to look for menial work, I'm afraid."

"Menial? What's that mean?"

"Simple tasks. Manual labour, that sort of thing."

"Manual labour doesn't sound like simple work to me. Sounds fooking hard."

"It doesn't require any skills, so it's classed as menial."

"Sounds a lot more difficult than sitting behind a desk being rude, unhelpful, and a bit of twat, don't ya think?"

Gareth ignored it. "What do you want to do, then? What are your skills?"

Rathbone pointed at his cape. Nothing more was forthcoming.

"I'm sorry, I don't follow."

Rathbone rolled his eyes. "I'm a fooking vampire, ain't I?"

"Yes, how could I forget? So that means you want to...?"

"Well, I want to do what me homies do. I want a job which requires vampiring skills."

"Vampiring skills?"

"Aye, vampiring skills."

Gareth scratched his head. "Erm...like fancy dress appearances, that sort of thing?"

"That's rather insulting. That's more than insensitive, you ogreish prick. I take it you want me to fooking work?"

"OK, Peter, what is it exactly you'd like to do?"

Rathbone nodded, satisfied. "There are a lot of women out there gagging to get into the pants of a vampire, you know?"

"Really?"

"Oh aye. They're all the rage at the moment. Vampires are on the telly, at the cinema, and the women are thriving on it."

"OK, so you want to be an actor?" asked Gareth unsure where Rathbone was going.

"That's the beauty, ain't it? I don't need to act. I'm already a vampire."

"So you want to star in films?"

"Not really, but the shaggin' sounds grand."

"Peter, the Jobcentre doesn't have any vacancies from Hollywood. However, Tesco is recruiting for trolley collectors. You could meet women that way, I guess."

"Are you taking the piss?" asked Rathbone.

"Peter, you've got to understand, Christopher Reeve wasn't picked to be Superman from a dole queue. If you want to get into acting, you can hand your extensive résumé to an agent. We can't help you."

"What else have you got? There must be something that will get me shaggin'."

"We have a position for a milkman. They have a reputation for being promiscuous."

Rathbone played with his cape in thought. "Yeah, they do do a lot of shaggin' now you come to mention it. Problem with that is it's morning work."

"You can't work mornings, then?"

Rathbone rolled his eyes and pointed to his cape.

"Ah yes, you're a vampire and allergic to sunlight. Guess that means you can't work with garlic or crucifixes, either?"

"Smart-arsed twat. That's the racist shit I've been putting up with ever since I got turned into a vampire. I didn't ask to be this way. This ain't a fooking choice. The least you can do is find me some decent work which involves me nailing a load of birds."

Gareth tapped his pen on the desk. "You do realise this is the Jobcentre, not casting for a pornographic movie. You need to think about this sensibly. We can help you find a job, and maybe then, you'll find it easier to meet a woman."

"What the fook you trying to say?"

"Do you want the trolley job or not?"

"No, I fooking well don't. I fooking came here, out of the goodness of my heart, to get a job—"

"You've been claiming benefit illegally for eighteen years," pointed out Gareth.

Rathbone ignored him. "—and all I get are insults and a shit job pushing trolleys. Well you can take that trolley and stick it up your arse," cried the wronged creature of the night.

"Do you want me to have another look in the system?"

"Aye, and if I can't get a job doing honest, decent vampire activities, such as shaggin', then it's a fooking outrage!"

Gareth typed into the computer and found something very unexpected indeed. A wry smile curled up the corner of his lips.

"You found some sluts?" asked Rathbone hopefully.

"Erm...no." The smile turned into an overly large grin.

"Useless twat. What've ya got?"

"I don't think anyone is going to be able to find you a job, Peter."

"And why the fook is that?"

"Because you're dead."

"Dead?"

"Yes, according to our records, you're deceased." Gareth swivelled the computer screen so that Rathbone could see.

"I guess it's 'cos I'm a vampire, like." The vampire pulled his cape around him. "The undead. The damned. You know?"

"Not really."

"Prick."

"Means you're off our records," said Gareth smugly.

"Well stick us back on."

Gareth shook his head with a smile. "I would, but you're dead."

"So that means ya can't get us a job?"

"Well, I'm sure we can donate you to medical research."

"Are there any chicks?"

"A lot of attractive, young medical students, yes."

"I've always liked me women educated. What do I have to do?"

Gareth tried not to grin. "They cut you up and find out what's inside you."

"That's rubbish."

"But you're dead." Gareth was enjoying this. Rathbone off the system, even through a cock-up, would mean Gareth wouldn't have to deal with him for months, possibly years if he tinkered with the computer.

"Fooking wanker!" Rathbone spat on the floor in protest and rose with a mighty (and well-practised) flourish of his cape.

Gareth smiled as Rathbone made his way out of the small office with a lack of vampire flair.

10

The funeral for the twelve scouts killed by scout leader Michael Walsh turned violent today when his wife turned up to show her respects. According to local residents, parents of the deceased hold her part-responsible for this terrible tragedy and many believe she'd covered for her husband for a number of years. Investigations into his alleged paedophilia continue.

—The Six O'Clock News

AT THREE HUNDRED years old, Patrick O'Flanagan was not old enough to appreciate life before the Agreement. He hated his appetite being suppressed by human politicians, and Borg Hemsman was going to give him the life his blood deserved. He was prepared to die for the cause, for life, at the moment, wasn't worth living. Borg was his leader, and he'd follow him into the daylight, even if he was harbouring his ridiculous grandson King.

It was a cold, windy night, much colder than his beloved Southern Ireland. Teesside was once a place of nightmares for the vampire, but with the death of Sid Tillsley, it was no longer a place to fear.

Patrick jumped down from his vantage point overlooking the chemical works and embraced the feeling of free fall. It was a long drop; one most vampires couldn't manage without breaking bones. Patrick absorbed the impact and used the spring in his legs to leap up again onto some nearby pipe work. He was born to run, and that's what earned him Borg's favour. He was an exceptional scout and an invaluable spy.

Borg had been fervently tracking the Coalition's movements since he'd lost his daughter. He kept his cards close to his chest, even from his most trusted allies, but the old master was convinced the Coalition had something up their sleeves. They were too quiet of late.

This was the third industrial site belonging to the Coalition Patrick had visited in the Northeast. His peers had performed similar tasks all over the UK. So far, he'd found nothing untoward, but that didn't mean he wouldn't scour this site to the best of his abilities.

He started running across the extensive pipe work around the great reactors, dodging the hissing steam exhausts and scaling great chimneys. None of the workers saw him; he was a shadow moving in shadows.

He reached a sudden end in the pipework and was surprised to find bulldozers clearing massive piles of rubble and steel girders sticking out of the ground, bent to the most acute of angles.

This isn't right, he thought.

Borg's informants had told him this was a Coalition research-facility site, and that may have once been true, but by the looks of the wreckage and the work being carried out, this hadn't been a planned dismantlement.

Patrick picked his phone from his pocket and accessed the Internet. Growing up during the Industrial Revolution had nurtured a fascination with technology and the power it granted. Technology was a rare interest in vampires, and the elders were mostly dinosaurs. Patrick quickly discovered the plant had been destroyed by a gas leak three months back.

Borg's spies had infiltrated deep into Coalition records to discover the name of this site, and if it was important, the chances of it being destroyed by a gas leak were slim.

He dialled his leader. "Sir, it's Patrick."

"Pat...HAVEN'T YOU HAD ENOUGH TO EAT FOR ONE DAY!"

"Sorry, sir?" said Patrick, pulling the phone from his ear.

"What? Oh, sorry. I was talking to the fat, useless grandson of mine. What is it?"

"I've reached the chemical plant at Seal Sands."

"That was quick, boy."

"Thank you, sir. There's a problem, though. The site isn't here anymore."

"I THOUGHT YOU WERE GOING OUT! Sorry, go on, Patrick."

"According to the local papers, there was a gas explosion here three months ago. It looks like humans are working around the clock to clear the site."

"I see. What happened there?" he asked rhetorically. "Pat, do some digging. We've found nothing at any other Coalition site, and there has to be something, there just has to be. That place screams suspicion at me. Use any force necessary. There's no need to be discreet. We are nearly ready to strike and take our—YOU'VE GOT MAYONNAISE ALL OVER YOUR FACE!"

SID HADN'T STOPPED Brian from getting on the Number Seven. He was driving back to the Smithson Estate. It was a good start. But, Brian could tell by the look on Arthur's face that things hadn't gone well.

"He's getting married in a week," said Arthur, nodding towards the portly, sweaty driver.

"You are fooking joking me?" shouted Brian.

This got a few tuts from some of the newer passengers who weren't from the Smithson Estate and classy enough not to have heard of Sid Steely, aka, Sid Tillsley.

"What the fook is wrong with that?" snapped Sid. "You not approve of a man and a woman showing their affection for each other?"

"Not when you've only been with her two months, and not when she's kicking the shit out of ya at night!"

"She's got cracking jugs, Brian, but I guess that's not what you want in a...partner."

"What the fook does that mean!"

"Apparently, that's what *you lot* have—partners."

"Sid, I'm not fooking gay," said Brian, closing his eyes with despair. "I just don't wanna see you make a mistake. I want you to settle down but not with the wrong woman. The sex will dry up, mate."

Arthur mumbled under his breath, "No sex before marriage."

"You are fooking joking me?" repeated Brian, holding on to the bus's handrail for support. His knees buckled with shock. "I thought that was illegal in Middlesbrough. Sid, what're ya playing at, mon? Ah fook, this is a disaster."

"Well, it's better than going traipsing 'round fooking Middlesbrough Memorial Park, waving me old fella at every windscreen in the car park, hoping some old slapper is gonna let me in for a jump!"

The conversation, or rather the shouting match, was causing much discomfort to the passengers.

"The Internet stuff was working though, weren't it?"

"Oh aye, and I nearly got put inside for attempted murder for throwing one of your *them lot* out of a window."

"I ain't fooking gay! And, anyway, didn't you meet this new bird through the Internet."

"So what if I did?"

"Well, you'll meet more, won't ya? Look, it's great you're happy, but she's got you working, off the booze, and off the fags. Mate, she's bad news."

"She's looking out for me health. Since meeting her, I've had no vampire shit; I haven't been shot at; I haven't had to smack anyone, much, either. Things are a lot simpler."

"Don't you miss The Miner's, Sid?" Brian banged his hand on the ticket machine with each syllable. "Don't you miss the Bolton?"

"Of course I do!" It was Sid's turn to vent his frustrations on the ticket machine. It didn't survive. "Of course I fooking do! But you turned, Brian. You turned into a *them lot*, and if it can happen to you, it can happen to anyone. I ain't risking it, mon. I need a shag, and in a week, I'm gonna fooking get one and live my life with a woman, Brian...a *woman!*"

"For fook's sa—"

Sid cut him off by slamming his foot down on the accelerator and sending Brian flying down the bus.

Arthur skilfully used his karate agility to dodge the airborne Brian and used his karate grip to grab his hand, plucking him out of mid-air.

"Sid, slow down!" yelled Brian.

"I've nothing more to say on the matter! And if you've gotta problem with the way I drive, then I suggest you travel in one of them Volkswagen Beetles with the fooking flower in the front, or whatever it is *you lot* drive!"

"Stop being a wanker!"

Sid was in full rant. "I know that the idea of holy wedlock between a man and a woman might upset you, but I ask you to respect my way of life. Now, fook off." Sid pointed at the door with a look in his eye that told Brian that the stubborn mule wasn't going to change his mind.

"You're going fifty in a thirty. How can I get off, ya twat?"

Sid turned around, enraged. "How dare you use such language in front of the general fooking public? I'm in a position of trust, and these people are in my care." Sid turned back to the road to see he was heading straight for a man on the pavement. This was followed with an almighty thud.

"Ah fook..." mumbled Sid.

IT HADN'T TAKEN LONG for Patrick to hunt down one of the operatives who'd worked the shift that'd seen the plant's destruction. Where possible, vampires had filled the posts, but human labour was hired for tasks vampires considered menial. One of the men working on clearing the site had taken little persuasion in giving the name of one of his co-workers and his haunts.

Unfortunately, the man Patrick was about to meet was a drunk and spent his leisure time inebriated in the pubs of Middlesbrough. Without Tillsley, pubs were no longer the lion's den, but that didn't mean the next few minutes were going to be enjoyable. Patrick opened the door of The Fat Cat pub.

"Norman Jackson?" he called out in the mostly deserted pub, and a young human, probably in his late twenties, turned from his pint glass.

"Who wants to know?"

"Landlady," he said to the ugly, ageing dragon behind the bar, "get this man a drink." Patrick decided to take the good-cop approach. He was young, but he wasn't brash.

"Do I know you?" said the human, supping his beer. The man had probably just started his session and was still coherent, but even with the Northeast accent, Patrick had trouble understanding.

"No, I was given your name. Nothing to worry about," he quickly added when he saw the worried look on the young man's pitted face. "I've got a few questions to ask you about the chemical works that went down a few months back."

"Why talk to me? Why not one of the bosses?"

"I want to know what really happened, not what they say happened. It's worth your drinks for the evening," he said, throwing a fifty on the bar.

Norman's eyes widened. He took the note and stuck it in his jeans. "Official report said it was a gas explosion." Norman looked around him and then to the landlady, who nodded at him to continue. "You may not believe this," he said.

"Try me."

"Vampires."

Norman was right. Patrick didn't believe what he'd heard. What sort of operation was the Coalition running if the general public knew about the lamia? "What do you mean?" he asked, testing the water.

"Place was run by vampires, it was. They were making some weird chemical thing."

Patrick took a seat next to Norman. "They were open with you about that?"

"Oh, no. They thought they were reet smart-arsed fookers. They didn't say 'owt to us. Treated us like shit, in fact."

"So how did you know they were vampires?"

"Oh, we were getting loads of the bastards kicking around town, a few months back," added the landlady.

Norman said, "Aye. Ol' Sid Tillsley's had a few run-ins with 'em. He knocked a few of the fookers out. They had the last laugh though when they turned The Miner's into a gay bar."

Patrick pulled awkwardly at his shirt collar. "I...I don't understand."

"The Miner's Arms was his local boozer, and he hasn't been in there since the vampires turned it into a gay bar." Norman laughed.

"I see. I guess death stopped him boozing all together, right?"

"Nah, mon. Death wouldn't stop ol' Sid boozing. The only thing that could is the battleaxe he's shacked up with. Got great norks though, or so me mate told me."

Patrick grabbed Norman by his coat lapels. "What did you say?"

"Great norks? Fantastic jubblies? Look, cool it, mon. She has nice tits, all right?"

Patrick wasn't worked up about Norman's derogatory comments, what confused him were Norman's references to Tillsley. "You're acting as if Tillsley is still alive."

"Well, yeah. That's 'cos he is."

For Patrick, the pub was suddenly the most dangerous place on earth. Tillsley had killed Sparle. Tillsley attacked the Occursus. If Patrick ever saw him, the first thing he'd do is run, and not just because he was young and hadn't yet reached his potential, but because no vampire could take him down, not without the use of a bullet, and even that hadn't been successful so far.

"Is...is he...in Middlesbrough?" he stuttered, relinquishing the human's coat.

"Aye," said Norman, looking at his watch. "And if you give it five minutes, you'll catch him."

"He's coming here!" said Patrick, in a high-pitched squeal.

"Calm down!" said Norman, smirking at Patrick's discomfort. "He ain't coming here, but he'll be stopping outside."

"Why?" Patrick couldn't keep his eye off the entrance to the pub.

"He's the local bus driver."

This wasn't a time for heroics. Patrick had to tell Borg, but safety first. He ran out of the pub.

As soon as his trainer came into contact with the pavement, his leg buckled and his femur burst from his inner thigh with a flash of red. Patrick was airborne before pain embraced him. Wind whistled through his hair. His body screamed, telling him his right side had been all but destroyed. Friction eventually brought him to rest, but at the expense of the skin being shredded from his back. For a second, he couldn't move, but then, his body began knitting back together, slowly. He was in a bad way.

Lifting his head, two headlights blinded him. A few spectators were watching, and thankfully, no one came to his rescue. The last thing he needed was human fuss.

"You fooking twat. He's probably dead."

Patrick could hear the Northeast accent from behind the headlights.

"It was your fault, Brian. You were distracting the driver. He'll be reet," said another voice.

"I think he's moving, Sid."

Alarm bells rang in Patrick's head when a huge silhouette drifted in front of the headlights. "You alright there, pal?" Patrick heard.

Patrick tried to get up to escape the bane of the vampire who had come back from the dead...to run him over in a bus.

11

Road traffic accidents have quintupled over the last couple of months in Middlesbrough. Speed cameras installed in the area haven't had the effect that Cleveland Police Force hoped for. A local AA representative said, "I've no idea why this is happening, but on a completely unrelated topic, I'd avoid taking the bus."

—*Middlesbrough Gazette*

"SEE, BRIAN, HE'S WALKING. HE'S REET."

"He don't look so reet to me," said Brian, noticing the bone sticking out of Sid's victim's leg.

"He'll run it off, I'm sure."

Brian shook his head at Sid's ridiculous optimism. "You're gonna be in for it, mate. He was on the fooking pavement when you hit him."

Sid paced back and forth. "Ah fook. I canna lose this job or the missus is gonna kill us."

"I'll have a word with him," said Brian, who jogged over and put his arm around the victim of another Tillsley road traffic accident. "Eh'up, mate, how you doing?" Brian couldn't believe just how big the man was. He was bent over with both hands on his knees, but Brian didn't have to lean down to put his arm round him.

"I'll...I'll be fine."

Brian blinked and shook his head. He could've sworn that the bone poking through the man's leg just snapped back into place. "Hang on a minute...Your leg..."

The man pushed him away, and Brian went flying. Something was fishy. There was no way he would be able to muster that much strength after being hit by a bus. Brian, being the smartest man on the Smithson Estate, put two and two together.

"He's a fooking vampire!"

PATRICK TRIED HIS BEST TO RUN. He could move now that his skeleton had reformed, but the muscles and ligaments were still a long way from full recovery.

"I don't know what you're talking about," he cried. He couldn't have had worse luck. He'd only stepped out of the pub and the bus had been upon him before he'd even seen it.

"Sid, he's a fooking vampire!" shouted the man in the hideous red suit.

"Shit!" cried the vampire's bane.

Run! Patrick's mind screamed, and he hobbled down the road. With each step, he felt the muscles knit together and his ligaments reattach. He heard more yells from behind.

"Sid, he'll tell the other vampire bastards about ya!"

"I canna catch him. Even the new, lean me canna run that far!"

"Well, you better do something!"

"I'll use my karate on him! He can tell me where my son is!"

"No, Arthur! I ain't risking Brian bumming another vampire!"

"For the last fooking time—"

"I'll kick his ass, man!"

"No, Arthur, I'll do it. I used to be a vampire hunter, you know."

SID CONSIDERED the fifty-yard distance between himself and the vampire who was picking up pace and who would, once again, plunge Sid into the world of vampire shit. It was time to finish the job with the thing that got him into this mess. Sid ambled back to the bus.

"Come on, lads. Let's take the fooker down the old-fashioned way."

Arthur and Brian followed.

Brian said, "You're gonna run him over when he ain't looking?"

"Aye," said the big man, climbing into the driver's seat before flooring it, much to the relief of the considerable tailback of cars that had accumulated behind the Number Seven. "Hold on everyone," he called back through the bus, "we're chasing down a vampire!"

This caused, as would be expected, a mixed reaction. Most of the bus passengers were from the Smithson Estate and knew everything about the vampires plaguing the area of late. They were excited about the prospect and knew there was nothing to fear as Sid was rock. Yet, there were quite a few people who weren't from the Smithson Estate, who hadn't heard of Sid Tillsley, his fight against the vampire, and his mission to get laid. These people were a little concerned.

"You back in the vampire-hunting thing, Sid?" came a shout from the back of the bus.

"Tonight I am," said Sid in, surprisingly, an action-hero sort of way. "And, I'm gonna smack the twat in the face."

PATRICK WAS BORN TO RUN, but not like this: being chased though a built-up area of Middlesbrough by history's most dangerous vampire hunter driving a bus. It wasn't long before he was caught. His broken leg brought agony with every step. Tillsley was taking no prisoners and Patrick threw himself to the other side of the road as the bus careered through the space he'd just occupied.

He lay on the cold, damp concrete, but quickly had to move again when the cars coming around the corner of a nearby junction failed to see him. He rolled onto the pavement and took a moment to regain himself before he saw the headlights of the Number Seven coming his way again.

"YOU'RE GOING TO KILL HIM!" screamed a well-dressed lady from the back of the bus.

"I'm fooking trying, pet," said the driver, not understanding her tone.

Brian and Arthur hung on for dear life at the front while encouraging their friend.

"You nearly got him there," said Brian.

"Look, man," said Arthur, "if you can just wound him a bit, then we can interrogate him and find out where they're keeping my son."

"I'll see what I can do, mate," said Sid, "but I canna risk him getting back to the other vampire bastards."

Sid made a beeline for the vampire lying on the pavement. Luckily for Sid, there were no parked cars. The lad was in trouble.

"RAMMING SPEED!" yelled the captain of the bus.

PATRICK GOT TO HIS FEET as best he could and broke into a run and then a sprint. He was healing but still wasn't well enough to scale the rooftops of the terraced houses and reach safety. If only he'd phoned Borg from the pub. Now, he concentrated on survival, which involved reaching a line of parked cars a hundred metres up the road.

"SID, YOU GOTTA GET HIM before he reaches those cars. You won't be able to follow him, and you'll never catch him on foot, baby," said Arthur.

"You're reet, mon. If only I had me Nissan Bluebird Turbo, then I'd have caught him ages ago, plus the heated seats would be a lot easier on me piles than this bastard," said Sid, squirming into comfort before dropping down a gear.

WITH ONLY TEN YARDS TO GO, Patrick felt the last of his wounds heal, and he kicked his legs, reaching top speed. Once past the parked cars ahead, he could scale the terrace houses at will and be away, a hero of the vampire ra—

"WHERE D'YA THINK YOU'RE GOING, PAL?" Sid growled.

"YEEEAAAHHHH!" came the cheers of the residents of the Smithson Estate as both sets of wheels bumped over the vampire.

"You murderer!" came the shouts of the non-residents who thought Sid had killed a member of the general public.

"Not yet!" he shouted back through the bus, before slamming it into reverse and adding another couple of sickening bumps to the disturbing evening.

He opened the door, and he, Brian, and Arthur quickly departed to see what damage had been done.

"Wait on here," said Brian to the bus. "We'll just clean up, outside."

"You murdering animals!" screamed a middle-aged woman.

"Shut up, ya soft twat," chastised the swordsman.

Sid reached the wrecked vampire first and felt a little queasy at the mess he'd made. "Fooking 'ell. They don't stand up to being run over by buses very well, do they?"

"No, it doesn't look like they do," said Brian looking at the mangled, bloody body.

"He's still moving, man," said Arthur. "Let's find out where my son is."

Sid shook his head. "Sorry, Arthur, but he's had enough, like. Let's put the fooker out of his misery."

The people on the bus couldn't see the body, but they did see Sid throwing a massive right hand to what some of them thought was a dead human being. Sid gave a satisfied nod when the body exploded into dust. "That'll do."

"What now?" asked Brian.

"No vampire shit, and more importantly, no bumming. Now fook off!"

12

Homosexuality is on the rise in Middlesbrough. Last year, in a poll of three hundred men, every single one of them stated they were straight and proceeded to threaten passersby in an impressive display of unquestionable heterosexuality. This year, however, although the three hundred men polled were straight, one camp customer admitted that if he saw Dale Winton in the street, he wouldn't even dream of setting him on fire.
—*The 'Boro Standard*

"THIS CAR IS RIDICULOUS," said Viralli.

"What are you talking about? This is a 1974 Cadillac Fleetwood Brougham." King floored the gas and overtook the car in front of them. "Yeeehhhhaaaah! Did you feel the pull, baby?"

"Not really."

King sustained the smile brought about by the classic car's burst of power. "This is one of the finest automobiles to ever grace God's green earth.

"It isn't God's earth, it's ours."

"Whatever, man," said King, uninterested. "I don't know why you all think you shit sunshine. Yeah, you drink blood, big deal. You can't sing for shit."

Viralli hated King and longed to kill him. If it weren't for Borg, he'd have ended his cursed existence a month ago. His respect for Borg stayed his hand. Viralli was a follower and needed a leader. Physically, he was one of the most powerful vampires left alive and had been part of the group that Michael Vitrago had assembled to bring down Sparle. He'd followed Vitrago and, as a result, the Coalition for three hundred years. But, with Vitrago's death, Viralli looked for strength elsewhere. Bwogi was weak, as were his attempts to lead the Coalition. Viralli was a loyal soldier, but only to the vampire race. Now, he spat on the Coalition.

Viralli had bitten his tongue when Borg had assigned him this mission. Babysitting was a waste of his talents. He didn't want to spend any time with King, let alone speak to him, but he couldn't sit back and listen to the nonsense he was spouting.

"How can you critique vampire music? The finest musicians throughout history have all been vampires."

King banged his fist on the steering wheel. "Bullshit, man. That's bullshit."

"Keep your eyes on the road," Viralli scolded when King edged nearer the centre reservation. "We don't know if you'd survive a crash."

"I'd survive any crash you would," said King to Viralli over his shades. "Anyway, you vamps can do all the classical shit, which is cool and all, but there's no soul in your music. It's all based on technical ability to play an instrument or sing in a certain key. There's no celebration of emotion. Nothing's sung from the heart."

"Human weakness you mean?"

"Beautiful music, baby, is all that matters. I don't care if it's human or vampire. I'm both. I'm impartial; I pick what's best. The humans, man, they've got soul."

Viralli sighed and looked at the scenery instead. The concrete rose ever upwards and the peace of the countryside was quickly waning. "Where are we going?"

"For a night on the town," said King with a toot of the horn.

"You're joking?"

"I'm gonna find you a woman. We need to put a smile on that miserable face of yours."

Viralli rubbed his head. "I'm not interested in your women."

"Well, I am. You're a good-looking fella, buddy. The shaven head and the stubble might scare off some chicks, but a lot dig the rough look. You're packing some awesome guns too. What do you bench press, man? Say, with a little bit of a makeover, we could pick you up some hot broads. The combat look is a little scary, but I reckon you'd look hot shit in a jumpsuit."

"I'm not interested in meeting women."

"Well, we ain't going to any places to pick you up a boy. Live how you want to live, brother, but you do that on your own time."

"That's not what I meant. Sex is something that doesn't bother all vampires. Our equivalent desire is that of blood."

"That blood shit is weird." King shuddered. "Making love to a sweet lady is so much more appealing."

"Have you ever tried blood?"

"Don't need it, man, why would I? I haven't needed it so far. I'm only three months old. What I do know is that I've been born with the horn." The sleeping neighbourhood did not welcome the accompanying blast of the car horn.

"And a hunger for saturated fats..."

King grabbed his belly. "Just need the fuel, man. I'm a hybrid, remember."

"What do you plan to do with your gifts, King? Are you going to live up to your grandfather's expectations?"

King's shoulders slumped. "Gifts? What gifts? I'm a hybrid, yeah, but I've no idea what I am. I've lost my childhood in a matter of weeks, and all I know how to do is sing, and my grandpappy doesn't want me doing that."

"You can walk in the daylight. Sometimes, I think I'd give my immortal life for that," said Viralli looking at the moon.

"I don't even know if I am immortal."

"Test yourself. Test your strength."

King pulled a cheeseburger from out of nowhere and unwrapped it, steering the car with his knees. "Not my bag, baby. Got the karate if I need it, but I'm a lover, not a fighter."

"The time may come when you don't have a choice. When we go to war with the humans, you're going to have to choose which side you are on."

King considered it. "Well, best we make the most of tonight before the shit hits the fan."

Viralli had nearly forgotten about the impending evening of frivolity. "Fuck."

A COUPLE OF HOURS LATER, King lazed against a bar, nodding his head to the beat of the music, his quiff reverberating with the rhythm. King loved nightclubs and nightclubs loved King. The place heaved with more chicks than he could shake his considerable stick at.

He pulled at the waistband of his blue denim jeans, which were a little snug. King assumed it was the combination of a little puppy fat and the big meal he'd just eaten, so he didn't feel guilty about digging out another cheeseburger from his pocket.

All the girls who walked past got the eye, and every single one returned it. Each went through the same routine. They looked him up and down, mesmerised by his perfect 'do, thick black hair, ice-white teeth, and unblemished skin, but couldn't help noticing the paunch he packed around his middle—before catching a glimpse of the monster held in captivity by blue denim. Each looked up again, a little flushed, and had the deal sealed by the baby blues winking from over the top of gold-rimmed shades.

He smiled, knowing the night would yield yet more loving. It was tough to get action when he was cooped up with his protective grandpappy, but when he did go out, he didn't stop a-rockin'. He turned to the bar.

"Pepsi cola, baby!" he yelled to the barmaid, who instantly ignored all of her other customers and fixed the man his favourite drink.

"I was here before you!" shouted some cat, his pint left under the beer tap, half-poured.

"Sorry, man, I didn't realise I was meant to give a fuck."

"You fat bastard!" screamed the balding troublemaker.

"What?" said King grabbing a couple of inches of flab. "Come over here and say that."

The man in his mid-thirties was well built and welcomed the chance to pummel the pudgy pretty boy. However, when he was within striking distance, his balls receded into his body faster than a sudden lack of testosterone could take them. The mouthy fatty had a mate so big he defied gravity when he walked.

He looked up at the shaven-headed mass of muscle, and even though the man was extremely handsome, the ferocity of the eyes encouraged the man to let go of his bladder. The troublemaker didn't say anything. The only option was to turn on a sixpence and leave the club.

King supped on a massive glass of Pepsi. "I'd have dealt with it, man."

"That's what I was afraid of."

Viralli was getting a lot of concerned looks from the door staff. Both he and King stood out a mile, but for different reasons. Viralli still had his huge overcoat on, making him look colossal. If they could see the muscles hidden beneath it, they would have been twice as scared. He was big for a vampire, and he dwarfed the entire nightclub.

"You wanna drink?" asked King.

"Vodka, straight."

"Sounds nasty, but it suits you, big fella." King turned to the barmaid. "Hey, baby, straight vodka." She left a customer, for a second time, but this time, it brought no aggrieved comments from the queuing punters.

When King gave Viralli the drink, the vampire downed it with a practised flick of the wrist and grimaced. "Watered down and full of toxins."

"Take that pole from out of your backside and lighten up. Enjoy yourself."

Viralli surveyed the drunken partygoers stumbling around. "This isn't my idea of enjoying myself."

"What is?"

"Mountaineering, hunting, swimming through the waterfalls of the Norwegian fjords are all things I consider fun. Being in the company of drunken humans is not."

"They ain't so bad."

"You like burgers, yes?"

"Who doesn't?" said King, reaching in his pocket for another.

"Would you choose to unwind on a dairy farm?"

"Depends on whether there were any hot milkmaids, baby."

Viralli ignored King's grin. "I don't like to socialise with my food."

"A few more vodkas will sort you out."

Viralli shook his head. "Drugs don't affect the vampire species. Our body destroys them before they can affect our central nervous system."

King gave Viralli a pat on his broad back. "It sounds really shit being a vampire, man."

"It is right now," said Viralli looking around. "Are you affected by drugs or alcohol?"

"I don't know. I'm only a few months old and have a million things to try before I die. There are more important things to life than boozing, and entertaining the masses is one of them. I'm going to sing a song."

"I don't think it's that sort of club. It's dance music they're playing. People are not here to listen to your version of 'rock 'n' roll.'"

King looked over the shades and winked. "We'll see about that."

AS THE EMBARRASSMENT MADE HIS WAY over to the DJ stand situated on a stage next to the dance floor, Viralli checked in with Borg who wanted to know everything his grandson did. The old vampire was a beast in his day, but his weakness, the love for his family, was unnerving.

The music blared out incessantly, so Viralli looked for somewhere quiet where Borg would be able to hear him. He yearned to leave and go outside but couldn't risk leaving the defenceless, fat waster.

He made his way out of the main room and into the entrance hall. The reek of stale urine and fresh vomit was overpowering even before he reached the queue to the toilet that stretched out of the door. He walked to the front and no one dared say a word. Viralli pushed through the door, crushing a human who stood behind it into the wall. The man went to say something—and then thought better of it.

"Out," said Viralli calmly.

All the men queuing quit the scene. The three men standing at the urinal continued to urinate, not knowing what stood behind them.

"Out," he said again, but this time louder. Two of the men turned to give him a piece of their minds but wisely decided otherwise and zipped up, wetting their trousers as they exited.

"I've started so I'll finish, so fuck off," said the one remaining human, dangerously ignorant of what lurked behind him.

Viralli thrust the ball of his foot into the small of the man's back. The acceleration nearly snapped the man in half and the ceramic urinal cracked and fell off the wall as he crashed into it. He fell to the floor and didn't move. He was conscious, but his spine was in tatters.

Viralli stood on his neck. There was no malice; he was simply finishing the job, although he did enjoy the purple colour the man produced. Once dead, he dragged the body over and placed it in front of the toilet door so that no one would disturb him.

He took a phone out of his pocket and dialled through to Borg who answered it almost instantly. Viralli shook his head. The old timer must be worried sick.

"Is everything OK?" asked Borg.

"Yes, sir, everything's fine."

"Where are you?"

"Sheffield. A human nightclub, unfortunately."

There was a silence from the other end of the phone "What's he doing?"

"I'm afraid to say that after eating a meal for six, he dragged me here and has been engaging with females. Now he is trying to persuade the DJ to let him sing a song."

"What is wrong with him? I'm starting to think there isn't any killer instinct in the boy."

"I think you're right. What are you going to do if there isn't?"

"He's my grandson, Viralli. Do you understand me?"

"Yes, sir."

Borg would march the vampire back to greatness, and for that, Viralli would gladly give him his life, even if it meant saving the pathetic thing trying to sing in the other room.

"He loves humans more than he does the vampires that look after him," said Borg. "Perhaps we give him a reason to hate them?"

"What do you mean, sir?"

"After we attacked the concert hall, the Coalition did an amazing job of covering up the whole ordeal. Only videos of King were leaked, and the bloodshed wasn't attributed to him. Perhaps, if it was to happen a second time...What is it the human's say? Lightning doesn't strike twice."

Viralli smiled. "What do you want me to do?"

"Turn the humans against him, and then punish them. If you can get him to join in the bloodshed, all the better. If not, leave a mess for the Coalition. The vampires are uniting and we are close to announcing ourselves. It's time for another sign of things to come."

Viralli put the phone back into his pocket and cracked his knuckles. King wanted to put on a show. It was time to see whose performance would be the most memorable.

"ARE YOU A FUCKING IDIOT, MAN?" shouted King above the din of the music.

"If you wanna do karaoke, then The Market Tavern is open till three in the morning," replied the young DJ.

"Karaoke? I ain't a karaoke singer." King unleashed an accusing chubby finger. "How dare you put me in the same sentence as the word?"

"This is a nightclub. People have paid good money to come here for dance music, and that's what I'm gonna give 'em."

"This shit?" King turned his finger to the speakers. "People pay to listen to this shit?"

"Now you're being a prick. Fuck off or I'll go get the bouncers."

Defeated, King turned to walk away, taking off his shades and placing them in the top pocket of his red flannel shirt.

Viralli put his heavy hand on his shoulder. "What's the matter?" he shouted in King's ear.

"That piece of shit won't let me sing."

"How can he stop you? You're half vampire. If you want something, take it."

King stamped his foot. "They should want to hear me sing! I am willing to give them five minutes of the greatest voice of the generation, and they don't want it."

"Then take it."

King advanced on the DJ stand once more. "Turn this shit off!"

"Go fuck yourself!" was the curt reply.

King retreated. "He told me to go fuck myself," he whined to Viralli, who looked down his nose at him.

"He can't stop you. You are more powerful than all of these people combined. Simply take it."

"That's not my style, man. I told you, I'm a lover, not a fighter."

"Are you scared? Are you scared you haven't got what it takes?"

"No, man, I just wanna be known as a singer first, not the guy who kicked the shit out of a nightclub to get his own way. You dig?"

"But no one will hear you, King. Sometimes, you have to use force to be heard. I'm going to give you a chance. I'm going to make you famous."

Viralli withdrew his arm from King's shoulders and strode towards the DJ stand with King trailing behind. Viralli didn't give the DJ a chance to say or do anything and drove his fist into the man's face, caving his skeletal structure into his brain. The DJ hit the floor in a flash, the back of his skull shattering, spraying blood across the wooden floorboards. With the DJ out of the way, Viralli pulled out all the cables from the computers. Soon, all that could be heard was the shouting and complaining of the partygoers.

"Now's your chance, King."

KING GULPED AND CLAMPED HIS HAND OVER HIS MOUTH. The cheeseburgers from earlier suddenly travelled north after he got a look at the DJ's face. It looked like a burger before it was cooked. King took a moment. This was it; he couldn't ruin it because he was squeamish. He unwrapped a burger to settle his stomach.

Showtime.

He sauntered to the front of the stage, but there was no chance of singing with the crowd jeering abuse at him. "IF Y'ALL KEEP THE NOISE DOWN, I'LL SING YOU A LITTLE DITTY!" he shouted above the din.

"FUCK OFF!"

"GET THE MUSIC BACK ON!"

"THIS IS A DANCE CLUB!"

King put his hands up to calm them down, but even his beautiful face couldn't calm the hostile crowd.

"WHO DO YOU THINK YOU ARE, YOU FAT BASTARD?" shouted a partygoer.

King grabbed at his waist. "HOW FUCKING DARE YOU? I AIN'T FAT!"

VIRALLI SMILED FROM BEHIND THE DJ STAND. It was the reception he'd hoped for. All he needed was for King to lose his temper and unleash whatever power he possessed on the baying crowd. Suddenly, a bottle flew from the shadows striking King in the face. King fell backwards, while Viralli stepped forward, keen to see how he'd deal with the wound. There was definitely blood, of that he was sure. A vampire wouldn't have flinched at such a pitiful missile, but King hit the deck and rolled around on the floor like he'd been shot. Viralli doubted King possessed any powers at all.

"Are you OK?" he said, standing over the victim.

King clutched his head and looked at Viralli through his fingers. "My pride is hurting me, man. They're meant to be my people. I was gonna give them everything, man!"

"Make them pay for what they did to you."

"No, man, I ain't ready for that shit." King rolled shakily onto his front and took a knee, only a standing eight.

"You may not be, but I am." Viralli jumped onto the dance floor and ripped into the congregation of clubbers who, in hindsight, regretted not opting to hear what the singer had to offer.

13

Fukkin bollox all over da telly. Only place wit the rite fax is the net and dis blog. The fukkers canna sensa us ere!!!!!1

I saw wot happnd. I waz dere. Fukkin kids???, bollox. No shooters or nun ov dat shit. Fukking vampires did it. Vampyres killed The Quest. CoulDnt take there triboot to da Prins of Darknes. Dey killd em cos dey were clos 2 da truf!!!!! Wat wil the guverment covr up nex????//
—Jonny Blagan's Blog. Hits: 0

"YOU WOULDN'T DARE, CHAMBERS. You pitiful dog. I could rip you in two."

"Is that right, Farouq?"

"Try me! TRY ME!"

Reece Chambers laughed and circled the vampire restrained on a steel surgeon's table with metal bands holding his limbs and head. Reece rubbed his finger slowly across the vampire's forehead, just below the metal band holding him fast.

Farouq thrashed, trying to rid himself of Reece's touch.

"I captured you easily enough. I could've killed you when I wanted. I am in complete control, Farouq." The calmness of his voice was testimony to his words. "Have I not killed dozens of your kind? Now, I am so much more. I'm beyond your primitive species."

"Press that button and we'll see if you live up to your boasts," urged Farouq.

Reece threw the remote control in his hand up and down, nonchalantly. "How long have you been here? Every day, have you lain awake in your prison, wondering what despicable torture or scientific experiment I had in store for you?"

"Fuck you!" Farouq thrashed some more, spilling blood from his wrists and ankles.

Reece laughed long and hard.

Dried blood covered the restraints. Farouq had spent his days trying to free himself, only succeeding in bringing more self-harm. Reece slapped the vampire around the face, laughing at the anguished grimaces Farouq pulled. "Even if you had escaped the restraints, how would you have broken out of the cell? None of your brothers and sisters ever managed it."

Reece left the vampire and ran his hand across the smooth concrete of the cell and walked its circumference before reaching the metal door. "Not even Vitrago or Sparle would have the brute strength to break out of here, and we can hardly expect you to match up to their magnificence, can we?"

Farouq had nothing to offer, but his wild eyes told Reece everything he needed to know: he was furious.

"I could've locked you up in the garden shed, couldn't I?" Reece leant back on the door. "It's strange, Farouq. I have often questioned how the vampire race benefits mankind. The Coalition believes the vampire have furthered our technological and cultural advancement by millennia."

"We gave you a civilisation," said the vampire.

"So, what about you? What have you managed with your lengthy time on the planet?"

"I've killed your loved ones, fed off your young, let the blood of your ancestors!"

"Quite." Reece picked some lint from his shoulder. "Ask yourself this: Why would I let you go? Why would I challenge you to a noble duel with nothing but my fists to protect me? Every vampire sees us as cattle. A man against a...what is it you all call yourselves? Gods?"

"You are food to us. I'd treat you no better than a lion would a gazelle."

"Is that so?" Reece paced the circular room once more. "Have you ever seen a gazelle turn to face the lion?" He stooped over Farouq, leaning on the table without a care in the world. "Bravery is for fools. You think I'd be here if I hadn't grown a set of teeth big enough to bite a lion in half?"

Uncertainty crossed the vampire's face, but it passed and the anger returned. "You're bluffing, Chambers. You haven't got the strength!"

"Sid Tillsley did."

"And he's dead."

"But his power is not." Reece took off his top so that he was bare to the waist.

Farouq laughed out loud. "Did you think pumping iron would grant you the power to take on an immortal?"

Reece flexed his considerable muscles, his chest contracting powerfully. He held up a keyfob. "Why don't we find out?" He pressed the button and the metal bracelets holding the vampire snapped free.

FAROUQ GOT UP SLOWLY. It had to be a trap. There had to be something waiting for him, unless Chambers really had lost the plot. He snarled at the vampire hunter. How he hated him. It pained him that he'd been trapped by a human, and this egomaniac had not stopped adding insult to injury all week.

Farouq had been slack with his precautions since Borg had started the uprising. Life was fun again and was only destined to get better once the accursed Agreement was shattered. Now, he had to get past Chambers, who'd have an ace up his sleeve, for sure.

As the two circled each other, Farouq took in the surroundings of the cell that had been his home for the past week. Chambers was right; there was no escape. The smooth, reinforced concrete walls stretched up to the unreachable ceiling. He considered the solitary door. His survival instincts told him to flee, but his pride made him stay.

Chambers paced in unison, poised with nervous anxiety. Farouq sensed his want for the fight. He could see the intensity in the cold stare of the old hunter that had seen sights not meant for human eyes. His heavily lined face had been etched with nightmares. His roughly cut, thick, grey hair showed that he took no pride in his appearance. He was a troubled soul, which the world had no need.

Farouq flexed his muscles that had atrophied from being restrained for so long. His body started to regenerate the muscle, causing his hunger to grow and his heart rate to increase. He snarled as Chambers mimicked his muscular display. Chambers' breathing picked up pace. The man was becoming anxious. It wasn't fear; he was dying for a fight. Farouq yearned for blood, and he yearned to kill this burden on the vampire race, yet he knew he should run. Bloodlust started to take him. He looked at the door; it was his last chance.

"Scared?"

Farouq made his choice and confronted the hunter.

Chambers applauded slowly, sarcastically. "So you've finally grown some balls."

Farouq charged. Chambers merely smiled.

REECE WELCOMED the adrenaline coursing through his body. His senses were tuned to notice anything and everything around him. He clenched his fists and listened to the bones crack; the tension of the sinews and the ligaments were straining, dying to rip into vampire flesh. This was power. This is what he'd wanted since a vampire killed his father all those years ago.

Farouq was nothing to him, just another bloodsucker in the wrong place at the wrong time who'd go down in history as the first vampire to be killed by the bare hands of Reece Chambers, the Destroyer of the Vampire Plague.

The vampire's footsteps thundered with the charge. Reece stood his ground. To him, the vampire moved in slow motion. This was too easy. The vampire's raging bloodlust made him rush in like a mindless animal.

Reece, standing firm, allowed Farouq to commit everything to his attack. At the last possible second, Reece pulled back his left foot, turning on his right, letting Farouq pass by. He was the matador taunting the bull. Reece threw a strong right hand into the vampire's chin as he passed, a sucker punch adding injury to insult.

The surprise and force was enough to make Farouq lose his footing and, with great momentum, skid across the floor coming to a violent stop against the concrete wall of the cell.

Reece regrouped. That wasn't what he'd hoped for. He'd hoped for an explosion of dust, just like when Sid hit them. Farouq wasn't moving, but Reece began to doubt himself. What if his experiments hadn't worked? Those weeks of agony, testing on himself for nothing...No, he hadn't connected properly; he couldn't have done. He'd seen Sid land shots without a fatal blow. He took a deep breath, trying to rein in his emotions.

He readied himself once more while Farouq shakily made it to his feet. He'd rocked the vampire, and it brought renewed confidence. He started to believe again. Reece sprinted the few steps to where Farouq had one hand on the wall, recuperating, and drove his knee into the side of the vampires head. The force smashed Farouq into the wall, his head bouncing off the concrete before he slumped into Reece, who took the opportunity to grab his head and drop elbows into his temple, taking him to the floor.

Reece straddled him and rained right hands down on the near-unconscious vampire. He had power, awesome power, but it wasn't enough to destroy wave upon wave of vampires like Sid could. He continued to drive his fist home, fuelled by the anger that his experiments and the endless days in the lab had been in vain. Tears streamed down his cheeks. "Weeks of work for nothing!"

Reece intended to keep punching until he could see brain.

Farouq, his face a mass of blood and exposed bone, suddenly caught Reece's hand in a vice-like grip and started to laugh, gurgling the blood that had found its way down his throat. "Things not going according to plan?"

Reece dropped a left hand, but that was caught just like the right, and Farouq drove his hips upwards, flinging Reece over his head. When Reece hit the floor, Farouq was above him crushing his stomach with his foot. Reece's organs screamed for relief.

"Did you really think you could take me?"

Through gritted teeth, Reece managed "Did you really think I'd have it any other way?"

Farouq lifted his foot to bring it down on Reece's head. As the foot descended, Reece screamed, "LET THERE BE LIGHT!" and slats in the metal roof opened, pouring daylight into the room like molten lava, searing and burning the vampire. The foot came down, but without force. The vampire had crumpled into dust all the way to the kneecap before his foot reached his target's head.

Reece lay panting on the floor. The voice-activated shutters had worked. He'd been a second from death, but that didn't bother him. Unravelling the mystery of how Bolton Bitter had given the men from Middlesbrough superpowers and harnessing it was the only thing that mattered in his tortured existence. The mystery was sending him insane, and he wasn't of sound mind to begin with. He started to cry harder, and the frustration brought forth a torrent. He pulled at his hair and writhed on the floor. Sid Tillsley had been the object of his torment for the last year, and he continued to haunt Reece from the grave. What was his secret?

14

Sheffield is the latest city to become a victim of a terrorist attack. Thirty-five were killed at The Garibaldi nightclub in the early hours of this morning. The club did not heed advice from local councillors and the club's CCTV cameras were not recording at the time. South Yorkshire Police are appealing for any witnesses to come forward.
—The Sheffield Standard

DAN SHIRE PUT THE KETTLE ON TO BOIL. He'd arranged all the furniture in his office into a circle and was almost ready for the next group. He looked down the list of Nazis, fascists, bigots, sociopaths, and...Sid Steely.

A smile cracked the corner of his mouth. There was no chance he'd be back, not after he literally ran out of the last session. In all his years as a councillor and his entire life as a gay man, Dan had never met anyone quite like Sid. Until meeting Sid, he'd never experienced the phobia part of homophobia in its purest, truest form.

It was surprising that a lot of men who came here didn't care that Dan was gay in the same way they didn't care that John who ran the anti-racism sessions was black. Some people came here because of gang and hooligan culture. Others were here because they harboured gay feelings. Were they here because they feared homosexuals? No. They were here because they feared other's views on homosexuality.

There was only one man who feared homosexuality's very essence and that was Sid Steely. The other thing that set Sid apart was that he wasn't here because the courts made him; he'd volunteered.

Sid was a monster the rest of the skinheads feared. Even though, by all accounts, he'd brought destruction to the neighbourhood through violence, drink-driving and antisocial behaviour, Dan could sense the child-like innocence in him. It wasn't evil that drove Sid's actions, it was stupidity.

Dan looked at his watch. They were all late, as usual. He wouldn't be surprised if some of them forgot for this was a particularly late session. Dan was proved wrong when the skinheads, forced to come here for part of their prison parole, trudged in, including one with a bandage around his jaw from last week's encounter with Sid. Dan went to shut the door and was shocked to see a man-mountain filling it. He suppressed the smile at the unexpectedness of it all.

"Sid, I didn't think you'd be joining us, today."

Sid didn't say a word or even acknowledge Dan's existence, but he took a seat while Dan made the tea.

"Good to see you all here, gentlemen, and on this late session too. We made good progress last week, with only a few minor mishaps." Dan saw Nigel rub his bandaged jaw. "Can we go round the circle as usual? Sid, can you start us off, please?"

Dan didn't expect anything from Sid, who sat sulking with his arms crossed, facing away from the group, but was surprised when he piped up, if grumpily, and said, "My name's Sid, and I can't stand *them lot*."

"Now, Sid, we've been through this before. 'I'm homophobic' are the words you're looking for. Will you please start again?"

"Fook off." Sid crossed his arms tighter.

"Sid, we're all in this together. All these men suffer the same issues. You did well last session, with the exception of your little fracas with Nigel." Nigel didn't look too convinced that a knockout punch classed as a *fracas*. "Together, we can work this out and reintegrate you back into society."

Sid finally unclasped his arms. "Every fooker is trying to change me. I'm reet as I am."

A general murmur of agreement went around the group.

"All the others are here as part of their parole. You signed up out of your own free will. So why are you here?" asked Dan.

"The bleedin' missus made me come here."

The other men shook their heads in disgust.

"And why did you agree to it?" asked Dan.

"She's got massive jugs." Sid held up his hands, his palms facing heaven, his bouncing movement indicating great weight.

"I see."

"Your missus made ya?" said one of the skinheads, mockingly.

"Yeah, what the fook is it to you?"

"She some sort of fag hag or summat?" asked the same skinhead who was farthest away from Sid's right hand, and closest to the door.

"Cool it, all of you," said Dan, sensing the tense atmosphere.

"What's a fag hag?" asked Sid, getting his tongue around the strange word.

"A woman who loves queers."

"What was that, Ron?" asked Dan.

The skinhead raised his eyes. "A woman who likes homosexual men."

"That's better." Dan gave a righteous nod.

"What're ya all talking about?" said Sid. "Women and *them lot* can't love each other. *Them lot* like...erm...*them lot*, don't they?"

"Women and gay men have an affinity towards each other," said Dan. "They feel comfortable around each other. There's no sexual tension."

"Eh?" asked Sid.

"Gay men don't try to have sex with them," Dan simplified.

"Why not? If the women are all over them, then they'll be on to a winner!"

"But, Sid, if you're gay, you won't want to have sex with a woman."

"Oh yeah...they're *them lot*."

"Maybe that's why Garforth got into the bumming?" offered the broken-jawed skinhead before entering the foetal position, just in case.

"You might be right, lad. Maybe he took one to give many. He's always been a clever one, has our Brian."

"The important thing here, gentlemen," said Dan, "is that it really doesn't matter if Brian's gay, bi, or straight. He's a human being and his sexuality makes no difference."

"Bi?" asked the big man.

"Bisexual people are sexually attracted to both males and females," said Dan.

"Are they stupid or summat? Canna they make their minds up?"

"No, they just find both attractive. Does it really matter, Sid?"

"This is fooking confusing, this. Life is so much simpler if you just find a lass with a cracking set of jugs and then squeeze them." He demonstrated the concept by sexually abusing the atmosphere in front of him.

"What about chick boys?" asked another skinhead, amused at Sid's philosophical dilemma.

"Eh?"

The skinhead explained, "You go over to Thailand and some birds have got great jugs. They've also got the ol' meat and veg' hanging between their legs."

"*Eh?*"

"Tits and a cock, mate."

Sid shook his head. "Nah, mon, that's just nonsense. It's tits OR a cock," he lectured. "You need your head examined, pal. Tits OR a cock," he repeated, clarifying it to himself.

"He's right, Sid," said Dan.

Sid wagged a finger. "No, he ain't."

"Have you heard the term 'hermaphrodite?'"

"Of course I fooking haven't."

"Biologically, a hermaphrodite is born with both male and female reproductive organs. It's rare in humans, but the phenomenon is common in the animal kingdom. Most slugs and snails have both sex organs."

"Slugs ain't got tits, dickhead."

Dan tried not to laugh. "Some people, though, Sid, feel they are born into the wrong body. They are born a man, but they feel that they are a woman on the inside."

"*Them lot?*"

"Not necessarily. I'm a man, and I like being a man; it just so happens

I'm attracted to men. Some people don't feel comfortable being a man and end up having a sex change."

"Aye," said one of the skinheads, "but some have the tit job and keep the cock."

"Fooking 'ell," said Sid, his head falling into his hands, "why can't people just keep things bloody simple?"

"Why does it matter, Sid? Why can't people just do what they want? It doesn't hurt you, does it?"

"My best friend bummed a man," he mumbled through his hands.

"So? There must've been something that happened to you before Brian's incident. You were homophobic before your friend's encounter, weren't you?"

Sid sat up straight. "I told you. I was born up North."

"And I told you that I was born in Leeds."

"Maybe that ain't north enough."

Dan changed tact after reaching a brick wall. "Your partner must think you have a problem if she made you sign up for this programme."

Sid said to one of the skinheads, "I guess she must be one of them 'fag bags' you were talking about."

"It's 'fag hag,' Sid," said Dan sternly, "and it's an offensive term, so please, for the sake of your improvement and the sake of these classes, don't use it."

Sid shrugged his shoulders. "No bother."

Dan was completely intrigued by what drove this man. *No bother.* He didn't mean to be offensive. He never tried to be. He just was, and it was through lack of education. Dan had to get to the bottom of what caused this man's genuine phobia. "Why does your partner want you to become more tolerant of gay men?"

"Awwww, she's trying to change fooking everything about me! She's got me quitting the booze, the fags, everything. She wants to turn me into, what was it again? Ah yeah, 'a decent man,' or some bollocks like that."

Dan sat on the edge of his chair. He sensed Sid's frustrations. "And why are you agreeing to it?"

"If Brian Garforth can be turned, any fooker can. My pub is now one of your—*you know*—bars, and my best friend is a *them lot*. I've had no luck with the birds for nigh on two fooking years, so now I've found one, I'm gonna fooking keep her...and she's got wazza jugs."

It wasn't the most noble of reasons, but it was a reason, nonetheless. Dan continued. "You're making so much progress. When you started here, you passed out when you realised the chair covers were pink. Once we pin down what kick-started your homophobia, we can heal the scars. We can make you a better person, and one your fiancée will be proud of."

"But, my best friend bummed a man."

Dan looked him in the eye. "And soon, you'll realise that it doesn't matter."

Sid broke the stare quickly. "Look, can't you just say I've passed the exam or whatever it is I have to do to prove I'm not against the bumming, and then, I'll be out of ya hair?"

"There's no exam, Sid. This is for you own good. Wouldn't your life be easier if you weren't affected by homosexual society? Look back through your life, aren't there times you regret? Things that you wished never happened?"

SID RECOUNTED HIS LIFE, which wasn't something he often did. The booze ensured most of his life was a blur. Most people would have regretted these "lost years," but Sid didn't. He was pretty certain he had a bloody brilliant time. Since he'd met the missus, he'd been introduced to, what she would consider the "normal" people of society, and Sid had come to the conclusion that they were all fooking boring.

"You got anything?" asked Dan.

"Eh? Oh, hang on. I've only just started thinking."

Over the last few months he'd got into a considerable amount of shit for punching *them lot*. It wasn't his fault that the vampire bastards all happened to be *them lot*, and it certainly wasn't his fault they'd always started playing silly buggers. It all stemmed back to that dogging outing, where two of the fookers had tried it on with him. One of them had got a big right hand, and it had all kicked off after that. Maybe if he wasn't— what was the word? Hobofoamic?—maybe he would have just given the lad a kick in the knackers and had done with it. His life really would certainly be a lot easier now.

"I think you're right, lad...eh?" His head darted to the empty chairs. "Where is everyone?"

"They left twenty minutes ago. We tried to get your attention, but you were in some sort of trance. It was quite bizarre."

"Aye, I don't often get into the thinking."

"And what did you find?" asked Dan.

"I think you're right. My life would be a lot easier if I wasn't so jumpy around *them lot*."

Dan smiled. "You really are making progress. Still, there's much to do. Have a think about your past life over the next few days. When we find out what caused all this, you'll be all but cured, and I bet your missus will give you an extra well done when you get home."

Dan gave Sid a wink, and Sid didn't even knock him out.

15

A Middlesbrough Bus Company has apologised to residents of the Smithson Estate whose motor vehicles were subject to vandalism caused by one of their drivers. An individual has been dismissed, but no charges have been pressed by the Cleveland Police.
—*A statement from "'Boro On The Buses"*

HARRY DEAN PARKED OUTSIDE The First Swallow of Summer and made sure he locked the car before going inside. He wasn't surprised to see the place hadn't changed since it was blown to pieces in a gunfight with Gunnar Ivansey and his followers. The same faces sat near the portable TV. The men were jaundiced, weak, and close to death, but they still puffed away on cigarettes and hammered down the booze. Apart from watching *Who Wants to Be a Millionaire?* it looked like bliss.

The sound of a breaking pint glass drew his attention to Kevin Ackroyd, the landlord, whose startled stare and ridiculous pink outfit were priceless. "What are you doing here?"

Harry was probably the last person the fat, greedy landlord wanted to see. He probably thought he was here to shut him down or kill him for real rather than faking it like he did last time.

Brian Garforth and Arthur Peasley were draped over the bar, bloodshot eyes and the occasional hiccup told Harry they'd been on a good session. Arthur was the spitting image of Borg's accomplice who had sung to the audience at the concert and been involved with the massacre at the nightclub a few days ago. Arthur had to know something.

"What are you doing here?" asked the landlord again, beads of sweat shining off his greasy, mirrored dome.

"Don't worry, your pub is safe."

Kevin breathed a sigh of relief. "Thank fook for that, like. Things have been bad enough."

Harry walked over to Arthur and Brian and laid a hand on each of their shoulders. "Maybe I can help the local economy with a pint for me, these two gents, and one for yourself."

"Coming right up, sir," said the suddenly polite barman.

"Send some vodka this way too. Make it a double." Harry pulled up a barstool and took a seat next to the lads. "How you holding up?" He hadn't made contact since he'd faked their deaths. He made sure Peterson, Sanderson's favoured agent, kept tabs on them since his actions wouldn't be under such intense scrutiny. Only Peterson knew these men were still alive, and if the Coalition discovered they'd both lied, they'd all be dead.

"Eh'up, Harry," said Brian. "Not so bad, really, pal. Survivin'."

"And you, Arthur?"

Arthur merely shrugged. "Cheers for the beer."

"No Sid?" said Harry, looking around.

Brian snorted. "If you're wanting him to smack vampires for ya, you're out of luck, pal, and there ain't nowt you can offer him to make him start, either. Booze, benefits, and tabs ain't his thing anymore. Not now some bitch is pulling the strings. You'll have to do it without him."

Harry was unaware Sid had moved in with a woman. He was certainly a sly one and difficult to track for such a big, recognisable man. It was good information to have. Sid could only be called upon under the direst of circumstances, and Harry's job was to ensure it never came to that.

"Aye, the missus controls him," said Kev, before pretending to whisper behind his hand, "And he canna stand the company of *them lot.*" He pointed, unsubtly, at Brian.

"You fat arsehole! How—"

Harry interrupted. "I'm here to see Arthur, actually."

"Yeah?" said the beautiful man with a questioning look, eyebrows rising above his shades.

Harry picked a printout of Borg's accomplice from the inside of his jacket and presented it to Arthur. "Do you know this...I'll be honest, I don't know if he's a vampire or a man."

Arthur took the sheet of paper, lifted his shades, and sat motionless, hypnotised by the photo.

"I'll take that as a yes."

Brian leant across and peered over Arthur's shoulder to have a look. "Looks like a fat version of you, mate."

"That's what I thought when I saw it," said Harry. "You know him, Arthur?"

"When was this taken?" Arthur managed weakly.

"Less than a week ago. It was taken at that concert where a bunch of school kids with automatic weapons blew it to shit. And he was part of the massacre at that Sheffield nightclub a couple of nights ago."

"It was on the news about that concert thing," said Kev. "Crazy little bastards killed the band and half the audience. It's them fooking computer games that makes them do that sort of shit."

Harry laughed but not with mirth. "Not this time. It was vampires, lots of them. We covered it up with the school-kid story."

"Bollocks. It were computer games, drugs, and fooking immigrants," said the barman righteously, bringing the drinks over.

Harry didn't care what Kev thought. He grabbed the vodka, hammered it back, and washed it down with the ale. "Same again."

"Was Borg Hemsman one of the vampires?" asked Arthur.

"Yeah, but how do you know that name?" Harry looked desperately at the optic, which bubbled as Kev dispensed some more liquor.

"Oh, man," said Arthur, holding the photo to his chest.

"What is it?" asked Harry.

"That's my son."

"I ain't got time for bullshit," said Harry, grabbing the vodka off Kev.

Arthur sighed, staring at the photo. A tear dropped from his cheek and landed in his empty pint glass. He nodded towards it and gave it to Kev before unleashing the greatest love story never told: "I was banging a hot vampire chick a few months back and got her preggers." Harry didn't interrupt, but Arthur held up his hands and said, "I know, I should have pulled out, but shit happens."

"You can't get a vampire pregnant!"

"And Sid can't kill vampires and my jizz doesn't make them explode, blah-di-fooking-blah," said Brian.

Harry nodded. "Fair play. What has Borg Hemsman got to do with any of this?"

"He's the grandfather."

"Lucia's the mother!" Harry pulled off his flat cap and rubbed his hands across his face and scalp. He was tired. This was a game that needed a young man's body and an old man's head.

"Was, man. Was. Kev, where's that beer?" The beer was on the bar before he finished the sentence and Arthur downed a medicinal half pint. "She died giving birth to my son."

Harry shook his head. This was big news for the Coalition, but he couldn't relay any of it back to them. "Wait a minute, the guy in the picture is in his twenties."

"A vampire should give birth after two years, I think, although I never really listened to Lucia 'cos she was always nagging. She dropped in six months and died during the birth. The baby came out perfect, though. He's the most beautiful thing I've ever seen."

Harry stubbed his finger on the photo. "He can't have grown that quickly, surely?"

"I don't know. It's not like you've anything to compare him to, is there? He's one of a kind, completely unique in every way." Arthur smiled at the picture. "He's beautiful." The smile faded as darker thoughts pushed their way to the forefront of his mind. "Has he...killed?"

"To be honest, I don't know. He didn't kill anyone at the concert, but he did sing a song, which is rather odd. The vampires killed enough innocent people to make up for it, and he did nothing to stop them. There was only him and one other at the nightclub in Sheffield, a tough, nasty piece of work named Viralli who used to work for the Coalition. Viralli's joined Borg's vampire faction. They're trying to end the Agreement."

Arthur nodded. "He doesn't know any better. Lucia's papa took him and swore to turn him against me. I guess he thinks we're dead now."

Harry nodded. "That should be the case, yeah."

"We ran into a vampire the other day," said Brian, trying to plug the awkward silence that followed.

"Where?" asked Harry quickly.

"He was walking out of The Fat Cat, a boozer just outside the Smithson Estate, and Sid ran him over in the bus he drives. We didn't have time to ask questions, but Sid made sure whatever he was up to, he wouldn't do again." Brian indicated with a wave of a fist.

"He wasn't with the Coalition, that's for certain," said Harry. "The only thing up here is you guys and the chemical works that was razed to the ground a few months back." Harry was suffering from information overload. Making sense of it all was a job for a sober man.

Suddenly, Arthur jumped off his chair and unleashed a sidekick into the air. "We need to get Sid back so we can go kick the shit out of Lucia's papa and go get my boy."

"Sounds like a plan," said Harry. "You got any idea where Borg is?" he asked hopefully.

"None at all. Lucia didn't keep that sort of information lying around. She didn't really talk about her papa. Can I keep this?" asked Arthur, holding up the picture.

"'Course." Harry deliberated before asking the stupid question: "I've gotta say, your boy looks remarkably like Elvis in his later years, and...come to mention it...so do you."

The whole pub laughed.

"That's a bit obvious, ain't it?" said Arthur. "Who do you think his other grandpappy is?"

"You're...Elvis's son?" said an unbelieving Coalition agent to Arthur.

"Ain't that obvious?" asked Brian.

"Well..." said Harry, weighing it up. "No. No, it isn't. I mean you look a bit like him, and...but...no, no, it ain't."

"I think most people worked it out, like, or at least they should've done unless they're idiots," said Brian. "There're enough bloody clues, you know, alluding to all the songs, yet never infringing copyright."

Arthur unleashed a barrage of karate punches. "What does that look like to you?"

"It looks like you know karate?" said Harry.

"I knew this from birth, man."

Harry shrugged. "Elvis wasn't even that good at karate."

"He didn't train hard because he didn't need to. My papa's karate was ingrained in his soul like mine is and like my son's will be."

"I guess you do look a bit like him, but—" Harry stopped. Arthur had burst into song. Harry sat enchanted by the deep, masculine tones washing over him, taking him on a ride of melodious majesty. Harry applauded. "That was beautiful."

Arthur snapped a knee back and forth. "I know, baby."

"How did you end up in Middlesbrough?" Harry sat forward on his stool, intrigued.

"I've always lived in Middlesbrough."

"But Elvis never visited the UK."

The boys shared quizzical looks. "What're you talking about?" said Brian.

"Elvis never visited the UK. OK, he landed in Scotland for about two hours..." said Harry.

"Think you've put a few too many of them voddies away, son," said Brian.

"Not enough more like." He passed his glass to Kev who flashed a winning smile before adding a quadruple measure. "So you're saying Elvis flew to Middlesbrough to knock up Mrs Peasley without anyone else knowing?"

"No, it was a chance encounter in Blackpool that led to sweet love. Blackpool is England's Memphis, baby. That's where the greatest musicians congregate for beautiful summers of music. Elvis Peasley, The Duke of Rock 'n' Roll played Blackpool Pier for thirty-seven summers straight before his demise." Arthur looked at his fists. "These ain't normal genes, baby. My son has the genes of a man who was almost a god, and they've been combined with an immortal, loving, beautiful vampire. Man, my son's gonna be one devil with the ladies."

"So your father...was an Elvis *impersonator*?"

The atmosphere turned so cold, frost appeared on the insides of the pub windows. "The question is," said Arthur. "Who was impersonating who?"

Harry wisely changed the subject. "He's a little overweight."

"Hey, my daddy liked a burger, but he still got the ladies."

All the men nodded in agreement.

Harry considered his next move. This was all useful information in his search for Borg Hemsman and...an Elvis impersonator's grandson.

"We'll come with you. We can help get my son back," said Arthur.

"You're dead, remember," said Harry.

"So? I can still kick ass!" Kicks like lightning seared the air.

"You're dead because I killed you. If you turn up alive, then guess what happens to me?" Harry ran a finger over his throat.

"So you're gonna do nowt?" asked Brian.

"No, I'm going to find Borg Hemsman, put a bullet in his brain, and then cut his damned head off."

"And my son?" asked Arthur.

"Arthur, I ain't gonna bullshit you, it all depends what side he's on. The Agreement is on a knife-edge, and the vampires are pushing the boundaries every day. It's only a matter of time before they gather enough followers to try and take over the country. If your son is on the wrong side, what choice do I have?"

16

"It's the same bloke. The fat bloke in the white suit who killed The Quest was at that nightclub in Sheffield. I saw his picture on the Internet. Looks like a fat Shakin' Stevens, he does. Do you know why he's kicking the shit out of the place? No, 'course you don't. You reporters are stupid. It's the immigrants. He's had enough of the immigrants taking our jobs."

—Someone's gran, Middlesbrough

ING LAY MOPING on his bed, reading through the Sunday papers. He
as comfort eating too, and who could blame him after the traumatic
perience a couple of nights ago. His duvet now contained more potato
ips than it did cotton. His picture was splattered over the tabloid
ess, and not for the right reasons. He wanted to hit the papers, sure,
t for his talent and his extraordinary ability to wow the crowds, not
cause he'd been part of a massacre ending in the deaths of thirty-five
man clubbers. He ignored his grandpappy walking into his bedroom
d stuffed his mouth with a custard donut instead.

"Are you still sulking, King?"

"I ain't sulking," said King sulkily.

"Really? One thing you certainly aren't doing is exercising. You need
You haven't been blessed with the vampire's body."

"How fucking dare you, man!" said the portly prima donna, grabbing at
man tits. "You never let me go anywhere, so how can I burn off the grub?"

'You could go for a run around the grounds. You could eat less."

'I get lightheaded if I don't eat. And, anyway, I'm still mad at you for
ding me out with that crazed lunatic Viralli. He's a fucking psycho,
n. Have you seen this?" He held up the front page.

'The Wonder of Food.' I don't get it," said Borg.

Elvis Presley sung 'The Wonder of You.'"

And you look a little like a fat Elvis." Borg laughed. "The humans are
e clever with their plays on words, aren't they?"

Clever? *Clever*? Read this one," he said, holding up another.

'A Big Hunk O' Flab?'"

Elvis sung 'A Big Hunk O' Love.'" King ignored Borg's amusement.

ry single paper seems to have forgotten it was that crazy-assed
li who did all the killing. I was trying to calm him down. The entire
an population of the UK thinks I'm a murderer!"

"We can bring down the undead sons of bitches, man. You ca pleaded Arthur.

"I kept you alive for a reason. I was ordered to kill you all and place to the ground, but after seeing you boys fight Gunnar Iv his followers, it was obvious what Sanderson saw in you."

"Where is he? He was a good bloke, he was," said Brian.

"Don't know, but I fear the worst. I would've heard from hin he was still alive. And, if I'm right, and he is dead, he was stal back because there was no one good enough to take him down boys need to do now is prove us both right. I hope I never ne just in case, get Sid back on side."

"Easier said than done, mon," said Brian.

"We'll do it for my son," said Arthur.

Harry nodded, turned, and left them to their beers. He was that the local kids hadn't debadged his car. It had taken all h to leave the pub and its top-shelf spirits. He took stock of t once inside his car, reached into the glove box, pulled ou vodka, and took far too big a swig of it.

It was time to head to Sheffield, the last known locatiot son. The Coalition had sent him all over the country, and th chase was pointless. If he ever found Borg, he didn't have bring him down. How had Sanderson lasted so long in this l took another shot of spirit to toast his old friend, and then a hell of it. Arthur and Brian had given him nothing. He hac backup, and no clue. All he had were nightmares waiting for closed his eyes.

"And a fat one, at that."

King ripped up the paper in anger, but it took him a couple of attempts, which ruined the effect. "It's out of order, man. You need to discipline that dog of yours."

"Viralli was defending your honour, King. The humans thoroughly disrespected you and refused to listen to you. He merely acquired their attention." His wry smile disappeared. "Remember, we're at war. Look how they treated you then, and look how they treat you in the papers. They hate you. *We* will always stand by your side."

"Stand by my side? Vampires hate me just as much. No one cares about me. Fuck this shit. I'm going out." King began the arduous task of rolling off the bed.

"You can't go out. It's still daylight."

King took a breather at the edge of the bed. "Well, I'm a mighty daywalker aren't I?" He rocked backwards and forwards a couple of times, and when he'd gathered enough momentum, made it to his feet.

"No one will be able to protect you." A hand came down on King's shoulder.

"And no one wants to, man! No one wants to!" King shrugged off the hand and stormed (very slowly) out of his bedroom, leaving Borg alone with his thoughts. A moment later, Viralli entered.

"You tried, sir."

"What else can I do?" Borg rubbed the back of his neck with both hands, exasperated. "I've tried to bring him into the fold. I've tried to involve him in the plight of our people, but he doesn't want to know. He wants the acceptance of mankind, and that is the one thing I can't allow in his life."

"There isn't much more you can do. You've turned mankind against him, and he hasn't reacted the way we expected. You hoped their animosity would cause him to bite back, but there is not an ounce of aggression in the boy. Forgive me, sir, but he is useless. And, he's bringing the morale of the troops down. You can't be seen to pander to his whim."

Borg closed his eyes. "You're right."

"The vampire race comes first. You taught me that."

Borg nodded slowly. "Is everyone in position?"

"Just give the word."

CAROLINE WASN'T LISTENING to the debate flying around the table. During the last week, there had been an attack every night, and each time, it'd stretched the Coalition's forces that much further. What scared the Coalition most was that last night nothing happened.

Nothing at all.

Flying around the table was pure speculation, and Caroline couldn't be bothered with it. Charles was more outspoken than usual, trying to put on a cool air, but his fat, flustered face told the true story. "Our spies haven't reported anything that indicates this huge offensive you've manifested out of nothing more than pessimism."

"They are no longer *our* spies," shouted Bwogi with a rare show of fire. "We sent vampires to infiltrate Borg's ranks, and now, they follow him. We can't share any information with anyone not sitting in this room for fear of it being leaked. It's a miracle that Haemo isn't on the front pages."

Unsurprisingly, Charles retaliated with sarcasm. "So what do you suggest, Great Leader?"

Augustus butted in. "I suggest we get out of here."

"Leave the Coalition headquarters?" said Charles slowly. He chuckled as he made eye contact with all the other councillors. "Nothing can infiltrate our building. Even if the vampire brought nuclear weapons to the fight, they wouldn't be able to touch us in here," he boasted.

Caroline decided to nip any more worthless rumour in the bud. "We can't run, not yet. Would you like to admit to the Prime Minister we've lost complete control?"

Augustus laughed heartily, shaking his head. "The Prime Minister, bless his soul, isn't the kind of man who'll disembowel you with a blunt knife. Borg Hemsman is. I don't want to think about what he'd do to us if he found out about Haemo. Fuck the Prime Minister."

"Don't underestimate what this government can do," warned Caroline with the wag of a finger. "We can't give up our position until Haemo is launched."

Bwogi nodded fervently. "How long before we can release it into the atmosphere?"

"Two days," said Rempstone, spinning a pencil between his fingers. "Garendon is performing the finishing touches to the delivery system, and then, it's just a case of charging the tanks before releasing the gas into every major city in the UK. Once Garendon gives us the nod, we're set to go."

"Excellent. Then why is everyone so glum?" Caroline asked.

"Have you seen the news lately?" asked Charles, unimpressed with her newfound optimism.

"Haemo will quell the hordes," she said calmly. "We stick to the plan. If vampirism reaches the public, then it's reported as a disease, and we, councillors, have the cure. Some eyewitnesses recounting tales of their loved ones turning in front of their eyes will do the trick."

"That simple, huh?" asked Augustus, shaking his head.

"Why shouldn't it be?" she challenged.

"I'll ask you again," said Charles. "Have you seen the news?"

Bwogi chewed at his nails. "Both sides are taking casualties out there. If Haemo doesn't work or the vampires get wind of it and the locations of the plants, this war will never end."

Caroline raised her eyes at the pessimism. "We'll find out in two days, won't we?"

"If we last two days," said Augustus.

"What do you mean?" asked Charles. "I told you this place is impenetrable."

Rempstone nodded his agreement.

"I'm starting to feel claustrophobic in this basement," said Augustus, looking at the exit.

"We stay until Haemo is released," said Caroline firmly. "Anyone who leaves will be hunted down as a traitor."

"No one can leave, anyway," whispered Bwogi.

"What are you talking about? Speak up," barked Augustus.

"The Haemo launch requires thirteen members of the Coalition to activate it. Majority rules." The African vampire kept his eyes firmly on the table in front of him, not daring to look up.

"When was this little failsafe introduced?" asked Augustus, his fangs slowly descending.

Caroline took over, tired of Bwogi's weakness. "When the Haemo project was re-initiated. I asked Sebastian to install it, which he agreed to before his unfortunate demise." The failsafe wasn't ideal. However, it was the only way she could manipulate Bwogi into re-initiating the project.

"And why weren't we consulted?" asked Charles, redder than usual.

"To initiate Haemo, we have to be utterly sure as a council," replied Bwogi weakly.

"And let me guess; we can only start the system from here?" said Augustus.

"Hindsight is a wonderful thing," said Caroline.

KING WALKED ALONE in the cold dawn of the day. This was his time since vampires couldn't walk here. This was where he came to think. It wasn't what he'd call "alone time;" every minute of the day was saturated with loneliness. No, he called this his quiet time.

His grandpappy lived on a beautiful estate. The manor house was set in acres of rolling hillside, deep in the Peak District National Park. It was rare that a walker would venture this far. It was even rarer they'd leave.

Every day, he found the trip down to the lake a more tiresome journey. If truth be told, it was getting hard to be arsed to walk at all. Everyone was waiting for some magical metamorphosis like some beautiful butterfly, hoping he'd transform into a dragon, one who breathed fire and brought terror to the human race. King knew it wasn't going to happen. He was slowing down. Something wasn't right and there was no one to help him. The only explanation he could come up with was that he was dying.

He unwrapped a cheeseburger and was disappointed to find it cold. He wolfed it down regardless, because he needed the energy. He had enough cheeseburgers to keep him going throughout the day. He'd sit here until the sun went down. Tears drenching his cheeks. His momma wouldn't have wanted this for him. He was so lonely.

17

Last night saw a respite in the violence that's haunted the UK over the last couple of weeks. The UK has been subjected to the highest rise in violent crime, including multiple homicides since records began. Criminologists remain baffled.

—Central Today

BRIAN GARFORTH AND ARTHUR PEASLEY didn't think they were in Sunderland. In fact, they weren't too sure they were anywhere near Earth. The boys were convinced that they were smack bang in the middle of an episode of *The Twilight Zone*, and a weird one at that.

They sauntered down from their reconnaissance positions to take a closer look. Shopping malls weren't familiar territory for the two heroes, or for any other red-blooded male for that matter. Shopping malls caused discomfort to any man over the age of eighteen. Younger lads got their thrills chasing the armies of teenage girls that spent the maximum time and the minimum amount of money in the vast corridors of these gigantic centres that had popped up across the land. Even though shopping malls were a relatively modern invention, the hatred harboured by modern man for these oestrogen-filled bastions of boredom ran deep.

Brian and Arthur wanted to get out of this place—fast—but first, they had to make contact with Sid. The lads heard it on the grapevine that Sid had landed a new job after being sacked as a bus driver. They'd heard rumours of his new position, and they'd expected them to be nothing more than that—rumours.

"That can't be him," said Brian.

"There's only one way to find out."

"Two for one on all Buddy Bear Burgers! Two for one!" came the unmistakable, deep roar of the former vampire hunter.

"Buddy Bear Burgers?" asked Brian.

"Buddy Bear Burgers," confirmed Arthur.

In some ways, Sid was one of the most qualified men to play Buddy the Bear for he was built like a grizzly. However, like a grizzly, it was best he didn't work with children.

Sid looked quite snug in his big, orange, furry outfit. It was obvious it was Sid, as the bear had all the mannerisms of a Tillsley. The shoulders of the outfit were taut, stretched by the monster contained within. A child ran up to the bear, ready to be enthralled by Buddy's famously charming personality, but quickly ran away in tears; the bear misjudging his audience with a filthy joke. The bear was paying special attention to the ladies, and Brian was impressed how Buddy's smiling face managed to give the impression of perving.

"Two for one on all Buddy...fook it."

Buddy the Bear gave up the ghost and took a seat outside one of the shops. He then set a bad example to the children of Sunderland Shopping Mall by lighting up a cigarette.

It was quite a feat, lighting up a tab while wearing giant, furry gloves. Sid managed to get a lit cigarette into Buddy's mouth and into his own mouth with some twisting and some turning.

"Let's go see him," said Arthur.

"Aye," said Brian, and they walked over to the offensive bear, now the subject of a lot of outraged remarks from shoppers walking past.

"Now then, Sid," said Brian.

"What the fook do you want?" Buddy patted down his cute little dungarees looking for more cigs.

"I need your help, man," said Arthur.

"What can I do for ya, mate?" said Buddy, happy to talk his hetero friend.

Brian let it go. If Arthur could get through to him, it was for the greater good.

"Harry Dean stopped by The Miner's the other day," said Arthur.

"Who's Harry Dean?"

"The bloke who got us out of all that vampire bollocks," said Brian.

"Oh aye, what did he want?" said Buddy to Arthur, ignoring Brian.

"He found my son. My poor son ain't a human or a vampire, and he's fell in with a real bad crowd. He was with them sons of bitches who attacked that concert. You might have seen him on the news. I think he may have killed some people."

"That's some bad shit, lad," said Buddy sympathetically.

Arthur took a seat next to the giant orange bear and grabbed a paw in both hands. "You need to help me get him back. We can't do it on our own."

Buddy considered it. "I get married soon, pal. I can't let anything get in the way of that. I'm sorry. She came this close," he indicated with his paws, "to calling the whole thing off when I lost me job as a bus driver, which was 'cos of *that* fooker mincing about on the bus."

"Shurrup, mon," said Brian. "You chased down a vampire and fooking beat the shit out of him in front of a bus full of passengers. That's why you got sacked."

Buddy waved him away with his paw. "Look, I was lucky to get this gig, and it's easy money. Plus, I get to eat the odd burger here and there, which is a fooking luxury now the missus has me on rabbit food." Buddy grabbed a handful of orange belly fur. "She's got me going to fooking Diet Darlings, you know?"

"Fook off!" said Brian, laughing out loud.

"If I don't drop down to twenty-two stone, she ain't gonna marry me, and you know what that means: No. Fucking. Shag." The word "shag" echoed around the mall. More children cried.

"You can't seriously be considering marrying that battleaxe?" said Brian. "You want this for the rest of your life? Do you think it will be any different after you're married?"

"Maybe not, but I'll at least had a shag. If I don't turn up on me wedding day free of all my flaws, then she ain't gonna let me do her. I ain't letting that happen. Besides, it'll get me out of the way of all them vampire bastards. I ain't getting turned like you did."

"For the ten thousandth time, I haven't been fooking turned!" yelled the swordsman. "Is this what you want?" Brian pointed at the ridiculous orange suit. "Is this what you really want?"

Buddy looked at his paws. "I just want the love of a good woman."

"Well, by the sounds of it, you haven't got it."

"What d'ya mean?"

"She sounds fooking terrible!"

"She's got great tits."

"Great tits ain't everything," Brian lied, crossing his arms.

"Well, you would think that." If Buddy's eyebrow weren't sown into position, it would have lifted.

"Pack in the bollocks," said Brian, standing in front of the bear with his hands on his hips. "Your life has turned to shit since she took over, and you know it."

Most bears would have been offended, but Buddy knew it was true. He took off his little blue fez and played with it in his paws. "It's a simpler life."

"It won't be for long, man," said Arthur. "We're gonna follow Harry Dean and get my boy back. Once the bloodsuckers and that shitty council thing know we're alive, they're gonna know you are too, and you're the one they really want."

Buddy twiddled his fluffy tail. "Ah, fook."

"And another thing..." Brian was interrupted by the screams of shoppers. The lads turned to see men, women, and children stampeding towards them, away from the entrance of the shopping mall. There was no order, no humanity, just raw fear. The shoppers trampled over each other, the young and the old alike. Buddy the Bear, sitting on the bench, parted the fleeing consumers, and Arthur and Brian took refuge behind the mighty orange mountain.

"What the fook is going on?" cried Brian.

"Dunno, but it's gone fooking mental in here!" shouted Buddy. "Must be a sale on or summat. I thought the vampire bastards were nasty pieces of work, but some of the women I've seen in there...Shit the bed," he said shaking his head.

"Ah, fuck no," said Arthur, craning his neck to see farther.

"What is it?" asked Brian.

"Vampire shit," said Arthur. "What shall we do?"

"Let's get out of here," said Brian, looking around for alternative exits. "We can't get mixed up in this too soon."

"Well, I ain't losing another job, I can tell ya that," said Buddy.

"I wouldn't worry about that, man," said Arthur. "Everyone's legging it."

As the crowds began to thin, the lads could see the vampires at the far end of the building, playing with the people they'd caught.

"It could be a trap, mon," said Buddy. "They're probably trying to catch me slacking."

"You were smoking a fag and looking up lasses' skirts when we met you," said Brian. "I don't think they'd need to go to so much trouble."

Security guards were the only ones travelling towards the entrance rather than away from it. They were greeted with mocking cries from the vampires. The lads watched as their brave, futile attempts were treated with utter disdain.

"Bastards!" said Brian. "We've got to get out of here. I don't want to get caught up in this shit before we're ready."

"It's only a matter of time, baby," said Arthur. "We may as well get the practise in, now." He jumped up from the bench and whirled his fists. "There are only about a dozen of them."

"I ain't got me Cumapult with me, mate."

Buddy pulled at his fluffy ear. "I'll sort this. You lot get out of here. I canna lose another job. And Brian?"

"Yes?"

"Keep it in ya pants, ya dirty bastard."

Buddy was not a liberal bear.

18

Breaking News: Shopping centres across the UK have suffered a coordinated terrorist attack, the worst ever seen in the UK. Gunmen are still raging through centres in London, Norwich, Sunderland, Bristol, and Nottingham. Many are feared dead at each location. We'll keep you updated through the night.

—*Sky News*

GERRAINT LE BOEL laughed raucously at the approaching security guards. "Look, they're sending the cavalry!" he shouted to his brethren, who all dropped the bloody bodies they were gorging from and joined in the banter, mocking the men with helmets and batons who'd no idea of the monumental task confronting them. The handful of guards slowed their approach. They were used to twelve-year-olds stealing makeup, not the dismemberment of limbs. To their credit, they advanced.

Like the attack on the concert, the vampires were striking deep into the heart of human society. A shopping mall was a place for the family, and Borg had sent his army to cause mayhem in shopping precincts all over the country.

Each of the vampires nearly jumped for joy when they'd been chosen for the mission. This was what they'd yearned for since the Agreement had been formed. Gerraint had lived his life as a prisoner, and now, this was the first step in breaking free. Borg Hemsman was a hero of the vampire race and would put to bed the travesty Michael Vitrago had conceived. They may lose, but it was better to go out fighting.

Gerraint took one more bite of his victim's neck and drew down the life-giving blood before wiping his mouth and turning on the overweight and underpaid security of the tacky, dishevelled shopping precinct.

He had never been one to make conversation with humans. Leaping at the nearest guard, he covered the ground between them in a split second. His hand darted out, grabbing the human's throat in one hand and tearing away the baton from his pitiful grasp with the other. Gerraint had never been interested in weaponry and never bothered using it, but then, he'd never attacked a shopping mall. Today was a day for new experiences.

The vampires burst into laughter watching him attack the security guards with the baton. There was no finesse in his moves. He was a thickset vampire, relying on brute strength in battle. Normally, he'd take great delight in pulling human beings apart with his hands.

Each security guard earned a single blow from the blunt instrument and the damage was devastating, each strike accompanied with the sound of breaking bones. Blood sprayed across the floor and up the shop windows until only Gerraint stood, twirling the baton.

He turned to his amused friends and, in the process, slipped on the blood-wet tiles and fell to the floor. This brought more hysteria to the vampires, and Gerraint joined in laughing until his ribs hurt.

"It looks like you have another challenger," cried a vampire, in between fits of laughter.

Gerraint lifted his head, the blood from his victims dripping from his hair. "What is that?"

The laughter waned as the vampires considered their next opponent, looking at each other to make sure they weren't seeing things. Once more, they all burst into hysterics.

Gerraint got to his feet carefully, not wanting to slip in the pools of blood. He was utterly intrigued by the...giant orange bear, cracking its—he could only presume—knuckles. "Aren't you adorwable?" he cooed.

"Fook off," said the bear.

Gerraint struggled deciphering the thick Northeast accent mumbled through a giant fluffy bear head.

The bear pointed at the entrance where the vampires had entered. "You've played enough silly buggers for one day, and if you go now, you'll all save yourself a bust nose."

Gerraint caught the gist if not all the words. "I see. Are you security? You're a little late." The sadistic vampire gestured at the broken bodies and chuckled.

The bear shook his head. "There was no need for that, ya bastards. Look, I'm on to a nice little earner with this job, so I'll let you off if you fook off now. Otherwise..." The bear indicated his violent intent with the shake of a big right orange fist.

"Oh really? Well what would happen if I struck first?" Gerraint pounced and, with all his might, swung the baton like a baseball bat into the bear's soft stomach.

The bear didn't budge an inch. Instead, he lazily reached into his mouth, pulled out a lit cigarette, and threw it to the floor, accompanied with a puff of smoke.

There was no cool, dry-witted comeback for this mammal was not smarter than the average bear. Cool-witted comebacks didn't matter when you had a right hand like Buddy the Bear.

BUDDY LANDED a big orange haymaker, but the massive padding of the paws absorbed most of the punch before his knuckles connected with the twat vampire's jaw. There was no explosion of dust like normal, but that didn't surprise Buddy. It wasn't a clean contact, but there was a satisfying crack when the vampire's head spun round at literally breakneck speed. The vampire fell to the floor, dead weight, and out cold. Still, it would be wrong not to give him something to remember his experience at Buddy the Bear's Burger Bar, and since Buddy didn't have any more two-for-one vouchers to give away, he went with an old favourite.

The rest of the vampires winced when Buddy's big orange foot crashed into their mate's knackers. The suit took some of the power out, but it was still a good shot. Keeping the uniform on would mean he wouldn't be recognised. He'd be dead set for employee of the month. He was confident of taking these pansies without the help of Arthur's karate and Brian's bumming. They both waited on the level above, ready to jump in if he got in trouble.

"Who's next?" he said, paw out, giving the vampires the come-on with his furry fingers.

The vampires piled in and the fur flew. Buddy was an orange blur in his outfit. He'd lost a lot of fat but not much muscle, and he was fast, real fast. The loss of fat almost meant Buddy didn't need a halftime break from the scrapping. He felt almost...healthy. Not only that, the orange suit was like armour. He couldn't even feel the pansies' punches or poncy martial arts bollocks.

Three of the nine vampires were out cold after a few swings of his mighty paws. He made a mental note which vampires hadn't been given the leaving present of a kick in the knackers. Buddy was having a lot of fun. A jab here, an uppercut there, and all without being seen and plunged back into the world of vampire shit.

"I'd put that down if I were you, love," said Buddy to a tasty little blonde piece who had drawn a knife. Buddy didn't like knives, but he was very keen on breasts, and the vampire who'd drawn the knife had an exceptional pair. Why was life full of dilemmas? Did he land a stiff jab to teach her a lesson, or did he go for a cheeky grope and risk being stabbed?

Buddy the Bear was a very naughty bear, indeed.

"You bastard!" screamed the vampire, looking down in horror at Buddy's paws, which, in all fairness, were excellent support.

Without hesitation, she plunged the knife into Buddy's head. Luckily, there were no children around to see a sight that would inspire incomprehensible nightmares.

Buddy was lucky; the knife wedged itself into the strong rubber material giving Buddy's cute head its shape. Sid was inches away from losing an eye. The assaulted vampire pulled desperately at the knife while Buddy the Bear worked both paws in a squeezing motion.

"Get off me!" she yelled, not able to push the knife deeper or free herself from the molestation. The remaining vampires ran to her aid and jumped on Buddy, trying to stop his unrelenting antics.

Buddy was having a wonderful time. He didn't often get the chance to smack vampire bastards while playing with titties. Not many people did, to be fair. Vampires jumping on his back meant it was time, sadly, to let go of the wonderfully pert breasts. He let go, and the vampire hotty fell back, ripping a massive hole in Buddy's face with the knife. This weakened the outfit, and the vampires, pulling at his cute little ears, ripped the helmet clean off.

"Fook."

"Oh, no...You're...you're dead."

Buddy despaired as the lass with the norks scrambled away on the floor, desperate to get away.

"Fook!" Buddy spun around and lamped the vampire who had pulled off his bear helmet, knocking him out. Buddy threw a searching cross at another, but the little whippersnapper was following the lass with the norks towards the exit. Buddy's punch missed by a mile.

Buddy put his head in his paws. This meant vampire shit. This meant lots and *lots* of vampire shit. All this trouble of avoiding vampires to stop being turned into *them lot* was all for nothing.

This was going to ruin his chances of getting a jump for sure.

Buddy was angry. Buddy was very angry. The closest vampire bastard got a mighty kick in the bollocks. The second closest got a mighty kick in the bollocks. And Buddy was going to repeat the process until the coppers came.

"SID TILLSLEY IS ALIVE AND WELL? Now that is interesting." Borg Hemsman sat in the hall of his manor house surrounded by fifty vampires, most of them old, powerful and, most importantly, all ready to act on his command. In fact, they were desperate to act. They craved violence and would rather die than abide by the Agreement any longer. "If the hunter is alive, then my daughter's mate will be alive too." His knuckles whitened as he gripped the arms of the chair at the mere thought of Arthur Peasley.

"Are you going to tell King?" asked Viralli.

Borg had been blinded by love for his grandson and his desire to see him leading the vampire race. But, his grandson was a disgrace, and Borg knew he'd been a walking joke for the past month. No one said anything to his face out of fear and respect. It was time to cut the blood ties and put what was most important first.

"No. We have work to do," he said confidently.

A chorus of "Here! Here!" echoed around the room.

Borg stood and paced around the hall, walking amongst his brothers and sisters. "Tillsley is not our concern, either. He is but one man who will be swept aside with the ferocity of our onslaught. Tillsley's survival shows yet more weakness in the Coalition. Their own people are hiding things from them, and they have completely lost control. We control the vampire nation, now." Borg let out a grunted laugh. "Control? No. We are setting the vampire free."

A murmur of agreement travelled around the hall.

"The time is almost upon us. There are houses like this one spread across the country, and each one is ready to strike. The attacks so far have been miniscule. Soon, we will decimate the human population. Our nation is unified. The Agreement is dead. All we have to do is announce it. My friends...our time has come."

The vampires stood and cheered, and the cheer turned into a roar.

19

The attack at Westfield Shopping Centre, Sunderland, left fifty-four dead, and many more wounded in the stampedes that followed the panic. An eyewitness said: "They attacked everyone—women, children, it didn't matter. We were saved, though. One stood up and fought. Who? Not sure. I was a long way away. We could see a big, old, orange body fighting with the maniacs. Must've been one of the lasses who does the makeup in Debenhams."
—Mackems' Daily

IN HIS TWENTY-SEVEN YEARS as a general practitioner caring for the community, Dr McAllister had never felt quite so unwillingly to help someone than he did now.

"I want you to sign me off on the sick. It's what you're meant to do, ain't it?"

Dr McAllister grimaced at the horrible, greasy bastard playing with the Newton's Cradle on his desk, leaving a greasy film on every metal ball he touched. "Well, if someone is unable to work due to illness, then, yes, one of my roles as a GP is to sign them off 'on the sick,' as you call it."

"Well, fooking sign me off then." Rathbone thankfully left the doctor's personal possessions alone and went back to playing with his ridiculous cape.

"Please, mind your language."

"You've seen up me arsehole before, Doc, are you really that bothered I said fook? Sign me off."

McAllister's insides contorted remembering that dark day when Peter Rathbone bent over the examination bed and pulled apart his buttocks. The general public often spoke out against GP's salaries. If they really knew of the sights, sounds, and smells that accompanied the role, they wouldn't be so quick to moan.

"You haven't even said what's wrong with you. What am I meant to sign you off for?"

"Are you fooking blind?"

McAllister took a deep breath. He wanted this over quickly, but he was a professional. "What are you talking about, Peter?"

"What does this look like to you?" Rathbone grabbed onto his stupid cape and raised it theatrically, like a pair of wings.

"It's a cape of some sort of description."

"Exactly." Rathbone was smugness personified.

McAllister massaged his temple. The emerging headache was not a surprise. "I don't understand."

"Thought you were meant to be fooking clever? It's a cape, which means...?"

McAllister held up his hands. "I've absolutely no idea."

"I'm a fooking vampire, ain't I?"

"Oh."

"And I can't get a job because of it. Therefore, I demand extra benefit money."

The doctor took out a pen and paper from his top drawer. "Why do you think you're a vampire?"

"For fook's sake, how many times do I have to point at the cape?"

"Wearing a cape does not make you a vampire, Peter."

"Well, yeah, but I'm wearing a cape because I'm a vampire. It's what we do."

"I see," said McAllister, trying to work out if Rathbone was taking the piss or was clinically insane.

"Then sign me off."

"Aren't you already claiming benefits?"

"Aye, but I can get shitloads more if I can get sick pay, and the bastards at the benefit office wouldn't give me a job I deserve. You wouldn't give me 'owt last time, either, ya tight bastard."

"It isn't normal practise to sign someone off sick with a pile, Peter." Dr McAllister held back some vomit after a flashback scarred his brain.

"Well you can sign me off now, can't ya?" said the vampire hopefully.

"Why?...Stop pointing at the cape!"

"Easy Doc, you're meant to be understanding, not a twat."

Dr McAllister didn't like Peter Rathbone. He looked ridiculous in his outfit, dressed like a vampire from a Hammer Horror film. It would have been comical if he wasn't such an unlikable, horrible, greasy bastard. He'd tried to slick his hair back like Dracula, but it just meant it was greasier than normal and strands fell over his face leaving an oily sheen on his pitted, pale skin.

"Why do you think you're a vampire, Peter?"

"Because I am a vampire."

"OK, why are you a vampire?"

Rathbone shook his head, sneering with his spittle-covered lips. "You're just like the other fooking racist bastards!"

The doctor massaged both temples with his fingers again. His head was throbbing. "What are you talking about?"

"If I was black, you wouldn't be asking me why I was black or why I thought I was black, would you?"

"I would if you were white."

"You smart-arsed—"

"Listen, Peter," said the doctor, cutting Rathbone off before he could utter any more obscenities, "vampires don't exist—stop flourishing your cape. I'm concerned you're suffering from some sort of delusion."

"Bollocks!"

"OK, OK," said McAllister, mentally exhausted after two minutes of the ten-minute appointment. "Prove you're a vampire. And no amount of cape flourishing is going to convince me."

McAllister sat intrigued as Rathbone rolled up his sleeve and presented him with his arm and reached over the desk separating doctor and patient.

Through gritted teeth, Rathbone said, "Go on, Doc. Give me the best you've got."

"What?" McAllister withdrew back into his chair.

"Come on, ya fanny, give me a Chinese burn. Whatever you can give, I can take it."

"How will that prove you're a vampire?"

"'Cos I can take it."

"So can a lot of people. By your logic, Hulk Hogan must be a vampire too."

"He hasn't got a cape, dickhead."

"You'll have to do better than that."

Rathbone withdrew his arm with a tut. "Reet."

"What are you doing?" asked McAllister, concerned that Rathbone was unbuttoning his trousers and unfastening his belt. Last time he was confronted with this situation, he'd been unable to eat for a week.

"I'm proving to you I'm a vampire."

"That isn't necessary." The doctor looked everywhere except at the vampire who was turning around.

"You believe me now?" said Rathbone, looking between his legs.

"No, but whatever you're going to show me, isn't going to convince me."

"Not even this?" Rathbone ripped down his Y-fronts.

"Peter, God, no!...Oh...now that is something." After the initial shock and fear of what he was going to see, Dr McAllister was pleasantly surprised. Perhaps "pleasantly surprised" was an exaggeration, but the anus in front of him certainly didn't make him want to rip out his eyes and stamp on them. "Your piles have healed quite nicely, Peter. Healthy living and good hygiene go a long way."

"Don't be daft, Doc. The vampiring healed 'em."

"Oh."

"Sign us off sick, Doc."

"Peter, this doesn't prove you're a vampire. I am not going to sign patients off sick because they've invested in a good brand of pile cream."

"But—"

"You'll have to do better than that, I'm afraid," said the doctor firmly.

McAllister appreciated the annoyed look that crossed Rathbone's face. He wondered what was going through his mind as the bloodshot eyes scanned the room before focusing on the wooden spatulas sitting in a cup on a shelf behind his desk.

"What are them things?"

"Wooden spatulas. We use them for pushing a patient's tongue down when looking at their tonsils."

"Chuck us a few of them."

McAllister obliged and gave them to Rathbone who placed three together and tested the structural integrity against his hand. "Wouldn't it be easier if I sent for some holy wat—FUCKING HELL!"

"Language, Doc."

Dr McAllister jumped off his seat and rushed around to where Peter Rathbone was sitting, quite comfortably, with a handful of spatulas embedded in his eye socket.

"Come, lie down on the bed. Quickly, man!"

Rathbone shrugged. "Why?"

A mixture of the eye's blood and vitreous humour oozed down his cheek; Rathbone should've been in agony, but his only concern was not dripping the fluid on his precious cape—so he made sure it dripped on the carpet instead.

"Does...does that not hurt?" asked the doctor, wincing at the thought.

"Sort of, but once you've had a cock knife driven deep into your lower intestine by a horny pensioner, nothing really bothers ya."

McAllister looked at Rathbone blankly.

"Long story, Doc. Just sign us off."

"You've lost the sight in your...you realise you just half-blinded yourself?"

Rathbone slowly pulled out the spatulas from his eye, and they eventually came free with a sickening squelch, like a boot being pulled from a puddle of muddy water. "Hang on a sec, Doc." He pointed at his newly formed hole.

McAllister found the whole ordeal almost as disturbing as Rathbone's last haemorrhoid visit. Almost.

"Any minute now," said Rathbone, calmly, drumming his fingers on the arm of the chair.

McAllister stared into the pit of gore. "I think we need to get you to the hospital, Peter."

"Ah fook, it ain't working. I don't need to go to the hospital," he said, holding up a hand. "I just need a few pints of Bolton Bitter. That'll sort me out."

"A few pints of beer?"

"Has to be Bolton, like, Doc. Only Bolton can regenerate me. Most vampires need blood, but I need beer," he said proudly.

"I see," lied the doctor.

"If you come down the boozer with us, I'll show you. Come on, you doctor-types are minted; you can get the beers in, like."

McAllister picked up the phone on his desk. "Peter, we seriously need to get you to the hospital."

"Just sign us off sick, and I'll be on my way."

"I can't do that."

"You prick!" spat Rathbone, reaching over to the phone and cancelling the call with his greasy finger.

"You need professional help, Peter. I believe you to be very unwell."

"You wouldn't say that if I was white."

"You really need help."

"Fooking 'ell. I'm fed up with being treated like shit by every bastard in the 'boro. You can stick your fooking benefit up your arse. I'm taking this to the fooking top!"

McAllister watched the self-harming—no—self-*mutilating*, delusional, paranoid, psychotic storm out of his office. If it was any other man, he would have called the police and an ambulance, but it was Peter Rathbone. McAllister considered the Hippocratic Oath he swore when he became a doctor and looked at the phone receiver in his hand. He considered the oath again before putting the phone down and wishing the horrible, greasy, little bastard would die on the way home.

RATHBONE WAS ON HIS WAY TO THE BOOZER, and against the wishes of Dr McAllister and most people who'd met him, he didn't die. Rathbone had come to the conclusion that vampiring was shit. He hadn't had any breaks. All the vampires he'd met were posh bastards, who weren't about to let him in their gang.

The benefit office and his doctor were meant to be sympathetic, but they were a bunch of bastards like the rest. Worst of all, he still hadn't banged a hot chick. There was only one place where justice could be done. There was only one place where the non-working class had their say, and Rathbone was going to tell everyone. Absolutely bloody everyone.

20

Police arrested three men for the attack on the Sheffield nightclub. The three brothers were all joint partners of a rival nightclub, and Yorkshire Police believe the attack was the culmination of a bitter feud that's raged for the past year in the city. Being taken into court, the three brothers were quick to proclaim their innocence.
—*South Yorkshire Gazette*

"I HAVE A BAD FEELING ABOUT THIS."

They sat on a bench in the middle of the lion's den: Middlesbrough High Street. The shopping centre in Sunderland was a cakewalk compared to this.

"It'll be reet, Arthur," said Brian. "What's the worst that can happen?"

"She sees you spying on her, she tells Sid, he gives us both a kicking, I never see my son again, and we get arrested."

"That sounds pretty bad, like, but hopefully, it won't come to that."

The two lads were in uncharted territory and way outside their comfort zone. Being real men, they'd never set foot in a High Street in the daytime before. Sure, they'd both stumbled along it back home after a lock-in and pissed on British Home Stores' window, but that was a standard part of a night out. In the daylight, High Streets were stalked by womenfolk, and danger lurked at every corner...

"Look, nowt bad is gonna happen," continued Brian.

"We're getting a lot of dirty looks, man," said Arthur, catching the glares of the passing women. "And not in a good way, either. They don't want us here. This isn't our place."

Brian thought the evils were reserved for him because of various misunderstandings in the past and lack of childcare payments, but Arthur was getting them too, and Brian had never seen a woman look at Arthur without carnal lust in her eyes.

"Just try to fit in," said Brian.

"How the fuck am I meant to do that?" said Arthur, panicked.

The use of the harsh swearword brought many tuts and more disapproving looks. Arthur now knew what the expression "She looked like she wanted to cut my bollocks off," which Brian used at least once an hour, meant.

"We'll have to do a bit of shopping or summat. They might leave us alone if we have some bags in our hands."

"Shopping? Aw, man, I don't wanna go shopping. There's nothing shittier!"

"Good point." Brian stood up from the bench. "Let's just get this over with and find her."

"I'm not convinced of your plan, buddy," said Arthur, staying put, not quite ready for suicide.

"Look, we're bashing our heads against a brick wall trying to talk to Sid. We have to go straight to the source. We need to scope out his missus."

"Sounds dangerous," said Arthur, noticing just how many FOR SALE signs were in the shop windows.

"All we're doing is checking her out and making sure there's nowt dodgy going on."

"Dodgy?"

"Aye. I don't trust her. Not one bit." He said, lighting up a fag.

"Why?"

"She's with Sid for a start."

"Harsh, man."

Brian put the lighter back in his pocket. "Oh come on, mon. Cracking-titted blonde stunners ain't been falling over themselves to get to him before, have they?"

"Good point. Maybe she's with him for his personality?"

"Fook off, mate. That personality bollocks ain't true. It's just made up for shite women's magazines. I want to see her for myself and make sure them vampire council bastards ain't trying to fook him over."

"You're right. We've gotta do this for the big man." Arthur put on his determined face. "Where do we start?"

"Marks and Spencer."

Arthur's determined face was replaced with one of confusion. "Why?"

"It's where all middle-aged women go in the day time."

The confused face was replaced with a can't-be-arsed face. "Where's Marks and Spencer?"

"How the fook should I know?"

"So, how do you know it's where older chicks go?"

"It's where Kev's missus disappears to in the day, apparently. She always takes her mother there too."

Arthur shuddered. "Aw, man! So, you mean we might bump into Kev's missus!"

"Mate, by the sounds of it, we'll be bumping into every middle-aged woman in Middlesbrough."

"Normally, that would be a good thing," Arthur said, disappointed. "Right. How we gonna find the shop?"

"You're gonna have to ask someone."

"Why me?"

"You're the pretty one."

Arthur nodded and grudgingly removed himself from the comfort of the bench. He tried his luck with the first lady who walked by.

"Excuse me, miss."

The scowl he received from the young mum ensured he wouldn't pursue the matter further. He tried again several times without success until he was run over by a pushchair. He fell back onto the bench, clutching at his shin. "She saw me, man! She fooking saw me and she went right through me!"

Brian watched the uncaring woman walk off, middle finger pointing to the sky. "I've seen a woman cause a fifteen car pile-up on a motorway to avoid running over a cancer-ridden hedgehog with AIDS. Give 'em a fooking pram, though, and they'd run over Brad Pitt's bollocks."

Arthur found his feet again and tested his weight on his bruised leg. "No one's gonna talk to us. Let's go in that shop and ask. At least the people working there will have to acknowledge us."

Arthur and Brian struggled to cross the pavement through the unrelenting foot and pram traffic to get into the store. Once inside, they discovered it was a women's clothes shop. Judging by the clientele, the target market were teens to early twenties. This was not the domain of the middle-aged man.

Brian cocked an ear. "What the fook is that?"

"I think...I think it's music, man."

Brian stuck his finger in his ear and wiggled it about. "Get away."

Arthur shrugged his shoulders. "Let's find someone and get out of here. I don't like it one bit. I ain't used to girls looking at me like this. This is how Rathbone must feel all the time."

"Yeah. Let's ask the lass behind the counter."

The boys traversed through the maze of multi-coloured clothing and display stands of stuff they couldn't identify. Brian coped with the journey better than Arthur, who followed close behind like a nervous child.

"Hey, man, did you hear that?" said Arthur.

"The quiet whispers of 'pervert?'"

"Yeah. What's that all about?"

Brian laughed. "This is what it's like in the posh bars in the 'boro. It'll be reet. You'll get used to it."

"I'm pretty sure I won't."

Brian took the lead and approached the girl behind the till who looked the most hospitable and the only one who hadn't given them a wanker sign.

"Eh'up, pet—" Brian couldn't finish the sentence because he was interrupted. Some would say "rudely."

"I'm not your fucking pet, you old, fucking pervert."

He pulled irritably at his goatee beard. "Can I speak to your manager, please?"

"JANE!" shrieked the cashier.

Her senior approached. She was probably only a month older than the foul-mouthed sixteen-year-old who grunted and nodded towards Brian.

"What d'you want?" asked the manager.

"Can you tell me where Marks and Spencer is, please?"

"You called me over here for that?" she asked, blowing a bubble into her gum and twiddling her hair.

"Yes, I did."

"Did you think I'd give a shit?"

Brian considered himself an educated man and a patient one. In reality, he was neither. He exploded.

"Well, you better fooking do! I would've asked that daft bint next to ya, but she looks thick as fooking pig shit! Now, tell me where the fooking shop is before I punch you in the face, you fooking twat!"

The entire store turned to watch the outburst, which, in all fairness to Brian, had been coming since these stores were invented.

"Get security," said the manager to her assistant, before announcing to the store, "These perverts have been looking through the panties, girls."

"No, I fooking haven't!" shouted Brian in protest. "I'm just looking for Marks and fooking Spencer! Will someone please tell me where it is?"

Various answers were flung back at him. None were helpful.

"Pervert!"

"Tell you? You'll only go perving on panties!"

"Granny panty pervert!"

Brian started to feel a little unsure of the direction the sortie was taking. Finally, into view came the white shirt and swagger of a security guard. A bloke meant someone Brian could relate to, or rather someone he wouldn't feel too bad sticking the nut on.

"Jimmy! Kick these two perverts out of here!"

"Jimmy the Barman!" cried Brian.

Brian hadn't recognised him from afar. He'd thought that the swagger was one a security guard put on to give the illusion of a tough guy—not the limp of someone who had been shared 'round fifteen horny vampires in a pub car park.

"Wh-what are you doing here?" came a shaky voice when the ashen Jimmy reached the till.

"Jimmy, mon, you don't look so good. How old are ya again?"

"Twenty-nine."

"Fook me! You look about fifty. What happened?" asked Brian.

"You're...you're joking right?" said Jimmy, wincing.

"Hey, Jimmy, what you wasting your talents here for?" asked Arthur. "You started keeping some quality cask ale, my man." He went to give him a manly pat on the shoulder, but Jimmy recoiled.

"Don't touch me," he whimpered, not looking the men in the eye.

"Hey, man, relax," said Arthur.

"Jimmy get rid of these men!" screamed the manager at the former barman.

Brian almost felt sympathy for the man. Almost. "Jimmy," he said, "I'm going to buy you a beer."

It was the closest a Northern man could come to compassion.

21

The Westfield Shopping Centre in Sunderland is a week away from reopening for business. The attacks on the other shopping centres, Bristol, Manchester, Birmingham, and Nottingham were more destructive, and it still isn't certain whether they'll reopen. Still, no terrorist group has come forward to claim responsibility for the attacks.

—Mackems' Daily

JIMMY HADN'T TAKEN much convincing to go down the pub. He'd lose his job for leaving his post, but so be it. Brian Garforth had a power over him that couldn't be ignored. Brian and his friends had caused him to lose two pubs, take numerous beatings from loan sharks, and experience what can only be described as an "ordeal" at the hands of fifteen randy vampires and an insatiable midget. That sort of impact leaves a scar on a man.

"So, what've you been up to, Jimmy?" asked Brian. His cheerful tone made the former barman want to cry.

Jimmy was on lager. He didn't drink ale anymore. It brought back memories of things, bad things, fifteen big bad things and one little bad thing to be precise. "Once I got out of hospital, I decided to get out of the brewery trade and got a job here. Working days means no more vampires, you know?"

"Aye, they're a bunch of wankers if you ask me," said Brian. "After all, look what they did to you!"

Jimmy choked on some lager, and Brian was quick to pick up on it.

"That's what that shit'll do to ya. Fooking lager, Jimmy, what're ya playing at?"

Jimmy couldn't look at Brian, even though he wanted to stick sixteen hot pokers up the man's arse, the only suitable revenge he could think of.

Arthur gave Jimmy a slap on the back. "You'd sorted out your beer a treat, man. You were good!"

"So why did you...? Doesn't matter." Jimmy realised there was no point. Brian was the reason he'd endured The Ordeal rather than some other fella, Reece, who was trying to kill them. Jimmy's only crime was to serve beer subpar to that of The Miner's Arms. His only crime!

"You can help us out, Jim," said Brian cheerfully.

"Help you out? Why would I want to?"

"I thought we were even?" said Brian. He held up his hands and looked genuinely surprised. "You made us drink shit beer for months!"

Jimmy was broken on the inside (literally in some places) and conceded. "What do you want?"

"That's better, like," said Brian.

"Jimmy baby, you must have a finger on the pulse of this High Street shit," said Arthur.

Jimmy played with a beer mat, tearing it into tiny pieces. "What're you talking about?"

"This High Street is weird, man," said Arthur. "The women don't act like normal women."

Jimmy nodded. "Aye, I know what you mean. They don't bother me. This uniform keeps me safe. I've seen other blokes on the street. If they're not with their wives or girlfriends, they don't last five minutes."

"Fook me," said Brian. "You seen Sid here with his missus?"

"Nope. Never seen her. Heard about her, like. The High Street is a strange place. News travels faster than the speed of sound. It's as if every shop is connected or the women have psychic links. There're no secrets here. They'll all know about your outburst in the clothes store already."

Arthur stared into his pint, trembling slightly.

"You're safe here, Peasley. This is like holy ground. The women won't come inside a pub in daylight."

Brian shivered. "Do you know 'owt about Sid's missus?"

"I've never seen her."

"I've got a picture of her." Brian reached into the top pocket of his red wool jacket.

"How did you get that?" asked Arthur.

"Done some recon, mate. Started banging one of the neighbours."

"Yeah?"

"She's a bit of a horror, like, but I'm doing her for Sid. I got a picture of Sid's missus from her lounge window." Brian pulled out a Polaroid to show Jimmy. "She's fooking hot, mon. It don't add up. Why has she gone for Sid? I mean, with them jugs, she could have any Northern bloke she wants. Why pick Sid Tillsley and change him into his complete opposite? If she wanted a challenge, she should have gone on *Krypton Factor* or summat."

"Yes, that's how she was described," said Jimmy, examining the picture.

"What do you know about her?" asked Brian.

"You hear a lot of things in my line of work. There're no secrets on the High Street."

"Enough with the bollocks, Jimmy, just tell us," said Brian.

"She's caused quite a stir around the ladies' sections. The women around here don't like outsiders, and she appeared out of nowhere. Another thing women around here don't like is good-looking women like Sid's missus."

"So, you're saying she just appeared?"

Jimmy nodded and put down some more lager.

"That sounds kinda odd, man." Arthur stroked his chin, thoughtfully.

"When did she turn up?" asked Brian.

"She's been kicking around ever since I got this job. The women said she turned up, probably about the time I went into hospital a couple of months ago."

"Fook!" said Brian.

"That means she turned up just to date the big man," said Arthur.

"Sure does."

Jimmy looked longingly at the picture. He used to be a bit of a ladies' man. Not now. "She is stunning. Sid's a lucky man...in some ways."

"What do you mean?"

"She's a ballbreaker."

"Aye, we know," said Brian sadly. "Anything else we should know?"

"As I said, I haven't seen her. I only work the day shift. I won't stay out at night since...you know." He looked at his watch. It was approaching dusk.

"So?"

"Well, that's why I've never seen her. She only comes out at night."

Brian paled.

"Fook!"

THE HORROR OF THE TEENAGE CLOTHES SHOP was over, and Brian and Arthur, a little oiled, entered the British institution that is Marks and Spencer, M&S, Marks and Sparks. They were far more at ease in the middle-aged environment. It brought comfort in a satisfying way that only cardigans and slippers could. Obviously, they'd have preferred to stay in the pub, but they had a job to do, and when Jimmy left, just before darkness fell, they finished their beers in order to give the shop a quick once-over before it shut.

"What now?" asked Arthur.

"Now we find Sid's missus and find out what she's all about."

"And you know she's gonna be here?" said Arthur, on tiptoes surveying the masses of pastel cotton, sensible shoes, and dignified customers.

"Of course, mon. She's a middle-aged woman, ain't she?"

"You really think she's a vampire, then?"

"Aye," said a certain Brian.

"And you really think she'll be here?"

"Well, depends if she's a middle-aged vampire. I guess middle-aged vampires have to shop somewhere, and Marks and Sparks is good a place as any."

"Do you reckon old vampires get saggy titties?" asked Arthur, feeling philosophical.

"Dunno, mate. Good fooking question, but we need to keep our mind on the game. We need to know what she's up to."

Arthur nodded. "Where's she gonna be?"

"The women's bit."

"You're fucking smart, man."

Brian twiddled his thin moustache. "I know."

Soon after, the boys spotted the blonde bombshell causing a stir around the store. The boys couldn't see what she saw in Sid, but they sure could see what he saw in her. She was absolutely gorgeous, and the jugs lived up to the rumours, and because the boys were drunk, they looked even bigger. The other women in the store were giving her evils, because she was flashing a lot of flesh. The boys hid behind some blouses while Sid's missus looked through some clothes a few rows away.

Brian whispered, "It don't add up, Arthur. Lass like that wouldn't go for Sid. Not just that, a lass like her would've been banged senseless, hundreds of times! She's dressed up like a tart too. No sex before marriage? Bollocks. It don't make any sense unless this is all vampire shit."

"She doesn't go out in the day. She's short, and she's pale. Real pale. She could be a vamp, man" said Arthur.

"I think she is, ya know." Brian made himself another viewing hole, parting a couple of items of women's crap. "We need to find out for sure."

"How we gonna do that?"

"What was it you said? Vampire tits don't sag."

"Did I? Anyway, Lucia's didn't. Man, I miss them," Arthur fought back a tear.

"Reet. We need to get a look at her jugs to see if she really is a vampire."

Arthur ducked quickly when Sid's missus turned towards them to look through a different rail of the same crap. "How we gonna do that?"

"Changing rooms. We sneak in, we take a photo with my phone, and leg it.

"A mobile phone, man?" asked Arthur, disgusted.

"Shut up," Brian snapped. "We get a pic. If the tits don't sag, she's a vampire and we tell Sid."

Arthur's drunken logic found nothing wrong with the plan. "Say if they do sag?"

"She ain't a vampire, and we're back to square one. She's gotta be a vamp. Look at her jugs!" Brian felt a little guilty at the blood flow to his groin.

"They are pretty mighty. This is gonna be some dangerous recon."

"Don't you think I know that, Arthur? This is all part of the plan," said Brian confidently.

Arthur poked him in the ribs. "You didn't even know where Marks and Spencer was."

Brian raised a knowing eyebrow. "Didn't I, Arthur? Didn't I?"

"No, you fucking didn't."

"Well, you got any better ideas?" he snapped.

"Pub?"

Brian had to admit it was a much better idea, but he didn't. "Look, Sid won't talk to me, and he won't listen to anyone. Something's up with that woman. We need him back. We need him back so we can find your son. We need to get rid of all this vampire shit and get back to normal life, and so does Sid."

"He needs a jump, man."

"And we'll get him one. Fook it, we'll just chip in and buy him a prossie. We should've done it months ago."

Arthur nodded.

"Good," said Brian, "Right. We need to get into the women's changing rooms."

"I don't like the sound of that."

"That's rough, 'cos you're gonna be the one going in."

"Why me?"

"Because I came up with the plan."

"How do ya know she's gonna try something on?"

"She's a woman, ain't she? She'll try half the fooking shop on."

"How we gonna get into the changing rooms?"

Two heads raised above a line of pleated skirts to survey the battleground. A pretty lady in her early thirties was checking through the items of clothes being taken in before giving the potential customer a ticket.

"I'll have to distract her, and you can sneak past," said Brian.

"If one of us is going to distract a lady, then it's best it's me. I don't know how to use that camera on that mobile phone crap, anyhow."

Brian didn't like to admit it, but Arthur was right.

"OK, fine," he said, a little frustrated. "We follow her, wait until she goes to the changing rooms, then you distract the lass supervising while I sneak in and take a picture of her tits."

"Let's do it."

"What can possibly go wrong?"

22

"The Dark Lord is coming, and there is nothing any of you can do about it. Pray and see where that gets you. The end of the world is coming, man. Revelations, fire, and brimstone is coming. Pray, Christians, it's all you're gonna be able to do once Armageddon comes and Satan rules once more."
—Some Goth twat with long hair and a shite tattoo.

SINCE BRIAN HAD BEEN CHASED by the vampire monster Sparle, he hadn't found the need to cover thirty yards, his specialist distance, as quickly as he was doing now. Dodging pensioners, hurdling shoe displays, diving through lines of skirts, he fled from the women's changing rooms with the deft agility of the most determined shoplifter.

It wasn't security that Brian was fleeing, well, not yet, anyway, it was the furious middle-aged housewives of Marks and Spencer. He burst past Arthur who was chatting up the shop assistant, a cute little brunette.

Brian couldn't tell how many women were hunting him down, but judging by the thunderous sound of sensible footwear behind him, he concluded it was every menopausal woman in the 'boro. He was knackered before he'd even left the blouse department. There was a whole floor to negotiate before he reached the freedom of Middlesbrough High Street, and that would offer the horrors and obstacles of prams, the elderly, and more haters of swordsmen.

"That pervert was taking pictures!" he heard in the background as other women joined the chase. They were closing in, flanking him down the aisles like hunting lionesses.

"PERVERT!"

"Oh, fook," he panted and forced his tired legs and tarred lungs to keep going. He made it to the escalator and dodged a pensioner, taking a clip on the ear from a swinging handbag. He took two steps at a time before one of the cruel witches pressed the emergency stop button and sent him sprawling to the bottom of the escalator in a heap.

"Are you alright, dearie?"

He looked up from the floor at a kindly old granny who looked on with, thankfully, a concerned look on her face.

Brian got to his feet shakily. His ribs had taken a battering and he'd landed funny on his ankle, but he had to keep moving. "I'm OK, thanks."

"He was taking pictures in the women's dressing rooms!" a woman screamed down the escalator.

The kindly granny's face turned from concern to one reserved for non-white, non-Christian paedophiles. "You filthy cunt!"

Brian received a thumb to the throat, as had been taught to her during her self-defence classes.

He couldn't take in the breath to tell her what he thought of her, and he limped off as fast as his injuries could take him.

"Pervert!" she screamed after him.

Brian wasn't making good progress, but the street was in sight. If he could just make it down the main aisle, then freedom would be his. He broke into a run and hoped that bastard Arthur was going to help.

He heard the pack approaching from the rear. Thankfully, they were forced into single file down the escalator, otherwise, he would've been done for by now. He had to get outside into a taxi or onto holy ground: the gents' in a boozer. Only Smithson Estate women would follow a man into such a place, and they didn't shop in M&S—but they did steal from it.

His throat began to regain its normal shape and he gathered momentum. He couldn't manage another thirty-yard dash. He was knackered and his ankle caused him grief, but he was picking up pace. He saw women enter the periphery along with a couple of security guards. They didn't bother him. He could knee them in the nuts and not incur the wrath of oestrogen.

"Fook!"

The women bounding past him on adjacent aisles could cause a problem. If they cut him off...

"Run, Brrrriiiiiannnnnn!"

Time slowed as Arthur's shout carried over the din of the baying hounds. A handbag swung in from the right, and Brian ducked as it whistled over his head. He managed to rearrange his 'do to cover up his bald patch and hurdled a high heel that'd been stuck out to trip him. One more woman to dodge. She went high to tackle him. He threw a big, swinging wild right, cracking her full in the jaw and sending her flying into the security sensors. He was a hero. He was a fucking hero, and he was going to make it.

"I'm gonna make it. I'm gonna fooking make it!"

Streetlights brought freedom, but they disappeared with the emergence of an impenetrable barrier. Brian crashed into a brick wall and hit the pavement like a sack of spuds.

"You...fooking..." he managed between wheezes, looking up to what had obstructed his bid for freedom.

Sid Tillsley stood with his arms crossed, and he didn't look happy.

"Sid, thank God! There's something I've got to tell you—"

Before Sid could say anything, Brian was surrounded by a sea of women. If they were naked, all his dreams would've come true. But, they weren't naked. They were going to kick the shit out of him. Stilettos landed on each gonad before, thankfully, he passed out.

BRIAN BOOGIED AWAY in the centre of the dance floor. He'd never really been much of a mover, but this disco was banging out tunes from the early '80s, and there wasn't a sausage in sight. Wall-to-wall fanny was heaven to a swordsman. His red woollen suit was in pristine condition and it was getting noticed. Every eye turned to him. He'd thought it was a lezza bar at first, but his "Swordy-sense" told him these women were cock hungry.

Deja vu, he thought. Eyes looked familiar. Faces began to push themselves into his memory. He knew these women. He turned with the rhythm, and it was the same story on the other side of the floor. He knew these women, because they'd all felt the fury of his sword, every single one of them.

The music intensified along with the looks Brian was getting. The looks were no longer lustful, but hateful. *Beer*, he thought to himself. When tension gripped the dance floor, you either smacked someone or got the beers in. Every woman he walked past, each a conquest, looked at him scornfully. He desperately tried to get past them, but the crowd was endless. He would've felt an ounce of pride if he wasn't so frightened. This wasn't what he was here for. He was here for something else, but what? The women appeared to grow, or he to shrink, and their hateful stares turned demonic. Red eyes bored holes into him and he lost his footing, falling at their feet.

"Must! Get! Out!" he sobbed desperately, and his prayers were answered. A door appeared in front of him out of nowhere and he quickly pushed it open, slamming it behind him. He leant against it panting. He had no idea why he was here.

He was in the bogs of a posh bar. Why was he here? Where was he? Was it just a piss he wanted? There were no urinals.

This was the ladies'.

A nagging sensation told him he was here for something, to look for something, and it was in this room. He took himself off to a cubicle and locked himself inside, racking his brains while having a lazy piss, sitting down. *Think, Brian. Think! Why are you here?*

A rustling from the adjacent cubicle disturbed his thoughts with a curiosity that couldn't be ignored. "Hello?" he called, but nothing came back, just more rustling. Never one to be shy, Brian pulled up his kecks, and climbed on the toilet to look over the divide and find out what was going on.

He peeked over.

"I know you! I know you! You're what I've been looking for!"

His eyes widened. "I don't believe it! SID!" he yelled. "SID!"

Suddenly, the door of his cubicle opened and an invisible force threw him through it and into the tiled wall beyond. Tiles broke and fell on top of him as he hit the ground, but before he could bounce to a rest, the main door to the toilets opened, and he slid through, dragged by the invisible force. Fear saturated him as he was dragged through the club, past the baying women.

"You're gonna pay for what you did to us, Brian," they said in one unholy voice. "YOU SEXIST PIG! YOU'RE GONNA PAY!"

"Next time I'll pull out! I promise!" he yelled.

Hell enveloped.

BRIAN CAME TO when a full can of Diet Coke was poured into his face. "Whassat?" he said spluttering before his brain informed him just how much damage he'd sustained.

"Foooookin' basttttaarrrds." He managed before curling into a ball. Every limb, rib, and extremity throbbed. He was glad to be rid of the nightmare but feared he'd landed in another. Thankfully, the women had backed off, not that they could do much more damage. Every nerve felt like it had been stilettoed and then nagged. He sat up groggily and wiped the Coke off of his face. The sharp pains told him there was a lot of blood mixed in with it.

"You should feel ashamed of yourself, ya dirty bastard," said a voice from the ring of women.

"Fooking pervert," cried another.

"I ain't done nowt wrong," he begged.

"You were taking pictures of us in the changing rooms, weren't you?" said a voice above him.

He turned his head to the middle-aged woman. "Well, not you, you ugly bitch. Aaaaarrgghhh!" She toe-punted his ear, crushing the lobe against his skull.

He clutched at his throbbing ear and prayed for a quick death.

"Brian, what were you doing?"

Brian recognised the deep voice of the wall he'd run into.

"Sid...stop 'em beating me, mon. For the love of God!"

"I did, Brian. I saved your life." Sid pointed up at the lamppost to a rope.

The blood rushed from Brian's head, and he felt dizzy. "They were going to *hang* me? That noose is pretty small."

"We were gonna hang you by your bollocks, ya horrible little toad!" came a scream.

Brian winced. Another angry spectator got involved. "You've been getting away with being a bounder for far too long, Garforth. If it wasn't for Sid here, we would've made you pay."

Brian felt at his throbbing gonads. "I think you already have."

"Bullshit. You deserve to have your nuts stamped on forever, and I tell you this: when you get to Hell, that's what'll be waiting for you."

He felt a pointy shoe part his ribs and he doubled up once more. The woman continued the verbal assault. "Sid saved you. It all makes sense why you're such a messed up soul and a womaniser. You wanted to get caught. You wanted us to punish you."

Brian, thinking his swimmers were finished, really didn't. "What are you talking about?"

"Sid told us you're a closet gay."

"I ain't fooking..." He considered the sack-sized noose. "Yeah... I love a cock, me."

"Brian Garforth!" The circle of women parted, and Brian felt compelled to turn and face the woman who'd spat his name with notably more venom than the rest. It was Sid's missus, and she didn't look happy. But, he didn't notice. He was looking at her breasts.

"Brian Garforth, you dirty little pervert!" she continued.

"Hang on. How do you know me?"

That stopped her in her tracks but only for a second. "Well, everyone knows you, don't they?"

"No," he said matter-of-factly.

"Well," she said, not so aggressively, "I heard the women calling your name."

Brian's eyes narrowed. Something wasn't right.

She turned to her man. "Sidney, what are you doing fraternising with...him."

"I was waiting for you, dear," said the big man obediently.

"Is he telling the truth?" Sid's missus asked of the rest of the women, who nodded his defence.

"Isn't that lucky, Sidney?"

Brian managed to pull his eyes away from her jugs as the blood flow brought more pain than he thought possible. Sid's lass was a cracker, but was she a vampire? Through the pain, he remembered the plan—and the changing rooms. He remembered peeking over the cubicle to where Sid's missus was getting changed, and...all that came to him was his nightmare and the beating he took in the dream, which, unfortunately, was happening in the real world. He must have taken some blows to the head. He couldn't remember.

"Fook," he said glumly, shaking his head, trying to rid himself of the cobwebs. The last thing he remembered was the announcement over the tannoy. Some bastard jobsworth security guard had caught him on the CCTV and announced it over the speakers.

Fooking Jimmy! The little bastard grassed me up!

"Come, Sidney," said his missus. "We need to discuss your behaviour, and also your progress for our big day."

"Aye, pet."

"Sid, wait!" Brian shouted in desperation. He had to try something. "Your missus is a vampire!"

"Eh?" Sid stopped, and it gave Brian a glimmer of hope.

"Come along, Sidney," she ordered, and he obeyed.

The circle of women closed in once more.

"Ah, shit."

Luckily, the sound of sirens dispersed the crowd. "Thank fook!" cried Brian when the local coppers pulled up next to the pavement.

An officer jumped out of the car and pushed his way through what women remained. "You're nicked, son. You perving little...Jesus, mate, are you alright?"

"No," said Brian before lying back down on the concrete. "No, I fooking ain't."

23

A pervert was chased out of Marks and Spencer in Middlesbrough today. The plucky ladies who were shopping in the store dealt with the middle-aged man who was creeping around the underwear section. One have-a-go hero had this to say: "We gave that dirty little pervert everything he deserved. He won't think about touching that thing of his for a while after the girls and me stamped on it. He's had this coming for years!"

—Loose Women, ITV

"GOOD MORNING, LADIES AND GENTLEMEN. I'm Colin Fitzpatrick, and I'm here to bring the nation together."

Colin smiled smugly as his non-working-class audience erupted in rapturous applause and hollering. He didn't try to calm them down. He didn't want to. He ran his fingers through his thick grey hair and marvelled at the technology keeping his hair implants in place. His new, beautiful barnet was a big "fuck you" to the tabloid bastards who'd ridiculed his wig.

Colin ignored the pleas ringing through his ears from his producer, telling him to hush the crowd and get on with the TV show. His producer was an ignorant fool, for these people were his people. They were only here to see him. They didn't care about the scum soon to humiliate themselves in front of millions of their equally scummy peers. They only cared about Colin Fitzpatrick's words of wisdom, oh—and not to forget the designer three-piece suits he was famed for.

Colin had a keen sixth sense that enabled him to anticipate lulls in audience appreciation, and when the applause and whooping began its natural diminuendo, he hushed the crowd. "Shhhh, come, my friends, we have people to bring together."

In a moment of professional brilliance, Colin's face turned from one of pure ecstasy to one of utmost seriousness. Only a true star could take the audience from a dizzying high to a formidable low with the mere lowering of groomed eyebrows.

Colin walked down the studio stairs that bisected the audience, talking into the camera as he went. "We have dealt with many issues on this show. We have ousted loverats, we've reunited lost lovers, we've brought together families, helped the addicted, and sometimes, we've helped the damn right weird." Colin pulled a funny face that brought forth hysterics from his studio audience.

"We have a special guest tonight." He raised his eyebrows and received the inquisitive "oohs" and "arrs" from his followers that he was looking for. "Yes, that's right, ladies and gents, but that's not all. Tonight, for the first time ever, *The Colin Fitzpatrick Show* is coming at you at six p.m., and as always—we're coming at you live!"

More applause. Colin felt a stirring in his pants. He was competing with the big boys now, taking this show to prime time. He was the man. He was the fucking man. "And why are we coming to you at six p.m.? Because our special guest can't go out in the daylight." He put his face in his hand and shook his head comically. "Because he thinks he's a vampire"

Sniggers filled the airwaves as Peter Rathbone made his debut live television appearance, walking in from the side of the stage. He was trying hard to rub off the face paint that'd been applied. The makeup artists had made a mockery of him with fake blood down the side of his mouth.

"Welcome, Peter," said Colin with open arms.

Rathbone straightened his cape and took a seat. He looked thoroughly uncomfortable on the hard plastic seat. The seats were one of the secrets to Colin's beloved show. They were so painful, they'd put the occupants in a terrible mood, meaning fighting was always a nudge away. Colin was always there to nudge.

"So, Peter, what brings you here?" he asked with a beautiful smile.

"You told me to come here." Rathbone was not suited to live television.

"You contacted us, Peter." Colin was a professional used to dealing with arseholes.

"I've been turned away by the local government, turned away from medical science, and that's left me one option: a slot on a crap TV show. I've had enough of being persecuted for my ethnic origin, and I want everyone to hear my story."

It took all of Colin's professional ability not to lash out when the horrible, greasy, little bastard dared call his TV show crap. Colin held it together, for he was amazing. "And what is your ethnic origin, Peter?"

Rathbone pointed to the cape.

"Can you be a little more specific, please, for our audience at home?"

Rathbone rolled his eyes. "I'm a vampire."

This brought much laughter from the audience and some jeering from the more hostile, drunken members that looked like an extended police line-up.

Rathbone pointed threateningly at the hundred-strong audience. "You can all go f—*BLEEP*—k yourselves, you bunch of cu-*BLEEP*-ts! Eh?"

The vampire scratched his head. His offensive tirade didn't have the bite he hoped for. He tried again. "You're all f-*BLEEP*-g inbred, ya f-*BLEEP*-g children of whor-*BLEEP*-s! What the f-*BLEEP*-k is going on?"

"Please, Peter, keep the language family friendly."

"It don't matter what I f-*BLEEP*-king say. I canna swear!"

"One of the crew censors any bad language, but, please, keep it down," said Colin, hoping he'd swear some more.

"Censorship? You're censoring me because I'm a vampire?"

"No, it's because you're using disgusting language and this show is going out at six in the evening, nearly prime time." The camera got a big smile with the mention of prime time. "Ladies and gentlemen, if you are just joining us, Peter Rathbone is from Middlesbrough, and he believes he is a vampire."

"You've just said that! And, who the fu-*BLEEP*-k are you talking to?" said Rathbone to Colin, who was enjoying some more Colin-time in front of the camera. "Hang on...What do you mean 'believes he's a vampire.'"

Colin averted his eyes from the camera, trying not to show his disdain for the horrible, greasy, little bastard. "When did you realise you were a vampire?"

"I was bitten by one of the bast-*BLEEP*-s a few months back, and when I woke up, I was a vampire."

"How did you know your attacker was a vampire?"

"Sid Tillsley, one of the lads from down the boozer, got involved with all that vampire-hunting bol-*BLEEP*-ocks, and one of the b-*BLEEP*-tards who was after him went and bit me."

"So, one of your friends is a vampire hunter?" said Colin sarcastically, looking at the audience for a laugh, which he got.

"Aye."

"You ever worried about him hunting you?"

"Nah, I'm f-*BLEEP*-ing rock, me," said Rathbone, flourishing his ridiculous cape. "Another vampire hunter tried. A twat—*BLEEP*— called Rich Chambers, and he got a kick—"

Colin interrupted, "Well, isn't that lucky for us? Otherwise, you wouldn't be here to tell us all about it."

"Eh?"

"We'll be back, after these important messages."

"Cun-*BLEEP*!"

REECE CHAMBERS SAT ON HIS BED, his unblinking eyes staring at the wall. He'd hardly slept in weeks, but he wasn't tired. The various DNA-altering injections he'd given himself during his research had given him both wonderful and terrible gifts; not needing sleep was one of them.

He'd turned the television set on to remind himself there was life outside the walls of his laboratory and zoned out for several hours. He'd concluded that it was a sort of meditation and did not fight it. His life was no longer governed by day or night but by his work.

He snapped back with a shake of his head. The clock told him it was evening. Haemo hadn't proved as useful as the actual viral carrier needed to transport Haemo into the vampire's bloodstream. He'd used the carrier to target his genes successfully, the ones that had been altered in the three men and a vampire from Middlesbrough. He'd found some success implanting some of the alpha acids that make up Bolton Bitter into his own genetic makeup. His muscular power had increased dramatically, and Sid's raw, brute strength was his. It had enabled him to give Farouq a damn good fight, but he wasn't able to finish what he'd started. He didn't have the power to knock the vampire into dust like Sid did, and that's what he needed if he was going to go down in history as the destructor of the vampire race.

Something was missing. Something else linked these men directly to the vampire through Bolton Bitter, and he didn't have a clue what it was. He'd tried to use Peter Rathbone's DNA to link the vampire's genes to his and hopefully trigger Sid's ability to kill them, but all that the horrible, greasy, little bastard's DNA did to him was shrink the size of his penis—considerably.

He'd obtained an increase in speed from Arthur Peasley's DNA, and thicker hair, but he hadn't investigated whether he'd added Arthur's prowess with vampire women to his arsenal. The idea of taking a vampire into his arms made him nauseous. Reece hadn't touched Brian Garforth's DNA. He wasn't risking the venereal diseases that were so ingrained in Garforth's body; they could be genetic.

There was more to the men from Middlesbrough than he'd originally thought, and there was no way for him to learn their secrets now they were dead. For all his despair, there was still no chance of—

"Another vampire hunter tried. A twat—*BLEEP*—called Rich Chambers, and he got a kick—"

The greasy voice was unmistakable.

It was nothing but luck that caused Reece to catch the worthless programme on television, and he couldn't believe his eyes. Rathbone was alive. This meant the others probably were too. He'd have given his soul for the chance to work on fresh samples from the four friends from Middlesbrough. This was a lifeline.

24

Shops on Middlesbrough High Street have drafted in extra security when local shoppers raised concerns after a pervert was chased out of Marks and Spencer this week. Security guard Jimmy the Barman told us, "Locals have nothing to worry about. We have it all under control. Hopefully, the pervert chased out of this store got his just deserts. Maybe he'll think twice in the future when he has a choice to make involving a rogering by fifteen randy vampires and an insatiable midget. NOW we're even, Garforth!"

—Sunday Star

"HELLO, LADIES AND GENTS. If you've just joined us, I am extremely pleased to introduce real-life vampire, Peter Rathbone."

"Stop f-*BLEEP*-ing repeating yourself, ya twa-*BLEEP*," said Rathbone in the background.

"So, Peter, you said you were being persecuted because you're a vampire. Do you want to tell us a bit more about your ordeal?"

"I f-*BLEEP*-ing told you, didn't I?"

"You told our researchers. Would you like to share it with us?"

Rathbone shrugged.

"I thought that's what you came on here for?" said Colin, struggling to hide his annoyance.

Rathbone sighed. "Benefit office wouldn't give us a job, and doctor wouldn't sign us off sick."

"That's terrible," said Colin, without listening. "What about your friends?"

"They're a bunch of tos—*BLEEP*—ers."

"Tell us a bit more, maybe?"

"Well Sid Tillsley is a vampire hunter, but he never really bothered me, to tell you the truth. Then there was Arthur Peasley, he got a vampire lass up the duff, what was her name...Lucia or summat. Anyway, it was his lad who attacked that concert and that nightclub, you know? It were all over the papers and the telly the last couple of days."

Colin looked directly at the camera while talking to Rathbone. "You know who's behind the attacks?"

"Not personally, but I know it was vampires, and the pictures in the papers are Arthur's lad, for sure."

"Those are rather grand allegations," said Colin, hoping the deranged individual would hopefully move back to light-hearted topics so he could be the figure of fun he was intended. "Have you contacted the police about this?"

"I'm from 'boro, we don't go to the police, ya soft Southern bast-*BLEEP*-d."

"Maybe after the show, the police will want to talk to you, Peter."

"Why would I give a f-*BLEEP*-k about that? Oh, and there's Brian Garforth, that dirty bast-*BLEEP*-d bummed a vampire. 'Ere, how come you didn't bleep that out?"

"I...I don't think anyone expected you to say it," said the bemused TV presenter.

"Aye, and that ain't all. His jizz kills vampires. Can I say jizz?"

"What's jizz?"

"Spunk."

"No," said Colin, disgusted, before calling his bleep man through his earpiece. "Make sure you censor that word in future, Barry."

"Garforth's bugg-*BLEEP*-d this mincey vampire and his jiz-*BLEEP* made the vampire explode. It all happened in The Miner's Arms' toilets. Well, it used to be called The Miner's, but now it's a gay bar called The First Swallow of Summer."

"What are you talking about?" asked Colin, hoping the camera didn't catch his confused look.

But Rathbone had started, and he was going to finish. "Kevin Ackroyd, the fat t-*BLEEP*-at-of-a-landlord who runs it, turned it into a gay bar. He always treated me bad 'cos I'm a vampire, but then, he's a weird one 'cos he keeps a lot of dolls up his allotment shed and goes up there to roger 'em, which is proper freaky if you ask me."

"Why are you telling us all this?"

"You asked."

"Peter, do you believe these people actually exist?"

"Well, I should do. They're all alive and well in the Smithson Estate, Middlesbrough."

BWOGI SAT WATCHING THE TELEVISION in his office in the Coalition headquarters. Ever since he'd sentenced Ricard to death, he'd tried to take the lead. He just wasn't strong enough, and whatever power he held had slowly diminished.

The only thing keeping him going was his love for his species. His life meant nothing, not to him or anyone else for that matter. Bwogi believed, in his heart of hearts, the Agreement was the best thing for the vampire. The human race would never understand their kind, and considering some of the uncontrollable animals he tried to protect, he could see why.

First, there was Sparle and his reign of terror in the Northeast. If a vampire was caught on video feeding, it could be passed off as a crazed human, which had been the case in the past. However, if Sparle, all twelve feet, six hundred pounds of him, had been caught on camera, there would've been no possible cover-up.

Then came Gunnar Ivansey, who was more dangerous than Sparle ever was. There'd never been such a radical change in a lamia. He killed the five vampire overlords who ruled outside the stronghold of Great Britain, and then, single-handedly, threatened to bring the Agreement down. But then, he changed into something quite different. After his bizarre metamorphosis, he started his own faction, something that hadn't been done since the Agreement was formed. Vampires flocked to him, even though his demands for their loyalty were extreme—and very peculiar. It was the sense of belonging they wanted, and it was something the Coalition hadn't offered.

Gunnar Ivansey's effect on the vampire world was greater than he could've possibly imagined. He gave the vampires who didn't believe in the Agreement a purpose, and the idea of belonging was an attractive one. Borg Hemsman pounced on this. The only reason for his reappearance was the disappearance of his daughter, and if Peter Rathbone was right, then that was due to another human from Middlesbrough.

Like a chain reaction, each disaster had amplified the next. Borg's rise to power had been perfectly timed. Vampires now flocked to him, and it was only a matter of time until he announced to the world that vampires walked the earth. Now, he didn't need to. Peter Rathbone had done it for him. The Agreement's only hope was that people thought this entire show was a complete farce.

Sid and his friends were alive, and Harry Dean had been lying to them. The Coalition's number one agent wasn't carrying out their orders, and the Coalition couldn't stop the tide from coming in. Bwogi hoped to whatever god was listening, that Haemo could save them from a holocaustic nightmare.

"SO WHAT DO YOU HOPE TO ACHIEVE by coming on this show, Peter?"

"I'm hoping to do some vampire sh-*BLEEP*-t. Hopefully nailing more red-hot sluts."

Internally, Colin breathed a sigh of relief. This was familiar ground. "Not been lucky with the ladies since becoming a vampire, Peter?"

"'Course I have. I've been nailing loads of birds in the 'boro, but I want to move on to some classier birds, you know, with me being a vampire and all."

"Has becoming a vampire improved your prowess as a lover?" Colin growled the word "lover." He was a god.

"I was f-*BLEEP*-ing mint before, pal, but yeah, I'm even better now."

"That's bol-*BLEEP*-ocks! He's f-*BLEEP*-ing rubbish, like," came a shout from the audience.

Colin turned to the back row. "I'm sorry? Have you slept with our vampire before?" He made his way to the back of the studio.

The camera panned across a row of gargantuan, tattooed, drunken women. Colin Fitzpatrick was now dealing with Maggie and her crew, the hardest of all the single mums on the Smithson Estate. Their frightening appearance didn't faze him. Every row of the audience consisted of similar ladies from around the country.

"Aye," said Maggie's mate. "He's f-*BLEEP*-ing crap, he is. Smallest pecker I've ever seen on a man."

"I told you," argued Rathbone, "it's average for a vampire."

"I see," said Colin, laughing at the unplanned priceless comedy. "So, let's summarise, shall we, Peter? Your friends have shunned you because you're a vampire, the authorities haven't acknowledged your status as a vampire, and you're not impressing the ladies as a vampire because you don't—*ahem*—measure up."

"F-*BLEEP*-k off!"

Colin's face turned from one of light amusement to one of concerned seriousness in the blink of an eye. He really was that good. "Now, Peter, we need to address something here. Do you really believe you're a vampire who needs to drink blood to live?"

"A," he pointed at the cape, "I am a vampire. B, I don't need blood, I need Bolton Bitter."

ALL THE COALITION LEADERS WATCHED THE SPECTACLE while their representatives were desperately trying to cut the broadcast. Caroline watched with utter amusement as the horrible, greasy, little man on the television spilled the truth that'd been kept secret for nigh on three hundred years. She'd suspected Harry Dean of foul play when he'd reported back that he'd erased the four friends from Middlesbrough, but she hadn't followed it up. They were of no concern to her plans. That was, until the little greasy man mentioned Bolton Bitter. She'd never experienced the feeling of sickness through worry, and she didn't like it. She couldn't shake the gnawing feeling that before the end, she'd need Reece Chamber's help again.

"DO YOU DRINK, PETER?" asked Colin.

"Of course I f—*BLEEP*—ing drink. I'm Northern, ain't I?"

Colin had given up trying to curtail Peter's language, not just because it was impossible, but because it was turning out to be unbelievable television. "Have you ever thought the reason you think you're a vampire could be related to the amount you drink?"

Rathbone closed his eyes. "I sometimes think it ain't worth wearing this cape at all. Fair enough, I'll show you, but if I'm gonna show you, I want double me fee."

When he wasn't on camera, Colin looked at the producer nervously. His producer made a cutting motion across his throat.

"Peter, we don't pay our guests to appear on the show. We're here to help people in need, not encourage people to come here for the sake of money. We do, of course, cover expenses."

"I want double me expenses covering."

"Done."

"Reet," said Rathbone, removing his cape and rolling up his sleeve. "You got the Bolton Bitter?"

Colin nodded. "Coming up."

An assistant wheeled out a trolley containing ten pint glasses of the magical ale. "This ain't tinned crap is it?" Rathbone asked her.

"No," she said, keeping the trolley between her person and the horrible, greasy, little bastard.

"Fancy meeting up later for a quickie?" he tried on the attractive blonde.

"Fuck off," said she on instinct, beating Barry the Bleeper, who kicked himself at not being able to predict her response.

"Racist lesbian!" said Rathbone and got back to the business at hand. He pulled out a tin of lighter fluid, much to the dismay of the front row of the audience, Colin Fitzpatrick, and his producers.

"What are you doing!" cried Colin, as Rathbone squirted it all over his arm. "Security!"

Two security guards ran on stage but looked unsure of the best course of action when Rathbone pulled out a lighter.

"Stop him!" shouted Colin, but before they could do anything, Rathbone's arm was a torch and he screamed so loud that some of the audience fainted and Colin Fitzpatrick worried that he'd finally gone too far.

"AAAARRRGGGHHHHH!!! YA BASTARDS!!!"

"'ERE, KEV, RATHBONE IS ON THE TV," said one of the locals sat round the TV in The Swallow. Kevin Ackroyd was surprised. He'd never heard the punter talk before.

Kev walked around the bar to have a look at the television, and there he was, bold as brass, Peter Rathbone with his arm on fire.

"Stupid twat. He's been on TV before...well, photofits of him on *Crimewatch* after he flashed his old fella at a busload of Mormons," said Kevin, before turning over to *Who Wants To Be A Millionaire?*

SECONDS LATER, one of the backstage staff ran out with a fire extinguisher and put Rathbone out of his misery. "Fooking 'ell, that hurt!"

Barry the Bleeper was too shocked to do his job, and everyone in the audience and all over the country was too shocked to care.

"Are you...are you alright?" asked Colin.

"Of course I ain't! I just set me arm alight, ya daft twat!"

"I thought you were a vampire."

"It still fooking hurts!"

Rathbone held up his arm for the audience to get a good look at his red, black, and withered limb. "This, I do for all the women who want to sleep with a vampire." Like most men trying to impress womenfolk, Rathbone drunk a lot of beer very quickly.

After the tenth pint was finished, Rathbone held up his hand. The crowd gasped at the arm regenerating in front of them. Skin crawled to cover the flesh, soot fell away to the floor, and the inflammation disappeared.

For once, Colin Fitzpatrick had nothing to say.

KING SAT ON HIS BED watching Peter Rathbone and a tear ran down his cheek. This was the only person on the earth who could feel his pain and understand his loneliness. Peter was the only one of his kind and was scorned by the people around him. King put down his plate of club sandwiches, before picking them up again and finishing them. Action was required, but he needed to fuel the fire if he was going to have to throw some devastating karate.

That wasn't King's only cause to cry. His papa was still alive. Mixed emotions spiralled uncontrollably around his chubby mind, and he couldn't decide if he was happy or sad at the revelation. He concluded that he was hungry and opened a packet of potato chips. Peter Rathbone was his soul mate, and he would lead him to his papa.

Before he could get up, his grandpappy burst into his room.

"The Agreement has been broken!" he announced grandly.

"Huh?"

"That vampire," he said, pointing at the television, "no matter how pathetic, is the first vampire to announce to the world what he is. This is not how I wanted it to happen, but this cannot be ignored. This can catalyse the uprising. This will be seen across the world. We need to get hold of this Peter Rathbone."

"I'll help, Grandpappy."

"Really?" Borg slapped King on the shoulder. "Good. At last, you understand your true purpose. Come. We must act fast. Viralli!" he shouted. "Spread the word. The Agreement is over."

HARRY DEAN SAT AT THE BAR of a seedy pub in Sheffield, downing shot after shot of vodka. He was a big man, and his body had soon built up a tolerance to alcohol of yesteryear. He'd spent weeks on a wild goose chase tracking down Borg, and it was all a waste of time. War was here.

Peter Rathbone had just sealed his fate, and Harry didn't care. Everyone on the Coalition would now know of his deceit and Peterson's too. The death of the scout leader was all in vain. There would be many more joining him soon. One life was insignificant in the grand scale of things but not to Harry's mental state.

He toasted Sanderson. How that man had stayed sane was a miracle. Harry always thought Sanderson had a screw loose, and perhaps, he did. Perhaps that had enabled him to live through the misery of the vampire's world. Harry wasn't cut out for it.

Another round of vodkas plonked down in front of him. The barman was under strict instructions to keep pouring until Harry hit the floor. Things would turn nasty if he didn't comply.

Harry raised another glass to Sanderson and hammered it back. Now, he was drinking to forget, and once he got through enough vodka, he was going to do his job. Fuck all this Coalition bullshit. So far, it had got him and the country nowhere. Once the vampires attacked, he was going to take his place on the streets. If he saved just one life before he was killed, it would be worth it. Soon, death would bring him the peace he longed for. He was going to go out unloading his revolver into the vampire masses, and the thought of it made him smile for the first time in months.

25

Public attacks carried out by terrorist groups usually come with a calling card. Over the last few weeks, the attacks on the general public have been numerous and horrific. Yet, no one knows why. We don't know why we're being attacked, and it makes it even harder to predict where the next attack will come. One thing is for certain; this government will not stop until the perpetrators are brought to justice.

—Prime Minister's Question Time

SID SAT WITH THE REST of his fellow homophobes in the office of Dan Shire. Strangely, he hadn't dreaded the session. He wasn't exactly happy about the whole prospect, but there was so much other crap going on in his life, *them lot* were the least of his worries.

Life hadn't been easy at home since he'd been sacked as a bus driver and losing his Buddy the Bear job. The missus had been kicking off every five minutes even though it wasn't his fault the burger bar had shut up shop after the vamp attack.

He knew he was done for when the vampires at the shopping centre saw him, and just before leaving the house, he'd seen Rathbone blabbing everything on the telly. It was only a matter of time before the vampire bastards showed up. The missus was in a mood because of that and because of the incident with Brian the other day. She'd threatened to call off the whole wedding, which would be disastrous after he'd put so much effort into getting a shag.

"How are we all doing?" asked Dan, taking Sid's mind off his domestic woes.

Sid didn't mind Dan. He seemed...all right. He was the first *them lot* that Sid had...not disliked. The lad was born up North and still turned out to be one of *them lot*. He must have been involved with some vampire shit to have been turned.

Brian was one of *them lot*, but he wasn't a proper *them lot*. Did Sid still like him? That was something he hadn't been able to think about until these sessions. He knew, inside, that Brian was still his best friend. But, things had gone too far, and nothing would stop Sid from shagging his lass, who, for all her faults, really did have a cracking set of jugs.

The other skinheads had said their piece and it was round to Sid, who instinctively said, "I can't stand *them lot*."

"OK," said Dan, "Firstly, I was just trying to find out if you had a good weekend. Secondly, I thought we were over using the expression *them lot.*"

"Eh? Oh, reet, err, yeah, had a good weekend, like."

"Good," said Dan, smiling. "This is the last session of the programme, and you've all done really well. In fact, most of you have made such good progress that you can leave now."

"And you'll sign us off?" asked the skinhead Nigel, still sporting a bandage around his jaw after Sid had lamped him.

Dan nodded, and Sid rubbed his hands at getting let out of the session early. The missus weren't expecting him back for another hour, so he'd time for a few pints. It was a rare opportunity to drink good, old-fashioned cask ale and not the tinned crap he hid in her wheelie bin.

The others got up to leave. So did Sid, but he was soon disappointed when Dan put a hand on his broad shoulder. "Sid, I have a few more questions for you."

"Ah fook!" Sid's head dropped and he fell back into his chair, which did a sterling job of not being obliterated under the force. "Why me?"

"I'm not interested in the others. I've seen hundreds like them. You are something different. I believe I can truly help you."

Sid needed to do well in this class. His missus would be checking up on him for sure. A regular job was her number one priority, and now that'd gone down the shitter because of the vampire bastards, he had to make a good job of number two: getting rid of his homophobia. He didn't understand why she was so bothered about it, but then, it was only just above boozing and smoking on the priority list. Basically, she hated him doing anything.

Might as well do me best, he thought. Who knows? Maybe he'd find a cure for Brian, and that would mean he could go for a cheeky pint down the boozer with him when the missus was out.

Once the rest of the group were out of the room, Dan shut the door and put the kettle on. "Well, Sid, have you thought any more about our discussion at the end of the last session?"

Sid looked blank. He hadn't forgotten on purpose; forgetting was what he did.

Dan reminded him, "You were trying to remember back to your first hateful feeling towards a homosexual, remember?"

Sid thought.

Dan rummaged through one of the drawers in his desk and pulled out a bottle of Scotch. "Winter warmer in your tea?"

"Oh, aye!" said the big man gratefully. "*You lot* drink whisky do ya?"

Dan laughed. "Of course. I love beer too. Apart from sex, there's no difference between us. I was a good footballer when I was younger, and it may surprise you to know, I was a bit of a scrapper too."

Sid smirked at the concept of a fighting *them lot* while Dan made the tea adding a healthy measure of Scotch.

"Relax, Sid, and try to think back," he said, passing the big man his brew.

Sid looked back at his life and tried to remember when he'd first felt any kind of fear or resentment towards *them lot*. He really did have a shit memory. "I think it might have been the first time I went dogging."

Dan's eyebrow rose.

"Aye, I was out for some action, and two of *them lo*...No, I mean *them homomo-sexuals* tried it on with me, so I lamped one of 'em."

"Why did you hit him?"

"I told him I didn't want any, and he wouldn't listen."

The cup on its way to Dan's lips froze. "He forced himself on you?"

"It never got that far."

"Ah, well it sounds to me you were harbouring some negative feelings before that," said Dan.

Sid got back to thinking, enjoying the whisky in his tea. He strained to reach much further back in his drunken memory banks, but there was something lurking behind the drunken blurs, the flashing rights, and the entire back catalogue of his favourite magazine, *Tits*. He'd buried the memory deep down, but it was always there, gnawing away at him, causing fear and ultimately violence against *them homomo-sexuals* for the past thirty-odd years. He didn't want to talk about it, but he'd come this far and was so close to getting a jump.

He finished the tea and put down the cup and saucer on the table in front of him. "I used to like playing a bit of cricket as a young lad."

Dan got up and put the kettle on to boil again. "Another?"

"Aye, mon."

Dan grabbed his cup. "Please, continue."

"Weren't a bad batsman, if truth be told. I didn't do any of the running crap, like. It was either a four or a six, or nowt, but I always could give a ball a mighty wallop."

"I can imagine," said Dan, pouring in the water and allowing the tea to brew.

"What was I? I must've been twelve at most. I was never good at school, 'cept scrapping, and the teachers didn't like me doing that. Cricket, though, I could've been good at cricket." Sid's voice faltered.

Dan strained the teabags. "What happened?"

"We got to the final of the county cup, and if we won, we would've been given a shot. Winners got a training session with the Durham county team. I reckon I could've made it, you know, if what happened...hadn't have happened." Sid choked up.

"Here," said Dan, giving him the tea before pouring a large slug of liquor in it. Sid nodded his thanks. He sat forward in his chair, his foot tapping nervously.

"We'd put up a decent total and had a fair bowling team, so were feeling confident. They were good though, real good. There was nowt I could do by that time. I never got into the bowling as it was fooking hard work. It all came down to the last ball. They needed two runs to win. Fooking tense, I can tell ya."

Sid was grateful when Dan poured a glass of neat whisky and handed it to him. This was tough. He'd never talked about it before. "My best mate was next to me at second slip. Always had a fantastic pair of hands, he did. Never dropped a thing. We were thick as thieves we were. Always getting up to mischief, scrapping and that.

"Bowler put down a peach and the batsman got an edge, straight to me mate...and he dropped it. He fooking dropped it, mon." Sid wiped away a tear.

Dan nodded. "Go on, Sid."

"It got worse," said Sid, actually sobbing. "He then made a complete fook-up of getting it to wicketkeeper. He picked it up and threw it in the *wrong fooking direction*. Worst throw I've ever seen. We lost. It was in the bag...and we fooking lost." The whisky was thrown down, and the empty glass longingly stared at.

"OK?" said Dan, questioningly. He refilled Sid's cup.

"Everyone was fooking livid. There was a big crowd, like, and they turned a bit nasty."

"You were twelve, right?"

"Tough up North, lad, especially when it comes to sport."

"Even so..."

"I took meself off behind the pavilion and bawled me eyes out. Reckon I was there for hours."

"No one comforted you?"

Sid guffawed. "It was up North, I keep telling ya."

Dan didn't say anything.

"After I'd finished playing silly buggers, I went back in changing rooms. Everyone had gone home, except for me mate who lost us the match, and our old school teacher. It was just them alone, and I didn't like what I saw." Sid paused and took several deep breaths. "I never told anyone."

"Oh, God," said Dan, starting to well up too. He put a hand on Sid's knee...and Sid didn't punch him in the face. "Was the teacher abusing your friend?"

Sid nodded, biting his nails, fighting more tears.

"Oh, Sid, I had no idea..." Tears now fell freely down Dan's cheeks. "It was a terrible thing you saw, Sid. Your friend didn't deserve that. No one does. The way he was punished—abused—was terrible. But you have to remember, it has nothing to do with sexuality; the same atrocities happen to girls too, Sid."

"Yeah, but it's meant to happen to them," said Sid, matter-of-factly.

Dan choked on his tea. "It's not meant to happen to anyone," he said, strongly.

"Eh?"

Sid's brow furrowed. Dan said, "I think there's a crossed wire. What happened to your friend?"

"Went off to public school. More fooking proof!"

"Sid, go back. What happened to your friend in the changing rooms?"

"The teacher was yelling at him, telling him he threw like a girl. He told him...he told him...*he'd caught gay!*"

Sid broke down and sobbed into his hands.

"And?"

"It went round the school in no time," Sid mumbled from his place of mourning. "Everyone knew he was gay by the end of the week. It was horrible. It was fooking horrible."

"Because he dropped a cricket ball... the entire school thought he was gay?"

"Girls can't catch!"

"And that's it?"

"He threw like a girl too! He never used to! He must have caught gay from somewhere!"

"Is that it?" said Dan, again, but slower.

"And then, he went to *public* school!" said Sid, whose cold, hard stare told Dan he was deadly serious.

"Sid, you were twelve. Not everything kids say is true, and it sounds like he was being bullied."

"You should've seen the throw, mon."

"Sid, listen to me. You can't catch gay. Secondly, a lot of gays and girls can catch, and throw for that matter. I played cricket for Yorkshire Under 16s. Sexuality and gender has nothing to do with it."

"W...what?" Sid grabbed the bottle of whisky from near the kettle and topped himself up.

"Listen, your friend might have been gay, but that has nothing to do with dropping a cricket ball. He didn't 'catch' gay. You've been harbouring these bad feelings towards homosexual men because of a schoolyard rumour? It seems you've confused homosexuality with poor sporting achievement."

"Well, Brian bummed—"

"So?"

"And he's shit at cricket."

"So?"

The tears stopped. Sid's most emotionally destructive experience didn't seem so destructive anymore; the time he arm-wrestled Belinda Carlisle at Blackpool Pleasure Beach was promoted to top spot. Sid clutched at some new straws. "I'm on for a jump, ya know? I've gone through a lot to fooking get it."

"So?"

"I...I canna be turned. I've been through so much to get a shag. You wouldn't believe what I've been through."

"I would. I know you're signed up for all the classes. I know how much you're trying to change."

"I miss me beer, like," he said, pouring a fresh whisky. "And I miss the tabs and the kebabs."

Dan gave a comforting nod. "Do you love her?"

"Don't be daft, mon!" Sid waved a hand.

"Why are you with her?"

"A jump. And to stop catching gay."

"But now you know you can't catch gay, don't you?"

Sid looked inwardly before coming to his conclusion. "Aye," he said, and he meant it.

"Is it worth marrying a woman, just for sex?"

Sid thought long and he thought hard.

26

In a public poll, sixty-three per cent believed the government knows more about the recent attacks than they're letting on, with a staggering eighty per cent of those convinced the government had, in some way, caused the terror that's been plaguing the UK.

—Conspiracies Uncovered

COALITION AGENTS ARRIVED at the studio broadcasting *The Colin Fitzpatrick Show* in record time. They'd been ordered to shut the show down at any cost and bring in Rathbone discretely. Five agents went to apprehend the greasy vampire while the same number went to pull the plug on the show. Phone calls hadn't been effective, because the television executives assumed they were hoax. They'd considered cutting the show themselves but quickly realised that something quite bizarre and incredible was taking place and any bad publicity would be outweighed by the good.

Peterson, Harry Dean's right-hand man, was in an uncomfortable position. He led the men tasked to apprehend Rathbone. He hoped Rathbone wasn't as powerful as a natural-born vampire. He'd no idea what he was dealing with.

Peterson arrived to witness the crowd's reaction to Rathbone having healed his arm. Now, they waited for the signal from the other team that the broadcast had been cut.

His eyes darted from Rathbone, to the audience, and the various exits. There weren't enough agents to usher out the crowd, and if they did get rid of them, they risked losing Rathbone in the mayhem. They had to do this in front of the audience, meaning eyewitnesses and more fuel to the fire. What did it matter? This had all been broadcast on live television.

On top of that, Peterson had the worry of the order coming down from above for one of his fellow agents to put a bullet in the back of his and Harry Dean's head for disobeying direct orders. They'd soon put two and two together.

"TV is off the air. Take him down," said a voice through his earpiece.

"STAY WHERE YOU ARE!" shouted Peterson, advancing onto the stage, pistol raised.

Rathbone turned to see five guns pointed at him. He just shrugged. "Get fooked, you lot," said the uncensored vampire. "About time," he said to the bleepman.

"OK, everyone calm down," said Colin Fitzpatrick, backing away from the firearm and nearer the exit.

"Keep out of this, sir," said Peterson, not taking his eyes from Rathbone.

"He's the wanker you ought to shoot. Reet annoying twat," said Rathbone pointing at Colin.

"On your knees, now," said Peterson, ignoring him.

"Leave him alone!" shouted one of the audience members.

"Aye!" said another. "That was a good trick with the beer. Leave him be!"

The situation was getting worse. "Look, Peter, there's gonna be vampires swarming down here in a minute. We have to get you out of here."

"Fooking Peter now, is it? Who the fook are you, anyway?"

"Coalition."

"Biggest bunch of wankers out of the—"

The crowd jumped with the sound of a single gunshot and decided against sticking up for the vampire with the bullet in his head. Rathbone tumbled back into his chair, his head lolling to the side, bringing with it the gush of blood from the entry wound.

Peterson placed his gun against the vampire's greasy head and gave the bullet already lodged in his brain some company. It would ensure no more backchat for a while.

"Let's get him out of here. Quick."

"This is going well," said one of the agents into Peterson's ear.

"With Borg Hemsman most likely on his way, I don't give a shit."

The agent nodded and grabbed a limb, as did the others, leaving Peterson to deal with the crowd.

"Folks, you best get out of here. Things are going to turn nasty."

None of the crowd had moved since Rathbone was shot. They all looked on, aghast, with exception to Maggie and her crew, who were used to it.

Peterson dealt with them. "When the rest of the vampires turn up, you're all dead." He didn't get a response, so he turned the gun on them. "GET THE FUCK OUT OF HERE!"

That worked.

BORG AND HIS CREW arrived at the television studio. The cars parked outside told them the Coalition were already here. A moment later, a sea of humans flooded out of the studio's entrance and screams of terror filled the night. The old vampire smiled. "This will be interesting television, indeed."

"Can I be on the TV, Grandpappy?"

"You'll need to wash the chicken grease from your face first, but yes, I can't see why not."

"Can I sing?" asked King, hope shining from his baby blues.

Viralli shook his head at Borg.

"If you kill a human, you can sing," said Borg, causing Viralli to grin.

King considered it and nodded. "I need to find Peter Rathbone, first."

"Very well. What's your plan?"

King looked into his bucket of fried chicken. There were seven pieces left. "I'm gonna wait in the car park, just in case he comes round the back way."

"Very well. I'll see you inside." Borg climbed out of the limousine, not wanting to look at the disappointment any longer.

Borg and Viralli left the hybrid with his chicken and marched into the studio with twenty vampires in tow. "I give up, Viralli."

"You've shown the patience of a saint, sir. You did your best."

"I tried. The human side is more dominant. We must forget him. He has no place in the new world, and I fear he won't last long on his own."

"You're doing the right thing, sir. Maybe when we have control of the country, you can try again, but first, let's take what's ours. Three hundred years we have lived in the shadows. I don't want to spend another day under this cursed Agreement."

"And you won't, my friend." Borg placed a reassuring hand on the huge vampire's shoulder. "It ends tonight."

"NNNGGHH," was all Rathbone could manage. He was aware he was being carried, and he was aware he was in pain. Suddenly, he wasn't aware of anything. Peterson had shot him in the head again.

"Borg is here. Hurry up!" shouted Peterson.

"How do you know?" asked the agent holding Rathbone's leg.

Peterson grimaced. "I just heard Summers scream into my earpiece."

"We have to go back," said another agent.

"It's too late. He told us to run. We've got to get this thing to the Coalition." Peterson wondered if bringing evidence of his lies to headquarters was such a good idea, but it was the only option he had. He needed to speak to Harry but feared he'd be found at the bottom of a vodka bottle.

They charged through the back corridors of the television studio, heading for a fire exit, the location of which was blurted at them by a stagehand when a gun was stuck in her face.

"They'll be vamps outside for sure," said an agent.

"Then don't miss," said Peterson. "We're almost there. I'll go first."

He sprinted ahead, kicking open the fire exit into the car park with his pistol drawn. He scanned the surroundings down the barrel of his weapon. Luckily, the car park was deserted. The only way of getting Rathbone away was going round the front of the building to where the Coalition's cars were parked.

"Clear," he called. The agents scurried outside with Rathbone in their arms. Peterson pulled out a blade from his jacket and drove it deep into the vampire's brain. "We can't afford to make any noise. This isn't gonna be fun. Let's go."

KING WASN'T A COWARD, no matter what his grandpappy thought. He was here to rescue Peter Rathbone and become buddies with the only other unique organism on the planet. But, he had a bucket of chicken to finish, and it was against his moral code to leave food.

"Fuck!" said King, when the final drumstick came and went.

The TV studio looked awful big. It'd be good to get on TV and rescue his future buddy...but there would be a lot of stairs, and he had no cheeseburgers to give him the energy he needed to climb them.

What's that? he thought when he spied movement at the corner of the building. He tried to hide below the level of the car window, but his belly made it difficult. Four men carried a lifeless body. His vampire vision allowed him to recognise the body of Rathbone.

Are they kidnapping him? he asked himself.

King had to act, and fast. He took one final look in his bucket and couldn't believe he'd missed a bit of chicken skin. He crammed it into his mouth. The vampire guarding the front entrance would see them. It would be fine and dandy. No point wasting any energy. Not just yet.

The vampire on guard dropped like sack of shit.

"Damn it!"

King searched desperately in the bucket for some more skin.

THE CROWD LEFT IN A STAMPEDE. Many had been trampled, and Colin Fitzpatrick knew the lawsuits would flood in tomorrow. The crowd was full of lowlifes. If they put this much effort into working as they did stealing and conning money from the government, they'd be very rich indeed. But not as rich as Colin, they'd never be that rich.

Taking off his makeup in his dressing room was always a bad time for Colin. Revealing the real him was not something he enjoyed. He wanted to be the man who appeared on the television, beautiful, intelligent, powerful, and irresistible to woman. He didn't like the reality of an old, saggy body, a cocaine addiction, and a string of broken marriages.

"Janie, get me a drink!" he yelled, and it irked him that it didn't appear instantly. Most of the staff had fled with the crowd but not him. He was a professional.

The dressing room door opened. "That better be a double...Who are you?"

"You present on the television, correct?"

Colin had no idea whom he was talking to, but a strange sensation told him that showing anything other than total respect for the massive, almost regal individual would not be wise. "Y...yes."

"Where is the one you called Rathbone?"

Colin stammered, "S-s-some men with guns took him."

"So be it." The frightening individual tapped at his chin in thought. "I want to appear on television. I want you to make it happen."

"It's not up to me. I...I..."

A flash of anger crossed the face. "If you can't make it happen, it means I have no use for you."

"I...I...can help."

A nod, and Colin was glad the giant left the room. His hope was short-lived. His stomach turned over when a shaven-headed man, twice as big as the last, filled the doorway. In one hand, he held the whisky that Janie was meant to get him, and in the other, he held Janie. Her lifeless eyes confirmed everything Colin needed to know.

"Your drink."

PETERSON POPPED HIS HEAD round the corner of the studio and scanned the vicinity, looking down his gun sights. There were a lot of cars and a lot of places to hide. Still, he couldn't see any movement, and time wasn't on his side. He put his hand up in a fist for the group to stop and ventured forward alone, slow and quiet.

When he stepped past the safety of his corner position, his legs disappeared from under him, and the air left his lungs as he crashed into the pavement. Stars swam across the cloudy sky and then across the face of Reece Chambers, whose fist, a moment later, filled his view.

REECE BEGAN DISPENSING with the four Coalition agents who carried Rathbone. His hands and feet were a blur as he ripped through the agents without the need to fire a shot.

He'd expected far more resistance than this. One vampire guarding the front? He thought Borg would be smarter, but then, he was always going to underestimate his human adversaries, and it would be his undoing.

The knife that the agents had left in Rathbone's head was a nice touch. He threw the vampire over his shoulder with ease, jogged over to his car, and threw Rathbone into the secure boot. He looked around, hopeful of some vampires to kill, found none, and jumped into the driver's seat. He sped back to his lab, eager for the research he was about to undertake.

KING PEERED OUT of the limousine window and watched the human throw Rathbone in the trunk of his weird-looking car. He quickly ducked when the human's gaze passed the limo he was hiding in. King wasn't a coward, but that was one tough son of a bitch. He'd made mincemeat of the cats in suits and showed no mercy messing up the vampire dude. King would've done something, but his fingers were slippery from the greasy chicken skin.

However, it was time for action. King couldn't let Peter down. He had dreams of hanging out together, singing some duets and shit. Once the tough guy's car pulled out of the studio, King hurried into the driver's seat of the limo. It was time to take care of business.

PETERSON CAME TO, and his hand instinctively reached for his jaw. He'd been hit hard. Chambers. His face and his fist were the last thing he remembered. He sat up, shakily. He'd been knocked behind some bins adjacent to the studio. The smell of dog piss and rubbish wasn't a nice one to wake to.

He wiggled his jaw from side to side, testing its integrity. Chambers had landed a punch he wouldn't forget in a hurry. Groggily, he got to his feet.

His colleagues lay beside them, all out for the count. There were still some expensive cars in the car park. The vampires were still here. He took out his phone and called Harry.

The call connected. "We're fucked now, ain't we kiddo?"

Peterson strained his ear. "I can hardly hear you, where are you?"

"Hang on."

Peterson feared the worst, and the beat of music faded as Harry made his way out of the pub he was camped in.

"Was just having a few drinks. Hear me OK now?"

"A few?"

"Don't lecture me, ya little shit. Now ain't the time," slurred Harry. "We're pretty fucked right now, me and thee."

"Borg's men are still at the television centre. There's still time to stop him."

"How many you got with ya?"

Peterson looked at his backup, all but one was fast asleep, and the one who was coming to groaned in pain. "Just me."

"Where are ya?"

"A few miles from Manchester."

"Listen to me, kid. The fight's almost here, and chances are, guys like you and me ain't gonna win. They're gonna hit us hard and we've gotta get ready."

"And you're gonna stop drinking?"

"Nah. I'm a good shot with a few voddies in me. Get out of there, now. No heroics."

"The Coalition will kill us."

"Well, I'm about to find out. They're on the other line. Now, get the fuck out of there!"

HARRY SWITCHED THE CALL. "Hello."

"Dean?" He recognised Charles' voice.

"Speaking."

"What did you think you'd accomplish?"

"I don't follow, sir,"

"Your orders were to eliminate Sid Tillsley and his friends, Dean. You told us they were dead."

Harry had no option but to tell the truth, and he was too drunk to make up any elaborate lies. "Sanderson saw something in these men and felt they were worth saving. He believed they'd have a part to play in all this bullshit."

"He was right too," shouted Charles. "Peter Rathbone just started a full-blown war on the streets of every major city of the UK."

"It would've happened anyway."

"You've let us down, Harry." It was Caroline's turn to rip into him.

"It's not like you've done any good, is it?"

"Don't you even dare," she said. "We'll strike soon. We have a plan, even for this."

"Then what do you want from me?"

"You're still the best we've got."

He hung his head. Saving Sid was the right thing to do. The bottle had just crept up on him. He was once a good man, but these vampires...they'd made him do unspeakable things. This council had sat back and expected him to take it all in his stride while they lorded it up in their swanky apartments.

Caroline said, "We need you to put down that bottle and be the soldier you were born to be. Are you still in Sheffield?"

"Yeah."

"Manchester has just been on the line and they've been hit hard. Real hard. Go take charge and make up for your mistakes. You owe the Coalition and you owe your country, Harry."

"Yes, ma'am," he said, throwing the glass of spirit he held into the gutter.

"And Harry?"

"Ma'am?"

"Don't fuck up again."

"I'll die first." He hung up. He meant it too. His life couldn't go on like this. He had a chance to make a difference and shooting things was simple. He dialled through to Peterson.

"I'm coming your way, kidda. We've been pardoned...for now. Let's take back the streets. If we make it through this, they'll stab us in the back, so we might as well go out killing some bloodsuckers."

27

Good evening, ladies and gentlemen. We are sorry to interrupt our regular broadcast of Who Wants To Be A Millionaire, *but we've reports of a series of violent, disturbing riots breaking out across the UK. London, Birmingham, Bristol, Newcastle have been hit, with riots in Manchester proving particularly destructive. What can only be described as madness has descended across, seemingly, random members of the public.*

—*ITV News*

BAD THINGS HAPPEN IN THE WORLD. Mother Nature can be a cruel bitch, but even she, on her time of the month, wouldn't be so vindictive to forbid Sid Tillsley from having a Stag Night.

Sid had moped for the entire night before his wedding day, gutted he wasn't drinking Bolton Bitter. It would've only been a small do. Brian wasn't an ale man anymore; Rathbone was now a Hollywood star; that only left Arthur, who was a good lad he'd loved to have sunk a few ales with. But no, he wasn't allowed. His only consoling thought was a jump at the end of it all.

Sid stood outside the registry office rubbing his hands. It was bloody cold, and the sun going down meant it was getting colder. Temperature affected Sid since he'd lost his puppy fat. He wore the outfit his missus had given him and hadn't spilled any dinner down it or nowt. He looked dapper in his suit, shirt, and tie.

"Married?" he asked himself, kicking stones across the car park.

He hadn't really considered marriage in its entirety. Sure, he was going to get a jump tonight, but since he'd got to the bottom of his homomofoabier after his chats with Dan, he'd been thinking about what else there was to holy wedlock. Taking the rubbish out, taking her to get her hair cut, and going on shit holidays—it was natural to get cold feet. He tried to concentrate on the positives: he was going to get a jump, at least once.

Negatives pushed their way back in. All the married men Sid knew said sex dried up when they got married. That worried the big man. He hadn't done any shagging before the wedding. It had been a barren desert, and it was likely to be a long trek before he reached an oasis—or at least got fingers and tops.

He looked at his watch. She was late, but then, she was meant to be. He'd never imagined he wouldn't have a best man at his wedding, but then, like most men, Sid'd never imagined his wedding before. Thanks to Dan the *homomo-sexual*, Sid was ready to forgive Brian, but after the little incident at Marks and Spencer, he'd be fighting a losing battle if he dared suggest Brian being the best man to the missus.

Sid kicked another stone, and this one dented the side of a fancy car parked and waiting to take the couple already inside to their reception venue. The chauffeur quickly got out of the car to give the vandal a clip round the ear, but after seeing Sid decided to buff the chrome wing mirrors instead.

It was time to stop kicking stones. He was to look smart for when she turned up. His timing was spot on; the car carrying his bride-to-be pulled round the corner.

ARTHUR AND BRIAN sat moping in The First Swallow of Summer, drinking beer so good it was a shame not to be sharing it with Sid Tillsley, the man on death row. The night previous had been a depressing affair for both men, who had drunk themselves into a paralytic state for the Stag-that-never-was. Sid's Stag should've been the ultimate piss-up. They should've partied so hard the whole world would've heard. They could've gone to Skeggy and everything, but no, they drank alone. Well, Kev was there, and the lads in the corner watching Tarrant, but essentially, they were alone.

"Can you believe Sid is actually getting married today?" said Arthur, finishing his pint and pointing to the glass.

Kev obliged. "I never thought the big man would settle down. Never thought a woman would take him."

"Especially one with such great tits." Brian smashed his fist down onto the table, and the pain reverberated around his whole body. After a copper had saved him, he'd been taken to hospital. The coppers knew his attempted murder would take a lot of paperwork, so they dropped the perving charge if he kept his mouth shut. Brian was more than happy to oblige...and made a mental note that he owed Jimmy the Barman a visit. Brian couldn't believe the little bastard had stabbed him in the back like that, not when they were even.

"Something's not right!" Brian tore at his thinning, oiled hair. "I fooking know something's wrong. I just canna remember what it is."

Arthur shook his head. "You've been saying that since Marks and Spencer, man. What the fuck did you see in those changing rooms?"

"I...I...can't remember."

"Come on, think! You were going in there for proof she's a vampire."

"I know." He massaged his temples. "But I can't fooking remember what I saw."

"They're getting married when it's dark. Surely that means something," said Arthur looking at his watch.

"Why would a vampire want to marry him, though? Surely they'd just kill him in his sleep or summat?" Brian slapped himself in frustration. "All I know is I saw something, and for the life of me, I canna remember what."

"Whatever it is," said Arthur. "It ain't right that Sid marries that battleaxe, tits or no tits."

"So what's she doing with Sid, then?" asked Kev.

"Exactly!" shouted Brian. "Fook me, there's something wrong. We've got to stop the wedding, no matter what."

"You can't just go in there and stop the wedding, man. Sid left you for dead at the hands of all those angry women in town—"

"So did you, ya bastard!" interrupted Brian.

Arthur put his shades on to avoid eye contact. "I was...erm...getting help. I can hardly use my karate on a bunch of middle-aged women, can I?"

"They fooking used worse on me!"

"It pains me to say it, but Sid is her lapdog, and if you go in there causing shit, the best it's gonna earn you is a broken jaw. He's only thinking about the lovin' now, man."

"Well, we've got to do something." Brian got off his barstool, taking a heroic stance.

"What are you going to do?"

"Eh? Oh, I'm off for a piss."

ONCE THE SUN SET, she stepped out of the car, and both of Sid's cold feet warmed up. She walked towards him, and she was a picture. Her tits looked magnificent.

Sid wasn't worrying how much the car cost, even though he knew he'd be working until he was seventy to pay for it. Tonight, he was going to get his hands on those puppies. It was all worth it.

He was surprised she was smiling. He didn't recall seeing her smile before. Out the other side of the motor stepped an older fella, whom Sid assumed was her dad. Sid hadn't met the old man, since there was no need to ask his permission for his daughter's hand in marriage. She'd told Sid they were getting married, and that was that. Sid wondered what the old man carried in his bag.

"Eh'up, pet."

"Don't call me pet," she said sternly. "This is Dr Stanley. He will be performing the tests."

"Tests?"

"You didn't think we'd be doing this if you hadn't changed like I asked, did you?"

Sid looked at her ample cleavage. "No, dear."

"Cholesterol check," she said in the same way a mechanic might tell his assistant to check the brakes during a MOT.

Dr Stanley pulled out a piece of kit from his leather holdall. "Please give me one of your fingers, Mr Tillsley."

"Pull that one."

"Do no such thing," ordered Sid's missus.

"Ouch!" said Sid, when the cholesterol tester pricked his finger.

Dr Stanley examined the kit and announced, "His cholesterol levels are extremely high."

A raised eyebrow from Sid's future bride meant trouble.

"But, it has halved in the last two months and passes your criteria, madam."

The eyebrow lowered. "Cigarettes?"

Dr Stanley, pulled another contraption from his bag, one made to measure lung capacity. "Please blow into this tube as hard as you can, Mr Tillsley."

Sid blew with all his might, thinking of blowing raspberries between titties.

"Very good, Mr Tillsley. Your lung capacity has significantly improved."

Sid smiled. One step closer. He aced the next test: the weigh-in. He'd invested in one of Jock the Turk's Jumbo kebabs. The special chilli sauce that gave the "Ulcer-Bringer" its name had once made a seagull explode. Sid had lost a stone overnight, a big "fook you" to those Diet-Darling bitches! The breathalyser, however, was borderline.

He rubbed the rolls of flab on the back of his neck. "I had a couple of whiskies, for Dutch courage."

"Why? Are you nervous?" she asked threateningly.

"I was only nervous that I'd fail these tests, my sweet." Sid had never thought faster. Maybe beer had been clouding his judgement through the years.

She nodded. Out came the last test, the one that would test both Sid's anger management and his homophobia. Sid had never seen ink blot cards before and had no idea that the Rorschach test would examine his inner psyche.

"Right, Mr Tillsley, I want you to say the first thing that comes into your head."

"Tits."

"Not yet," said the doctor. "I'll show you the card, and then, you say the first thing you think of, OK?"

"OK," said Sid.

"Go," said the doctor flashing the card.

"Tits."

"I don't think this is going to work," said Dr Stanley.

"You're a fucking professional. I want to know if he's changed for the better," spat the future Mrs Tillsley.

"OK, Mr Tillsley, I want you to say the first thing that comes into your head, after I say it, OK?"

"OK."

"Right," Dr Stanley paused before hitting Sid with it. "Gay."

"Cricket."

"Rimming."

"Second slip."

Dr Stanley's brow furrowed.

"OK...Brian Garforth."

"435 for six, declared."

The doctor paused for a second. "OK, let's try a standard question. What do you think of homosexual relationships?"

Sid didn't say anything. It wasn't something that inspired any emotion in him at all. A year ago, he would have fainted. A month ago, he would have floored the doctor, but now...nothing. Dan Shire had completely cured him. Sid was still an idiot, but he wasn't a homophobic idiot.

"He's fine," said the doctor, giving Sid a slap on the arm. "He's passed everything."

Sid looked hopefully at his future partner, who sighed.

"Might as well get this over with," she said.

28

The police have quickly lost control, unable to determine whom they are trying to apprehend. Reports say hundreds are dead in Manchester. The army is being drafted in. Anyone in an affected area should lock their windows and doors and not leave their homes.

—Public Broadcast

Brian stood in The Swallow's fancy toilets. Kev had gone to town jazzing them up at the Campire's request. This was a place that brought nothing but bad memories to the swordsman. He stood at the urinal in the most manly position a man could piss in: legs spread wide apart, one hand shaking the snake, the other stretched high above, palm of the hand on the wall, bracing the gentleman from the force of his stream.

He relived the events that took place in these toilets a few months ago every time he stepped through the door because lavender air freshener puffed out at him. The Campire was a low point in the life of Brian Garforth. Not the lowest—but definitely in the top ten.

Everyone on the Smithson Estate knew Brian as a scholar, if a gay one, but now, he had to prove it to himself and remember back to the day in Marks and Sparks. There was something not right in that dressing room, he was sure of it.

Everything pointed to a vampire, but that, in itself, didn't make any sense. Sid's only other enemy had been the benefit office, but not now since he was officially dead. That just left the council thing. What was it? The Coalition. Was the woman a spy?

"Come on, Brian, what did you see in those dressing rooms?" Brian wrung out the snake, and, as he did, it hit him.

"Oh, God!"

NEWLYWEDS RAN OUT from the registry office, confetti following them through the doors. They were an older couple, just like the future Mr and Mrs Tillsley, but Sid was pleased to note the bride didn't have jugs half the size of his lady. They looked so happy. He turned to face his future, and she looked miserable as sin...but the jugs...the jugs. Sid put his arm out, and the lady took it. There would be just two people at this wedding. Not a single friend on the groom's side was allowed to come...The bride had no friends.

It was just what the bride intended.

BRIAN DOUBLED THE SPEED LIMIT down the tight streets of the Smithson Estate. There was no danger of any children being killed since the mighty roar of the Capri could be heard for miles around, and the kids of Middlesbrough knew that Brian wouldn't stop if they ran out to get their footy. Brian and Arthur were in a race against time.

"Once you eliminate the impossible, whatever remains, no matter how improbable, must be the truth," said the scholar.

"That's deep, man. Is that some sort of quote or summat?"

"Aye," said the well-read Northerner, "Columbo."

"Cool. So what does it mean, Brian?"

"It's quite elementary, my dear Peasley. It means that Sid's missus has a cock."

Brian's epiphany caused Arthur to pause. "They're some mighty allegations you're making, man."

"It sounds far-fetched, but it's the only possible explanation."

"And you distinctly remember seeing it?"

"It's...erm...hazy."

"Fuck," said Arthur, "One minute you think she's a vampire, and the next you think she's got a dick. You're clutching at straws, man."

"What other explanation is there?"

"Probably a different one."

"Look, those jugs ain't real—they're plastic—they've just gotta be. She's got him in these homophobia classes so that he doesn't kick off. She's a bloke who's had a sex change, I'm telling ya."

"I thought you said you saw the cock."

"I said it's hazy." Brian took a moment to give a wanker sign to an old lady attempting to make her way over a zebra crossing. "Look, it all makes sense."

"So what about the booze, the fags, and the job?"

"Women change men. It's what they do. A bloke having a sex change is gonna try and take on every aspect of what being a woman is and exaggerate it. He/she's taking it to the extreme."

"And why pick Sid?"

"I..." Brian's fingers tapped on the steering wheel. "I don't know."

"Are you sure about this?"

"No, but we're gonna find out." Brian slammed on the brakes.

They'd reached the registry office.

"DO YOU TAKE SID TILLSLEY, to be your lawful wedded husband?"

"I do."

"And will you, Sid Tillsley, take—"

"Stop everything!" cried Brian bursting through the door to the ceremony.

The registrar raised his eyebrows but did not look surprised. This was Middlesbrough's Registry Office. There were at least three fistfights a day in this grimy, dated office. Every other wedding was stopped for some reason or other, often due to alcohol-related vomit.

Brian clutched at his ribs. The dash from the car had been a hard one and had aggravated some of his wounds. "Stop..."

"Brian, what the fook are you doing here?" demanded Sid.

"You can't marry her, Sid."

Arthur followed in close behind. The two paid witnesses announced they were off for a fag while they let another domestic run its course.

"Brian fucking Garforth," spat the venomous bride. "I thought you learned your lesson outside M&S."

"Sid, you can't marry her."

"Brian, I know what you're going to say." Sid raised his hands, trying to calm his friend down. "Listen, I owe you an apology. I've had counselling, mate. I was wrong to treat you the way I did. There's nothing wrong with being gay."

"I ain't fooking—"

"You haven't got to say it anymore," interrupted Sid. "Look, I know why you're here."

"No, you don't."

"I know you don't want me to get married, because you think I'm getting married for the wrong reason, but this is what I want, Brian."

Brian cut to the chase. "Sid, she's got a cock!"

"What?" exclaimed Sid and his bride in unison. The registrar didn't bat an eyelid. He'd heard the same line twice this week already.

"She's got a cock, mate."

"Outside M&S, you reckoned she was a vampire," said Sid.

"I thought she was. She never goes out in daylight. I went to the changing rooms to prove she was a vampire. I saw something else though, and it was wiped from my memory when them crazy-arsed bitches kicked the fook out of me, but it's come back to me...sort of."

"Are you going to get rid of him?" said Sid's missus.

Her cool, calm voice made Sid extremely nervous of losing titties. "Fook off, Brian," said Sid. He'd hoped his friend had burst in to see him get married, or at least try and stop him for a decent reason, like a pint.

"Come on, Arthur. He's too far gone," said Brian, turning to go.

The registrar looked at his watch and the witnesses came back. "We'll continue then?"

Bride and groom nodded.

"Do you, Sheila Fishman..."

"SHEILA FOOKING FISHMAN!" screamed Brian.

"Take another break," said the registrar to the witnesses, who gladly obliged.

"That's fucking right, Garforth, you horrible, disease-ridden bastard."

"Ain't that the psycho who tried to get Sid done for benefit fraud?" asked Arthur, pointing disbelievingly at Sheila.

"Aye," said Brian, staring at Sheila with his mouth open. "But...but she never looked like...that."

"I may have had a little work done," she said, adjusting her nose.

"Sid, what the fook are you doing? She tried to have you killed, mon!"

"But look at the jugs, Brian."

Sheila jumped up and clipped Sid round the ear.

"Do you really want to spend the rest of your life with *her*? She'll have you working until you fooking die. There'll be no booze, no fags, no kebabs, and all the time you'll know that if you step out of line, she'll try to have you killed like last time."

"I...I..." stuttered Sid.

"Fooking 'ell, woman. What do you want to marry Sid for anyway?" asked Brian.

"Can't a woman change?" she said, doe-eyed, fluttering her eyelids at Sid.

"But you hate him," said Brian.

"I saw the error of my ways, and now, I want to settle down."

"Bullshit, man, Brian saw your cock," said Arthur, confusing matters.

"Sid," said Brian. "You can't do this. This will be the end, mate. If you marry her, there won't be any coming back."

"I...I've got to."

"For a shag? All this for a shag?" The look Sid got from Sheila said there was no chance of him getting any tonight.

"I...I'm sorry, Brian. I'm going my own way. I've no problem with the path you've chosen. I don't blame you for what you did. You homomo-sexuals are alright by me."

"Then, you leave me with no choice," said the swordsman, drawing the weapon from his suit jacket.

"What the fuck are you doing!" screamed Arthur when Brian pointed the Cumapult directly at Sid.

"Brian, calm down," said Sid slowly. "Put that thing down. You can't give me homomo-sexual. It doesn't work that way anymore."

"You've forced my hand, Sid."

Arthur winced at the thought.

Brian pulled the trigger.

29

"I don't know what's happening! People have gone insane. I watched two women kick my neighbour's front door in. The screams...you should have heard the screams! I heard them leave, laughing, boasting of what they'd done. I...I...plucked up the courage to...to see if anyone was left. They'd been drained of all their blood, the whole family. Cannibals are stalking the streets at night, and the army can't stop them because they don't even know who they are."

—Eyewitness, Manchester

RATHBONE WASN'T ENJOYING his time being a hostage. The last time he'd been a hostage was pretty shit too, but at least the Allotmenteers weren't a bunch of pretentious wankers like his current captor. Even when Rathbone was a human, he'd thought Rich Chambers was right up his own arse. Since Rathbone'd been turned into a vampire, Rich, the Southern twat, had really gone to town. But, the thing Rathbone would never forgive, or never forget, was the day Rich made him get piss on his cape.

The cape was gone. There weren't even any clothes to hide Rathbone's dignity, not that he had any, mind. He was naked to the world, strapped to the same table that, unknown to him, had held Farouq hostage a few weeks ago. Rathbone didn't know he was a guinea pig. Not that it would have worried him if he did. He was more concerned about why Rich had tied him up with his cock hanging out. Rathbone very much doubted that there were prostitutes behind the thick steel doors in front of him.

The cold, hard restraints burrowed into his wrists and he wriggled, trying to get comfortable. His back was clammy and sweaty, more so than usual, from lying on the steel bed for so long. He needed some Bolton, and fast. He'd taken a lot of bullets after being kidnapped from the orange-skinned bastard's television show. Again, Rathbone very much doubted that if there were prostitutes behind the doors, they'd be holding pitchers of Bolton Bitter. Life wasn't fair.

The whirring of metalwork from behind the steel doors indicated he was going to be bothered by that wanker Rich. He was right. Rich strode into the room when the gap in the door was big enough for him to fit his frame.

"Why ain't you got a fooking top on!" shouted Rathbone, starting to worry more about his uncovered pecker.

"Look at the wonderful gift you bestowed upon me," said Rich flexing his muscles.

"Garforth's the one you want. Garforth is into all that shit, not me. You've got the wrong man."

"Man? Oh no, Rathbone, you're a vampire, remember."

"Doesn't mean I do that shit." Rathbone wasn't enjoying Rich's manic grin.

"I thought you were dead. I thought I'd lost you. I thought I had everything I needed to gain the ultimate power, but I didn't. I need you, Peter." Rich ran his hand coyly through Rathbone's hair causing Rathbone's old fella to defy biology and shrink even further. "You will give me the specimen I so desperately need."

"You dirty bastard!"

Rich walked out of Rathbone's field of vision. "Now, all the answers I seek are in that white, pasty, yet powerful grease pit of a body of yours."

Rathbone heard the trolley before he saw it. He didn't have a clue what was going on, but he certainly didn't expect Bolton Bitter to be wheeled in front of him. "Howay the lads!"

"A whole keg of your beloved beer."

Rathbone cut himself on the metal restraints; he was so drawn to the Bolton. "Givvus some then, ya tight bastard."

"All in good time, Peter."

"Now's a fooking good time," he said desperately.

Rich's wry smile indicated trouble afoot.

"What are ya up to?"

"First, you are going to take part in a scientific experiment." Rich turned the trolley round to unveil the terror-inducing syringes that the keg of Bolton hid from Peter's view.

"Does it involve hookers?"

"No," said, Rich, picking up the most monstrous of the needles, long, thick, and glinting in the artificial light of the prison. "We might as well get the worst one over with," he said, walking over to where Rathbone lay.

Rathbone screamed as the syringe pierced deep into his stomach.

GRITTING HIS TEETH, King tried to ignore the pain, but it was impossible. Panting like a pregnant woman didn't help either. He'd landed himself in a predicament. He'd come this far and followed the man who'd kidnapped Peter all the way back to this warehouse, or whatever it was, only to be thwarted at the end. He had to try, one more time, even though the pain was excruciating and the chance of being stuck forever was high. With one mighty effort, he pushed, unable to hold in the scream that tore itself from his body.

King had managed to get his belly past the steering wheel.

Exhalation was orgasmic.

Once out of the car, he took a minute to regain himself. He'd built up a hell of a sweat and was seriously regretting the choice of a black jump suit.

"Aww, shit." He'd ripped the buttons and most of the sparkly Diamoniques off the front when he'd taken on the wheel. Soon, even getting into a car would prove impossible. He pulled out a crushed cheeseburger and quickly munched it down. He needed to be at full strength if he was in for a hoedown.

It'd been easy to follow the crazy old man in his weird black car, and King was ready to land some karate on him if the need presented itself.

A few minutes later, King completed the arduous twenty-yard walk across the car park to the metal doors of the warehouse and wished to God he'd parked closer.

AFTER WHAT SEEMED AN ETERNITY, Rathbone stopped screaming. This was revenge for the time Rathbone hurled a toilet brush into his mouth. Reece ripped the syringe, now filled with stomach fluids, out of the vampire's gut.

"Now, will you givvus a pint?"

Reece wasn't expecting that, and he didn't like it. He picked another syringe from the table and drove it into Rathbone's ear, not that he needed to extract any more brain matter. Another scream echoed round the circular concrete room.

"All in good time. First, I need to analyse the wealth of bodily fluids you've so graciously given me. Then, I'll feed you your Bolton, and then, I'll be back to repeat the whole process."

"As long as I get the beer," said Rathbone.

Reece wondered if he hadn't captured Rathbone, would he have agreed to the testing for free beer anyway?

KING STRUGGLED to get through the warehouse door. He had no idea how to deal with the levels of security expertly implemented to stop any intruder—he wasn't gifted with the technical ability to break into a tenner. However, none of this was a problem, because Reece hadn't turned on any of the security systems. He hadn't even shut the door. King was struggling because he was going through a repeat performance of the steering wheel situation and struggling to get through the warehouse door. He regretted that last cheeseburger.

Eventually he stumbled through to the other side, crashing through a pile of boxes that went flying with the tremendous momentum he was carrying.

"WHAT WAS THAT?" asked Rathbone.

"What was what?" replied Reece.

"That almighty crash. Sounded like it came from behind me. It might be an intruder here for the Bolton. Go check it out!"

Reece's eyes narrowed. After he'd captured Rathbone, he'd hoped he'd be in a constant state of fear, but he didn't look bothered at all. That would change when he tortured him with sunlight, just for the fun of it. "I'm going to start my analysis. I'll be back for more samples soon."

"And you'll crack open the Bolton?"

Reece nodded grudgingly.

"Champion." Rathbone settled back and made himself comfortable.

"AH, MAN, THIS IS TROUBLE," whispered King, flat on his back after tripping over the crates. At this moment in time, making it back to his feet seemed impossible.

"Ah, man. It must be really shit being a tortoise."

He unwrapped a cheeseburger for a power boost and tried to remember some of the television he'd watched, his only education. He'd watched a lot of Chuck Norris films. That's where he'd honed his karate skills. McDonald's adverts were where he discovered he liked burgers, which reminded him. He reached into his jumpsuit pocket and pulled out anoth—

"Nooooooo!"

His desperate cry shook the warehouse. The element of surprise had been lost, but he didn't care. He was out of burgers! Panic set in. He could feel himself wasting away. If he couldn't get up, he wouldn't be able to eat more burgers. He needed to summon the will and strength from deep down and make it to his feet. He was the only vampire/ human hybrid. Surely he had some powers hidden somewhere.

"Shit, man, I only wanna get up."

REECE LOOKED AT HIS WATCH. He couldn't understand what was taking Arthur's Peasley's son so long to find them. He'd left every door open and made enough noise for the most inept tracker. The warehouse wasn't very big. He would have stumbled across the room even if he wasn't looking for it.

The security cameras showed nothing, and the hybrid couldn't hide his vast bulk. Vampires didn't store fat; their body had no use for it. Maybe the hybrid's body wouldn't prove useful in the search for vampire-killing powers after all.

Reece looked back in his microscope. Rathbone's DNA revealed many missing building blocks, more so than when he'd tested it a couple of months back. He needed to feed. If he was a normal vampire, he would have craved blood after the injuries he'd sustained. He needed Bolton Bitter.

A flask of the clear brown liquid caught his eye. He'd tested it to death. There was nothing in it out of the ordinary. The only thing that separated it from the three hundred other beers he'd tested was the different levels of hops and basic components. There was nothing untoward about it at all. Nothing! He picked up the flask and threw it across the room.

BEHIND THE JOWLS, King was still devastatingly handsome, and the look of pure satisfaction of a job well done painted across his face would have made most weak at the knees. He felt and looked utterly heroic.

He'd made it to his feet after an Olympian effort. He'd seen Chuck Norris do the move in one of his films, and King remembered being awestruck watching Master Chuck call upon his limitless power to perform "the sit-up." King was immensely proud to have followed in the footsteps of the Black Belt for it meant he could rescue Peter Rathbone, his soul mate...After he'd stocked up on enough burgers to get him through the mission.

Getting back in the car was possibly a mistake after how long it had taken to get out last time, but he couldn't risk another burger shortage, the last one had nearly finished him off. He would rescue his future friend, but after a trip to the drive-thru.

"FREEZE!"

Reece had heard the blob wheezing from half way down the corridor and wasn't surprised when the hybrid wobbled into Rathbone's prison. Reece had positioned himself so that if he needed to, he could jump behind Rathbone's steel bed. But, he didn't think it was going to be necessary and chewed on an apple, nonchalantly. He was in complete control.

"Freeze? Why?" Reece asked.

"What? Oh, yeah." King realised he hadn't pulled out his revolver.

Reece had never seen slower reactions. The blob went for his gun but went for the wrong pocket and then patted at all the pockets of his ridiculous jump suit, twice patting the pocket where the gun was obviously stored, before pulling out a burger, unwrapping it, and devouring it as if his life depended on it.

"Oh shit, yeah!" The satisfied look was replaced with one of determination as he tried to figure out where he stored his gun. Again, he patted every pocket three or four times before eventually finding the firearm. It took him longer to prise the weapon from his skin-tight outfit than it did to find it in the first place.

Reece readied himself. He could've drawn his gun in a heartbeat.

Finally, the firearm came out when the hybrid added some gusto to his pulling, but unfortunately, he dropped it.

"Who the fook is this twat?" asked Rathbone.

"I'm King, and I'm here to rescue you," said King through strained breaths, reaching to the floor to pick the gun up.

"Aren't you a little fat for a...for anything, really?"

King's belly made picking up the gun difficult. His hand trembled with the effort to reach it. He still had two feet to go when he gave up. Slowly, King regained full height, wheezing with his hands on his hips. He turned on Reece. "Freeze!"

"You took your time getting here," said Reece.

"You were expecting me?" King looked shocked.

"You were following me in a limousine, and you tailgated me most of the way."

"You were driving like a granny, man. I wanted you to speed up."

"In answer to your question, I was expecting you. It's an honour to finally meet Arthur Peasley's son in the flesh, and lots of it, by the looks of it."

King's eyes narrowed. "You know my daddy?"

"Why of course. So does our friend here," he gestured at the naked form of Rathbone and took another bite of his apple.

"Peter's coming with me."

"You got any Bolton Bitter with ya?" asked Rathbone.

"Bolton what?"

Rathbone rolled his eyes. "That'll be a no then. Fook off, I'm staying here."

"Why do you want him?" asked Reece.

"He knows where my daddy is."

"So do I."

"But, he's suffered the same pain I have. I saw him on the TV. Humans have treated him like crap because he's different, and vampires have treated me like crap because I'm different. I just wanna talk to someone who knows how I feel."

"You gonna get the beers in?" asked Rathbone.

"I'm minted, man," said King.

"Class. Knock that twat out and I'm all yours."

"I guess that's where the problem lies," said Reece, deciding to test the hybrid's reactions and make sure he wasn't bluffing with the display of complete ineptness when handling a gun. Reece threw the rest of the apple at him and King watched it all the way, not that he had much choice—it hit him in the eye.

"You bastard! Arrrgghhh, it kills! That was a juicy one! Man, the acid—it burns! It kills!"

Reece was close to laughter. This thing's accelerated growth was worth researching, but he was weak and slow. Reece had all the time in the world to take a syringe, walk the considerable distance around the temporarily disabled hybrid clawing at his eye, and take a blood sample from a vein on the back of his leg. But, he only managed to suck fat into the barrel of the syringe.

"AAAAAAAGGGGHHHHHH!" King screamed to the heavens. "Are you trying to kill me?" He grabbed for the back of his leg with one hand while holding his eye with the other.

Reece put the sample on the table with the Bolton Bitter. It was time to have a little fun. He may not be able to take down vampires yet, but he could certainly take this fat oddity. "I'm not just *trying* to kill you; I'm *going* to kill you. Now, what are you going to do about it?"

King put up a guard. "Don't make me use my karate on you, man."

Reece laughed. "Just like your father."

"My daddy knows karate?"

"He does. He's very good."

King fired off a punch, but only got half way before running out of steam.

"Unfortunately, it doesn't look like you are."

Reece flexed his muscles and advanced on the lardo. It was still best to keep his distance. The blob would be strong, very strong, if not powerful like his pathetic excuse for a punch had proved. Reece decided to use his feet. He'd always been good with them, and after his genetic alterations, the newfound power in his legs was lethal.

Reece moved closer. He could blast out a sidekick when he wanted, but he wanted to see what King would. He soon got his answer. Nothing. Reece was just out of range and Peasley's son was too lazy to even move a foot to close the gap.

Reece laughed before stepping forward and snapping out a sidekick. He felt it drive through the mounds of fat and flesh, and then, he felt nothing. Nothing at all.

30

The army hasn't been able to stop the violence raging across UK cities. Riots continued throughout the night, but with the coming of dawn, rioters dissipated. Forces were hopeful until dusk brought a wave of violence that equalled the night before. This has led to a countrywide curfew being enforced by the Prime Minister.

"Regretfully, we are enforcing a curfew affecting everyone one in the UK. Anyone seen at night will be shot without question or warning. Scientists believe a virus is inducing psychosis and leading to this madness. Do what you have to do to protect your family if your residence is infiltrated."
—*Prime Minister, public broadcast*

IF THERE WAS EVER a cause to celebrate, then this was it. Kevin Ackroyd was the jolliest pub landlord pulling a pint in Middlesbrough. His cash cow was here: Sid Tillsley sat at his bar, where he belonged.

"That'll be two quid, please, Sid."

"Stick it on the tab, Kev. I'll pay up at the end of the night, like. I haven't got time to be putting me hand in me pocket. I have two months of boozing to catch up with."

Kev didn't think twice. Sid had racked up shed loads of cash in the vampire-hunting business, and he'd gone through a string of legitimate jobs too. On top of that, he hadn't been drinking much so he'd be absolutely minted. A tab meant Kev could whack a few extra on for himself and the big man would never remember.

"Fook me, that hit the spot," said Sid, banging down an ale. He lit up a tab. "I'm gonna have to start getting these knocked off. They cost a fooking fortune."

"All in good time, buddy," said Arthur.

"I knew you couldn't resist the Bolton, mon, not this stuff, anyways," said the smartest man on the Smithson Estate.

Sid nodded. "I didn't have a fooking clue what was going on when you fired that gun thing at me, but when the water balloon hit me in the face and covered me in Bolton... I knew I was making a mistake." Sid clinked glasses with his bestest friend. "Keep these coming, Kev. I need to drink, not just to enjoy the ale, but to forget the woman I left at the altar and who I should be shaggin'—" He looked at The Miner's clock. "—About...now."

Brian gave him a pat on the back. "She'd never have put out, Sid, even if she didn't have a cock. She was stringing you along to ruin your life and ours."

"You may be reet, but I've still got shaggin' on the mind."

"Right. Prossie, on me, mate."

Sid rubbed at the fat at the back of his head awkwardly. "Not really my style, mate."

"What are ya talking about, mon? You've been with loads of prossies through the years."

"Aye, but, you know I like fanny, Brian."

Brian banged his pint on the bar. "I ain't fooking gay."

"Brian, don't try and change what you are. You haven't got to put on a macho front in here," said Sid soothingly. "You lot all listen," he announced to the bar in general, which only consisted of him, Brian, Arthur, Kev, and the lads watching Tarrant, but he had something to say. "Anyone giving Brian a hard time for bumming, answers to me, you hear?"

Everyone pissed themselves except Brian, who went red with embarrassment.

"So, what are you going to do now, Sid?" asked Arthur.

Sid pointed at his empty glass, and Kev got to work. "Once I get the boozing out of my system, who knows? Number one priority will be a shag, and then, I may go back on the benefits, like."

Arthur laughed. "I can't really see you getting the boozing out of your system, buddy, but I have a favour to ask you, and you may not like it."

"How can I help, mate?"

All joviality diminished. Arthur took off his shades and summoned some emotional strength. "My son, Sid. I still haven't found my son. We've been in contact with Harry Dean, the cat who's been hiding us away from all the vampire bastards. Sid, my son's out there with them bloodsuckers. He's been all over the news branded as a killer. I've gotta find him."

Sid nodded. "Now, I know I ain't going to catch *them homomo-sexuals* off the bastards, I'll help you, buddy." He patted Arthur on the shoulder and turned to Brian. "You can bum as many of 'em as you want, Brian. Sow your wild oats, and all that, lad."

"I'm not fooking gay."

"Me *them homomo-sexuals* councillor told us loads of *them homomo-sexuals* go round beating *them homomo-sexuals* up because they are angry about being *them homomo-sexuals* themselves."

Brian couldn't decipher the Tillsley code. "What are you talking about?"

"Just rubber up." Sid gave Brian a mighty slap on the back that took the wind out of the swordsman. Sid turned his attentions back to the pub and surveyed The First Swallow of Summer. "You gonna turn this place back to the way it was, Kev? It's proper shite, like."

"Don't be daft. I canna afford that sort of money, plus the missus likes it."

"Would have thought the fancy furniture would be worth a few quid, like," said Sid.

Kev hadn't thought about that. He was the sort of landlord who gave the customer what they wanted. "I'll see what I can do, like. Main thing is the beer though, ain't it?"

"Sure is, Kev. Another round over here."

Kev grinned. "Right you are." He set about pouring a perfect pint.

Sid held up his pint to the light and smiled. "It's fooking great to be back, mon!"

"Great to have you back," said Arthur.

"Do you know where your lad is?" asked Sid.

"Harry's been hunting down his bastard grandpappy, and he'll let us know if he finds him. Now we have you, I'm sure he'll look that little bit—"

Arthur was cut off mid-sentence when the vampire in question appeared on the portable TV. Sid, Brian, and Kev turned to see what had caught his attention. Borg's face filled the screen.

"Who's that twat?" asked Brian.

"That's Lucia's papa."

"Turn it up!" shouted Brian.

One of the lads reached over and twiddled the volume knob:

> "This message is for mankind. I am Borg Hemsman, and I am a vampire. Today marks the end of our captivity. We have been hiding in the shadows for three hundred years. We are throwing off the shackles and taking this country back. For the last two nights, you have witnessed my brothers and sisters rising up in your towns and cities, showing you what it means to fear the vampire."

The camera panned back from Borg's face to the studio. The boys recognised vampires when they saw them. The birds were tasty, and the blokes looked like *them lot* but with a decent set of shoulders on them. Only one human sat with them.

"That's that twat off that daytime TV chat show shite!" said Brian. "I can't fooking stand him. The guests they get on that programme are the lowest of the fooking low."

"They had Rathbone on t'other day," said Kev.

"Exactly."

"Looks like he's not so full of himself now, man," said Arthur.

The camera zoomed in to Borg who grabbed Colin Fitzpatrick and lifted him up by the scruff of his neck. The TV presenter retained his orange hue, even though there was no blood left in his face.

"YEEEAAHHHH!" Brian raised his arms aloft when Borg bit deep into Colin's throat. Borg's eyes almost glowed as he took Colin's life. The camera caught it all, and there was no mistaking the reality.

One of the lads at the bar checked his watch and turned it over to Tarrant. There were some things a man just couldn't miss.

"He's a crazy son of a bitch," said Arthur. His sneering lip told the pub he was thinking of using karate.

"At least he killed that daytime TV twat," said Brian.

"I'm glad my son wasn't with the sick bastard. I hope he's safe."

Brian placed a friendly arm over his shoulder. "We'll find him, Arthur, don't you worry."

Sid shook his head. "I ain't ever going to shake off this vampire shit. Fooking 'ell. I've been drinking for twenty minutes and the bastards are getting in the way of me ale time. They ask to be smacked, fooking *ask* for it! Tonight, we drink," he cried. "Tomorrow, we—"

"CERTAINLY WON'T BE DRINKING!"

All heads turned to the doorway filled by a figure in white, Sheila Fishman.

"Ah, fook."

"Tillsley, you *bastard*!" she spat.

"Ah, fook." Sid turned back to the bar and looked into his pint, a place of solace that all Northern men turned to when the nagging came.

"You bastard, Tillsley."

"Fook off, ya mental bitch!" shouted Garforth. Brian would have put the nut on her weeks ago, but not Sid, he had a heart of gold.

"You fucking worm, Garforth. You horrible, fucking worm!" She ground her teeth until a filling cracked. She despised Brian nearly as much as Sid.

Brian shook his head, turned away, and adopted a similar stance to Sid, staring into his pint glass.

"Can I get you a sherry or summat, love?" asked Kev, used to hostile women and never one to turn out the chance of a bit of trade.

"Fuck you, Ackroyd, you sexist pig."

"Pint?"

Sheila stuck her finger up and stormed over to where Sid pretended nothing was happening. She tried to pull his shoulder back so that he'd face her, but she wasn't strong enough. She tried kicking him in the leg with her pointy shoes, but she couldn't kick him hard enough. She took a different tact.

"How about we just make love, for old time's sake?"

"Howay the lads!"

He spun around, and she stamped into his stones—and he went down like a sack of them. Vampire killer or not, a shot to the stones was something no man could ignore, and Sheila had a knack for perfect placement.

She stood over him and screamed, "That's all you ever think about! You were only with me for sex, you filthy bastard!"

Sid groaned, trying to massage some life back into his throbbing jewels.

"I was willing to give everything, Tillsley. And you threw it all away for these losers!"

"You hate Sid," said Brian, coming to the rescue. "Why the fook did you want to marry him?"

"Get me that sherry," called the jilted bride, and Kev obliged. "He'll pay for it," she said, and Kev added a triple measure to Sid's tab. "I hate Sid Tillsley more than any other man, including Hitler and Alan Titchmarsh. Tillsley sent me over the edge. I lost the plot trying to send that lazy, drunken bastard to prison."

"You should've left him alone, then," said Brian.

Sid wasn't bothered with arguing. He was too busy tending to his bruised gonads. Sheila was the past, pain was the present, Bolton was the future.

"It was my job to send that bastard down, and do you know what thanks I got? I got sectioned. I got sent to a mental home. Three months I spent there, before finally pulling it together. I lost my job, my cats, my home; I lost everything because of him."

"So why fooking marry him?" asked Brian.

"I'm getting to that!" she screamed. "They let me out, and I was finished. I had nothing except the clothes on my back and a few hundred in the bank. I'd spent my life working and had nothing to show for it. But Tillsley...Tillsley had everything given to him without ever lifting a finger. Where is the justice in that?"

"Well, for a—"

"It's a rhetorical question, you arsehole!" she yelled at Brian. "But, I'm pleased to say there is some justice in the world. I decided to take a chance. I had nothing to lose. I took all the money in my bank account and bought 250 lottery tickets, and do you know what? I fucking won."

"Well done, now fook off," said Brian.

"I won the lottery and that's when I knew that revenge could truly be mine. I had the money to change myself into this." She grabbed her breasts and suddenly the men were like putty in her hands. "You men are so easy to manipulate, it makes me sick. You're weak."

Brian came out of his trance when she let go of her boobs. "Well, Sid got away. He wasn't as weak as you hoped, was he?"

A wicked grin split her plastic face. "Well, I'm going to have the last laugh."

"I ain't fooking laughing," groaned Sid on the floor, still holding his nuts.

"Sid made me ruin my body with these," she grabbed at her massive fake breasts and again inspired blood flow in all onlookers with exception to the incapacitated vampire hunter. "I had these implanted to woo you, Tillsley. I desecrated my female form for you." She ripped off the wig (which didn't bother the lads in the pub who were still looking south) to reveal patchy, limp, mousy-brown hair. "I wore this because you bastards like blondes, and after all that, you still left me."

"I haven't done nowt wrong." He managed to get to his feet but remained bent over, hands on knees. The pain migrating through his stomach was overpowering. He thought about how many vampires he'd fought and was glad they simply weren't bright enough to hire prossies to kick him in the nuts. He would have packed in vampire hunting on day one if they had.

"*You've done nothing wrong?*" she squealed.

"I did everything you asked when we were engaged. I did nowt wrong."

"You illegally claimed benefit for nigh on thirty years!"

"That's got nowt to do with you."

"It was my job to stop bastards like you! Then, you grabbed my breast at the despicably sexist Ladies' Night, and that was the start of my journey into insanity!"

"I think you've always been round the twist, love," said Brian. "Why not use that money to have Sid killed or beat up rather than go through all this palaver?"

"I had grand plans. When I won the lottery, I had a private detective follow Sid and find out everything about him. I didn't know his homophobia was so...intense. Gunnar Ivansey—" she spat on the floor, "— and his transformation taught me a lot about Tillsley, and I knew I could break him."

"Why marry him?"

"I'm getting to that, Garforth, now shut up! The plastic surgery was excruciating. I won't be able to go out in direct sunlight for another month. The work I've had done is so extreme and the materials so cutting-edge, the scientists were worried the plastic would react with sunlight. I did it all in order for Sid to marry me."

Brian laughed. "You should have just had the tits done. Sid would bang a lamp post if it had tits like them." He got back to the point at hand. "Why all the classes then? Why all that bollocks?"

"I had to change him. When I worked for the benefit office, I had never failed, not once...until I met him. I had to get him working, and to do that, I had to keep him sober."

"And the diet?" asked Sid, belly rumbling.

"It was fun watching you come back from Diet Darlings a broken man." She laughed.

"And the anger management and the homophobia classes?" asked Brian.

"I needed to calm him down, but the course didn't work. As for the homophobia, I had to break down his sixth sense. He seemed to know when a gay man was within half a mile of his vicinity. The classes took this sense away and I was able to have the operation without his knowledge. The only problem was that it made him more accepting of you, Garforth, but I had him on a leash. It was only the evil beer that freed him."

"Operation?" said Brian. "What the fook are you on about, woman?"

"Tonight, on our wedding night, Sid was going to get the full brunt of this."

She lifted her dress to gasps.

"I was fooking reet! She's got a cock!"

"That's right," she said, covering her member by dropping the dress. "And you, Garforth, ruined my wedding night."

Sid didn't really know what to say, so he ordered another beer. A cock definitely added closure to the relationship.

"I was going to drug the bastard, and in the morning, the pictures of the wedding night would be all over Middlesbrough!"

"So why bother to marry him?" asked Brian.

"For the papers. After Middlesbrough, the world would know of our love and Tillsley's torment would last forever because I'd refuse a divorce. Officially, he signed up for homophobia classes, and I'd tell the world he knew of my penis and was struggling to come to terms with it."

"You evil cow," said Brian. "But it looks like it was all a waste of time, ey?"

Sheila laughed, and the pub knew it didn't bode well. "I have one final surprise for you, Sid Tillsley."

"Surely the cock was enough?" said Brian.

"I needed a backup plan... and I have devised one so ruthless, you will not recover from it."

"Two cocks?" Brian ventured.

"With my millions, I was able to buy something else; something dear to your heart, even if I am not." She held her hands aloft, theatrically. Her moment had come. "Sid Tillsley, I OWN THE BOLTON BREWERY!"

"Champion!" he said. "Can I get a discount, like?"

"And I am going to shut it down!"

The shot to the stones had hurt, but that was physical. This was something else entirely. Nausea rose from the pit of his stomach. This was worse than the most brutal of hangovers. Sid collapsed against the bar. No more Bolton Bitter.

His friends looked just as bad. Kev cried. Brian looked distant, his mind numb. It was hard to imagine a world without Bolton. Arthur was singing to himself, trying to soothe the pain. The lads in the corner, they just watched Tarrant, who looked a little bit sad himself.

There was nothing to say.

There was nothing to say, and there was nothing anyone could do that would make this better...except one.

"Pint of Bolton, please, Kev," said Sid.

"Wake up, ya fat twat!"

Slowly, King's eyes opened to the ugly, greasy face of Peter Rathbone looking down on him.

"What happened?" asked the hybrid groggily.

"You got into a scrap with that arsehole next to ya."

King turned his head to see the bloody, mangled face of Rathbone's captive. "How did...?" King was confused. "How did you get free?"

"I heard a click when he sat down. He must have a remote control for the lock in his pocket or summat."

"What happened to his face?"

"He kicked you in the gut, and you doubled over like you'd been shot in the nuts. You caught him with the nastiest headbutt I've ever seen, and then, you hit the deck."

"And you waited for me?" Through the grogginess, a warm sensation of belonging filled King.

"Nah, I finished off the Bolton and was going to fook off in that motor of yours, but you're sat on your keys, and even me vampire muscles canna pick you up, ya fat knacker."

King didn't feel quite so warm inside anymore, just a little hungry. "Help me up."

Twenty minutes later, King was on his feet, and Rathbone was in need of more Bolton after such a monumental task. "Thanks, man. Thanks for the help. Cool get-up you're wearing, baby."

Rathbone flourished his cape, giving King a glimpse of the beautiful lining. "Aye. Glad Rich didn't throw me clothes away, like."

"Why did he kidnap you, Peter?"

"Bastard was doing all sorts of scientific experiments on me. He took a sample of bloody everything, he did. Stuck needles in my eyes, my ears, my nose, my mouth, my stomach. He even did both bollocks...fooking *twice*. Dirty bastard."

"Sounds bad. What are you gonna do?"

"You're buying the Bolton, ain't ya?"

"Yeah, baby."

"Well, I'm gonna drink some Bolton."

"What about him?" King gestured to the unconscious vampire hunter.

"There was one bodily fluid he didn't extract," said Rathbone, unzipping his pants.

"Ah, man, that's nasty. Whizzing on a guy...geez," said King disgusted.

"Guess again," said Rathbone, turning around.

31

Colin Fitzpatrick has been blasted, yet again, for his tasteless follow-up to his absurd show revealing a real-life "vampire." Fitzpatrick is now in the custody of the Metropolitan Police and will face terrorism charges in light of the situation.

Station officials have announced that the show was never sanctioned and couldn't apologise enough for the insensitive nature of the programming considering the violent, inexplicable riots that are plaguing the city.
—The Independent

THERE WAS A LOT OF SULKING, moping, and irritability in The First Swallow of Summer. Brian, Arthur, and Sid sat one side of the bar, chins on fists, elbows on bar, staring into their pints of perfectly clear Bolton Bitter. Kev stood on the other side, running his finger down the beer pump that had brought him so much hard cash through the years.

"What are we going to do?" asked Brian forlornly.

"You're the one with the fooking answers!" snapped Sid. "You're the one who ruined the wedding! If I'd got married, I'd have got me end away and been drinking Bolton on me honeymoon!"

"She was gonna dangle her old man in your mouth when you were asleep, take a photo, and stick it on the Internet!" Brian yelled, "I should have left you to it."

"Cool it, you two," said Arthur. "This ain't getting the Bolton back." Brian and Sid both backed down. It wasn't personal, but desperate times were upon them. "Things are getting worse. Lucia's daddy is kicking off all sorts of shit, and that means those council bastards are gonna be on our tails now they know Sid's alive."

"I don't want no more vampire shit. They're a bunch of twats," said Sid.

"There's gonna be a heap more coming down on us, baby. We need to get my boy back. That hasn't changed."

"I canna fight vampires if I have no beer to look forward to."

"I know. And I can't bring my kid up in a world where he's got no decent beer to drink." Arthur nodded slowly, realising what had to be done. "We need to get our brewery back first."

"Fat chance," said Brian. "Two months ago, we saved that no-good, sell-out brewmaster Buggleswaite's life. The Campire was going to cut his nutsack off, and we stopped him. Look how the twat repaid us?"

"We've got to try, Brian," said Sid. "If that doesn't work, then we're gonna drink the place dry before they shut the place down."

"One last hurrah!" said Brian, coming round to Sid and Arthur's way of thinking.

"And then we go find Arthur's lad and give his granddad a smack."

"Yeah!" said Arthur.

"But first," said Sid, looking like he meant business. "We drink this place dry."

Kevin rubbed his hands with glee.

THE COALITION SAT in their great underground hall, their last stronghold. The war they'd tried so valiantly to avoid now raged hundreds of feet above them. Borg had been testing them for months with varied, brutal attacks before turning loose his vampire army in every major city in the UK, starting a panic around the world.

With martial law now imposed, some of the civilians were proving as troublesome as the vampires. Now, there was nothing the Coalition could do to save the Agreement. This was a war that wouldn't be forgotten by mankind, and when Haemo was eventually released, man wouldn't be able to forgive or allow vampires to live side by side. This war would rage until the end, until mankind was enslaved or the vampires were wiped from the face of the planet.

"Everybody loses," said Bwogi. He no longer tried to hide his tears.

No one responded.

The council watched regional newsflashes from around the country, helpless. Their agents were trying to lead the army. The only reason they'd contacted the traitorous Harry Dean was because they didn't have a choice. It was almost impossible to fight the vampire who could blend in with the rest of the population with nothing more than a hat.

"What can we do?" asked Charles. He couldn't pick fault in others anymore. The entirety of the situation had knocked all the pompous stuffing out of him.

"Wait for death," said Augustus forlornly.

A slit of light formed on the wall, and the door to the Great Hall swung open. In walked Caroline with her head held high. "Good evening," she said before sitting down.

"What are you so fucking jolly for?" Charles' profanity caught her off guard, although she didn't show it. She turned to the door she'd just walked through, and Garendon followed her in. "Haemo is ready."

"Hooray!" Augustus mocked, clapping slowly.

"We knew this was coming," said Caroline over the echoing clap.

"Now, we have to deal with it, and because of Haemo, we *can* deal with it."

"Death is coming to us all," said Bwogi.

Caroline ignored him. "We chose this path many months ago. We all did." She looked every councillor in the eye, in turn. "We have no option but to finish what we started and bring order."

"You sound like you wanted this," said Bwogi with narrowed, accusing eyes.

She looked at him with contempt. "You were the one who brought this project back from the grave. Vitrago would have ended your life for it, but this council agreed it was the best course of action. Now, we must use it."

Augustus leaned forward in his chair, staring at Caroline with murderous intensity. "Mark my words, woman. Haemo isn't going to stop this war."

Caroline stared back with fire. "It will give mankind something to fight for, and it will give the vampire cause to reconsider their actions. The war is here. You're all leaders of this country, and what you do now will decide its fate. If we don't initiate Haemo, this battle will be to the death."

"Then let's do it," said Charles.

"No." Augustus' defiance carried a weight bringing silence to the Great Hall.

"Get a grip of yourself," Caroline snapped.

"Borg won't just kill us for this; he'll make us yearn for death."

"Isn't it a little late for a change of heart?" she asked.

"Now the war is here, everything changes." Augustus turned his attention to Garendon who was tapping away at a console. "Stop whatever you're doing."

"Why?" Garendon didn't look up. He was only concerned with the task at hand, occasionally pushing locks of unkempt brown, curly hair out of his face.

Augustus rapped his fingers on the table nervously. "This can't happen."

"It's the vote of the council," announced Charles.

"He will spare us if we stop this." Augustus said desperately to the other vampire councillors.

Bwogi shook his head, laughing but not with mirth. "That's absurd and you know it. Don't lose your head, Augustus. Even if the Haemo project didn't exist, Borg would torture us for merely sitting on this council."

Garendon finished inputting commands into the console, and where each councillor sat, a console screen flipped over from the seamless black marble.

"It goes to the vote," said Caroline. Her insides contorted while each of the councillors considered their choice.

"Every human in this room will vote against us." Augustus stood up, desperately searching the eyes of his fellow vampires for support. "We can't do this."

"Vote," announced Bwogi, placing his thumbprint on the console, registering his choice. Each member followed suit, inputting their vote. Augustus sat back down and entered his, shaking his head.

The computer announced the result: "Haemo initiated."

It took Caroline's breath away. She'd come so far, and now, she was one step away from realising her ultimate goal. She took a deep breath; she still had to be the rock.

"What have we done?" said Augustus, falling back in his chair.

"What we set out to do, months ago," said Caroline. "Right now, Haemo is being released into every major city. Without knowing it, every vampire's bloodlust will be quelled. Once we control the masses, we can regain order."

"Control? After this war?" Augustus scoffed. "Everyone knows vampires exist. Are you hoping everyone forgets?"

"That is why we'll announce that vampirism is a disease—and we have the cure. This was a clinical trial gone wrong. We'll make sure there's another disaster for the media to focus on soon after."

"Borg will chase us down for this." Augustus' head lolled over the back of his chair and he stared up to the ceiling. "Our deaths won't come quickly."

"Then I suggest we all get out of here," said Charles.

The only light illuminating the room turned scarlet red.

"Doesn't seem like it's going to be possible, now," said Caroline, her heart sinking. She was so close to getting away and starting the next phase. So close. There was still hope. There was always hope.

Rempstone was out of his seat and at the main console in a second. "Report!" he shouted.

A voice shouted through the speakers, "Sir, we're on lockdown! We've sealed off the building's entrance! Borg's men are leading a huge offensive against us!"

"They can't break through our defences," said Charles confidently. "Why would they even try?"

"Perhaps they're bored of killing humans and want some bigger fish to fry," said Augustus.

"It doesn't matter," said Rempstone. "We've enough supplies to last us decades, and this stronghold could withstand a direct nuclear explosion. They can waste their time attacking us. It will mean less work for the troops trying to take back the city."

Caroline's mind raced, but right now, all she could think of was just how much she despised every living vampire.

"I...FOO—HIC—FOOKING LOVE YOU, BRIAN."

"I...foo—*hic*—fooking love you too, Sid."

Brian, Sid, and Arthur's attempt to drink The Swallow dry was looking likely. "I...I don't give a shit if you love the bumm—*hic*—ing, mate."

"I...I..." Brian wanted to protest, but it was proving hard work.

"You can...bum anyone, fooking *anyone*, and I won't care 'cos you're my—*hic*—mate."

"I ain't..."

"If you want to—*hic*—get into musical theatre, then...then I don't care, Brian. You can, you can bum—*hic*—bum—*hic*—bum all the musical theatres in the world." Sid threw his arms out in a depiction of a gay world, nearly falling off his stool. "It won't bother me, Brian, 'cos you're my mate."

"I...ain't...I..."

"If you want to—*hic*—dance—*hic*—dance on that fooking ice—*hic*—wearing one of the fooking costumes they wear, watched by millions of *them homomo-sexuals*—*hic*. Then it's alright by me, 'cos you're my—*hic*—mate."

"I...ain't..."

"And, if anyone, and I mean fooking *anyone* has a problem with it—*hic*—then they answer to me."

"I ain't...I—*hic*—ain't..."

"I won't hear another— *hic* —fooking word." Sid went to put his finger over Brian's lips, but missed and poked his eye instead.

Brian grabbed his temporarily blinded orb but couldn't stop Sid stumbling off his stool and venturing out into the cold night air to make sure that none of the locals had a problem with Brian's choice.

"LISTEN!" shouted Sid for all to hear. "IF ANY OF YOUS BASTARDS HAVE A PROBLEM WITH MY FRIEND BRIAN, THEN YOU'LL HAVE TO ANSWER TO ME. HE CAN—*hic*—GO ICE-SKATING WHEN HE WANTS, AND NONE OF YOU WILL JUDGE HIM! YOU HEAR? YOU FOOKING—*hic*—HEAR?"

Brian shouted from the bar. "Shurrup, mon! For fook's sake. I— *hic* —ain't...Fook it! More Bolton, Kev." He banged his fist on the bar.

"Coming up." Kev had kept relatively sober through the evening. He had a relatively short supply of Bolton, and he'd confirmed with the brewery that production of the finest best bitter in the world had indeed stopped.

He pulled three pints and pushed them over the counter. Sid heard the wonderful sound of 568 millilitres of beer hitting the service side of the bar and stopped offending the entire Smithson Estate with his attempts at political correctness and zoned in on the ale. Sid put down the pint as if it was his first of the day. It disappeared and hit every taste bud on the way.

For Kev, it was time to put an end to the night's festivities. It was late, and the bar bill was staggering. Any more booze would lead to much vomiting. A good landlord knows the signs, and Arthur having thrown up down himself was one of them.

"Right, that'll do for tonight, lads. It's midnight and there's plenty of Bolton for tomorrow."

"Just a couple—*hic*—more, man?" asked Arthur who was lying on the floor.

"Nah, you've had enough. Fook off."

"No one tells me when I've had—*hic*—enough." From the floor, Arthur threw some rubbish karate shapes.

"Right, Sid, you gonna pay up?" said an excited barman.

"Eh?" said Sid, heading on his way home.

"Your tab, mon," said Kev, beads of sweat forming on his bald head. "You've run up a 300 quid bill."

"I'm—*hic*—very sorry, Kev, but Sheila—*hic*—took all me money."

"She was a fooking millionaire!" he screamed.

"Aye, but I didn't know—*hic*—that. She made me pay for—*hic*—everything."

"So you can't pay me?" said Kev, nostrils flaring, knuckles white from gripping the bar.

"I'll pay you to—*hic*—morrow?"

"And where are you gonna get the fooking money?"

Sid shrugged.

Kev pulled out a shotgun from under the bar and aimed it at his patrons. "I've put up with you bastards for too long, and now, the Bolton's gone, there's no fooking reason to put up with this shit any longer. I want my 300 quid!"

"Calm—*hic*—down, Kev," said Brian, swaying on his bar stool.

"Give us what you've fooking got," said Kev, one eye shut, looking down the sights.

Brian got up to leave. "You're not gonna rob—*hic*—us, ya fat bastard."

"Rob *you*? You're robbing me! I want my money." Losing the brewery had all been a bit much for Kev, and this was the last straw, but he wasn't ready for murder just yet. "Get the fook out of my pub, you bastards! You're barred! You're all fooking barred, and I hope I never see you again! GET OUT!"

Time was called on The Last Swallow of Summer, and without Bolton Bitter, it was possibly forever. No one was going to go to a gay bar on a homophobic council estate that sold shit beer.

REECE AWOKE WITH A SPLITTING HEADACHE induced by his head being split. He didn't dare open his eyes for the pain the light would bring. He'd never been hit so hard in his life, not even by Sid. The back of his head was wet and his nose was numb. Whatever hit him in the nose had caused catastrophic damage, which, in a way, was lucky because his sense of smell was out of action.

He opened his eyes, and when sight didn't return, he worried he'd been struck so hard that both optic nerves had ruptured. It was only when he clutched at his eyes in panic that he discovered that something covered them, something soft and slimy.

Reece screamed until he could scream no more.

32

At this moment in time, we haven't identified the cause of this illness, this infection, and we do not believe it to be contagious. Our scientists are working around the clock to find a cure, and until they do, do not make any unnecessary journeys. Anyone seen on the streets an hour after the streetlights are illuminated will be shot without warning.

The working class should be shot in the daylight as well. What?... My microphone is still on? Bugger.
—Field Marshal Montgomery
Smythe-Montague-Windsor III

BOLTON WAS THE CENTRE of the universe for the three individuals getting out of the Ford Capri. "Woooowwwww," said the awe-inspired worshipers, looking up at the gargantuan plant that mixed a harsh, metal landscape with mind-blowing aromas. This wasn't brewing beer; this was creating life. The boys hadn't been here in years and had forgotten just how special this place was. And, it was all coming to an end.

"Lads," said Brian, weighed down with emotion, "this is a sad day, and there's gonna be many more like it in the next few weeks, months, maybe years if we canna find a decent drop of something else. However, it's our duty to send Bolton Bitter off with the piss-up it deserves."

"YEAH!" shouted Sid, warming up his right biceps, for the downing of pints.

"Let's just hope Buggleswaite lets us at the ale," said Arthur.

"We saved his knackers. He owes us, and if he doesn't..." Brian pointed at a salivating Sid.

Arthur nodded. "Let's take care of business."

The lads marched to the front entrance of the brewery. Freddy Buggleswaite and the whole of Bolton had no idea what it was in for.

"HOW DO YOU FEEL, SIR?" asked Viralli, taking a deep breath.

Borg smiled. "I feel fine. The view helps."

The two vampires looked across the River Thames from an office in the Houses of Parliament. Fire ravaged the city, searching for fresh meat, licking the tallest towers and suffocating the streets with its toxic breath.

Human looters had caused a lot of destruction themselves, risking the bullets of the army and the Coalition to steal meagre sums of money.

Borg had instructed the vampires to leave London's landmarks intact, and he was pleased Whitehall and Westminster were not lighting up the sky. The old lamia didn't need to be told, but the youngsters were often unaware of their own history and didn't know of the vampire's influence on the great city. The foreign contingent would have gladly attacked London's monuments if it weren't for respect, or rather fear, of the old warlord.

Viralli nodded. "You're right. This is the most wondrous thing I've ever seen." He turned to Borg. "Do you think our spies are telling the truth, or have they turned?"

Borg laughed. "Oh, I'm sure Haemo is pouring into our bodies as we speak, my friend. I knew the Coalition was planning something. I've sent spies to every building and plant that the Coalition has ever thought of occupying. Patrick O'Flanagan disappeared last week while investigating a chemical works in Middlesbrough. After that, I sent more spies, and they uncovered what the Coalition so desperately tried to cover up."

"If you don't mind me asking, sir, why haven't you done anything about it?"

"It's a scary thought, is it not, that a molecule can influence our bodies. It makes you think just how delicate man really is. Everything kills them. Their cowardice is somewhat understandable."

Viralli's brow furrowed. "Sir?"

"If I'd told the nation about Haemo, it could've gone two ways. It could've spurred them into action, rebelling against it, or it could've sent them scurrying back into the woodwork they've called home for three hundred years. I couldn't risk that. We didn't need the extra ammunition to turn our brothers and sisters against the Coalition. Sitting around their precious table, they became so engrossed in Haemo, they allowed this to happen." Borg opened up his hands at the magnificent view.

"Are you going to tell the nation about the Haemo project?"

"Once we infiltrate the Coalition, we will find out the location of every Haemo station in the country and tear them down. Haemo may have had a chance before we took to the streets but not now. Let me ask you this: when was the last time you were thirsty?"

"I'm always thirsty."

"Even now?"

"I've never been without blood for more than a day. My body has never craved it, yet my mind needs the kill."

"Yes. I should imagine they didn't test their drug on lamia with appetites as vivacious as yours." Borg laughed. "For the Coalition to control the lamia with Haemo, they'd need an army like the one Vitrago led to the slaughter against Sparle. There'd be no need for us to feed and they could enforce a law. Predators desire the kill. Haemo may take the need away, but the addiction is still there. Haemo is too little too late."

Viralli nodded. "Sir, your plan couldn't have run any smoother."

"Well, not everything has gone to plan." Borg bit his lip in frustration.

"There's nothing you could've done about King."

"He will be with his father now. Once we have control, I will scour the earth and punish them both. King spits on his mother's grave by following Arthur Peasley. We will destroy him and his friends. Sid Tillsley's head on a stick will rally the troops. The Coalition couldn't stop him, but I can."

"I've wanted to face him since the night I was ordered by the Lamian Consilium to escort him to a battle with Sparle. I will bring you his head."

Borg patted his Viralli on the shoulder. "I'm sure you will, but there are more important things to attend to. It's time we met with the Coalition. I've been looking forward to this for a number of years."

"BOLTON!" shouted Sid once he was inside the brewery reception.

Most people didn't know what to do when a monster skinhead charged into their office and aggressively shouted the name of their hometown, but this secretary did. She'd seen this skinhead before. It was difficult to forget the last time he'd entered the building shouting the same word. That infamous brewery tour a couple of years ago hadn't ended well, and she had a strong feeling that today wasn't going to end well either.

"Hello, Mr Tillsley."

"Bolton!"

"Calm down, big man," soothed Brian.

The secretary's eyes narrowed at the weasley, little man patting the ape on the shoulder. She would remember him as long as she lived.

"You!" she said with venom.

"Eh? Do I know you, pet?" said Brian.

"Don't play games with me, you bastard."

"I don't wanna play fooking games with ya," said Brian, disgusted, "women are shit at sport."

"It took me three visits to the clinic to sort out whatever it was you gave me." She was red with anger, not embarrassment.

"Eh? I ain't ever given you one, have I?"

"You don't even remember?" she shrieked.

"Must have been a few years ago, like. You've clearly let yourself go, pet."

"Get out!" she screamed, getting up and pointing to the door of the snug reception.

"Fook off. We're here to see Freddy Buggleswaite."

"Oh yeah, like I'd let you through after the last visit, and, not to mention, he specifically told me not to, under any circumstances, let you lot through."

"Bolton!"

"Look, love—" started Brian before he was swiftly interrupted.

"Don't you call me 'love!'"

"Look, you horrible cow." Brian's misogyny had levelled up since the beating he took outside M&S. "How are you possibly gonna stop Sid getting through to that beer?"

Sid stood, eyes transfixed on a point on the wall. He wasn't looking at the wall; he was looking through it, at the brewing room. The secretary knew Brian was right. "I'll...I'll call the police."

"You'll call the police? Do you really think they're gonna give a flying fook there's an intruder in a brewery that is closing for business when there are armies of vampires a few miles away on the streets of Manchester kicking the fook out of everything?"

"Well...," she started weakly.

"Now let us through."

"I hate you!"

"Don't you all?"

"Bolton!"

The lads pushed past her and wandered through the maze that was the Bolton Brewery. Sid knew exactly where he was going. He was like a child at Disneyland, except he wasn't going to be sick because he'd eaten an ice-cream and been up Space Mountain; he was going to be sick through alcohol abuse, the best kind of sick.

There was no staff to be seen. The boys weren't worried. Sid's nose told them there was enough to keep them here for days, and they weren't going anywhere until the last drop was drunk.

"The brewing room isn't far," said Sid, picking up the pace.

"I still can't believe Freddy did this to us," said Arthur.

"Well, he did, and he's gonna regret it," said Brian.

"Aye," agreed Sid. "If he starts playing silly buggers about us staying here till the beer's gone, then I'm gonna punch him in the face."

Brian agreed. "He's an old man, but it doesn't mean he's exempt from a pasting. Could mean trouble from the rozzers, mind."

"I've been arrested for a lot over the last few months, Brian, but I'm sure that if I smack a few vampire bastards next week, it will all be forgotten about."

Sid could practically taste ale before he threw open the double doors separating him from his destiny.

"Bolton!"

"OH, GOD!" Freddy Buggleswaite dropped the bottle of beer he was showing to a group on the last-ever tour of Bolton Brewery. With the arrival of Sid Tillsley, Freddy realised he hadn't saved the best until last.

Freddy stood shaking. This was the worst thing that could've happened on this day. Freddy looked like a kindly old man, like someone's granddad, even. His soft features and round belly, pushing out his brewmaster's jacket, made him instantly likable to anyone who cast their eyes on this legend in the world of ale.

"YOU DOUBLE-CROSSING, GREEDY WANKER!" screamed Garforth, much to the dismay of the tour that consisted of dignitaries and honourable members of Bolton's society.

"I-I-I'll call the police if you don't leave," stammered Freddy.

"Go on then," said Brian. "They won't give a shit with them vampire bastards flying around."

The dignitaries looked uneasy, and not just because of the face of rage and language of filth Brian brandished. The vampire scourge hadn't affected Bolton and had concentrated its attacks on Manchester. It was only a matter of time before the vampires made the short journey to their own little town.

"You lot here for a mammoth session too?" Sid asked an elderly lady who was accompanying the mayor of Bolton.

"Sid, please—," started Freddy.

"Don't you 'Sid, please' me, ya fooker. We saved you, and then, you sold out. If it weren't for us, that vampire, the one Brian bummed to death, was gonna stick a knife under your knackersack and make you a fooking woman. You fooking gave away the only thing we asked ya to keep."

The mother of the mayor of Bolton fainted on the spot.

"You scumbag!" cried the mayor.

"Fooking right!" agreed Sid. "See, Buggleswaite, even the old, posh fella thinks you're a wanker for selling off our beer!"

Freddy looked from the mayor to Sid to the potentially dead O.A.P. and back to Sid.

"Far from it!" said the mayor. "Freddy Buggleswaite has served the town well over the past thirty-five years. No one can blame him for taking such a marvellous opportunity."

"You're fooking joking," said Brian.

"No, I'm not. Freddy has struck an extremely good deal, and in the process has pumped fresh revenue back into the town and is starting up a new business with the money he's made."

Sid screwed up his face. "Eh?"

"Freddy is upsizing."

"Eh?"

"This brewery will soon become the biggest producer of lager in the UK."

Sid had never headbutted a mayor before. It probably wasn't the finest moment in his fighting career. He'd taken on twenty vampires at a time and had a fistfight with the most dangerous carnivore since the T-Rex, so headbutting a frail, spectacle wearing, sixty-year-old man who wasn't looking, was a little low.

"He'll be reet," said Sid, not too convincingly.

33

You want to know what's out there? You leeches, the fucking press, thrive on this. Well, I'll tell ya what's out there, not that it matters, as you're dead, just the same as me. They ain't ill. There ain't no disease. They're fucking vampires! I saw them take some poor bastard down on the street and tear his throat out. Everyone knows what they are. The government are trying to cover the whole thing up, but it ain't gonna happen. This is beyond a disaster. I've got fifteen minutes to get home before they start shooting. I'm getting out of here. The army hasn't got a chance. None of us have. Get out of my way...
—Eyewitness, London

THE SIEGE was twenty-four hours old and Caroline was desperate to make one telephone call. Just one. She'd never anticipated Borg and his troops would sweep through the capital's defences so quickly. Things were starting to unravel. With Borg's troops camped out above the Coalition building, the council had spent virtually all their time in the Great Hall, heatedly discussing nothing. Now, lockdown had been initiated, there was no way to escape the building.

"It's only a matter of time before they break through," said Augustus. "They won't rest until we're punished."

"They can't infiltrate this fortress. We're too well protected," said Rempstone, irritably playing with his tie. "I'm fed up repeating myself."

"A monster once protected this cave, and nothing would've dared enter its lair," said Augustus. "Without Vitrago, all we have are a handful of vampires and a few guns. They've only got to breach the upper gates."

"And they can't. Can't you understand fucking English?" said Rempstone. "Nothing can break through."

"Watch your tongue, boy, or I'll tear it out."

"Enough!" cried Caroline. "This isn't helping. Be professional. We're safe." She tried to stay calm. She'd lived amongst these animals for years and couldn't let the façade drop now. She had to stay strong.

"You don't know Borg," said Bwogi. The old vampire leant back into his chair, appearing calmer than he had in months, like he'd already accepted his fate.

"I've spoken to the Prime Minister," said Charles. "Surprisingly, we're not high on his list of priorities."

"What did he say about the Haemo launch?" asked Caroline.

Charles stared over his half-moon glasses at Caroline. "'Too little, too late' were his exact words."

"Has the drug had no effect whatsoever?" asked Garendon, desperate for some feedback on the effectiveness of his baby.

"You've seen for yourself," said Charles, laughing at the ridiculous question. "The violence hasn't stopped. It grows every day. Your magical formula has done nothing. Absolutely nothing, you useless fool."

"It won't stop the violence, but it will limit their feeding. It's not a pacifier, but the effects will gradually affect them psychologically. It will work. I'm hundred per cent sure of it. I need to speak to a vampire on the surface," he said, looking at the door of the Great Hall.

"That isn't going to happen though, is it?" said Rempstone. "We're airtight down here, and that's the way it's going to stay, so don't get any ideas." He pointed at the vampire threateningly.

A murmur went around the group, agreeing with Rempstone's sentiments.

"We wouldn't be in this mess if you hadn't created that abomination," said Augustus.

Garendon was a ball of nervous energy, almost jumping up and down in his seat. "I just want to know that it works."

"You've doomed us all!" shouted Augustus before storming out like a pubescent teenager.

"You thought he would have grown out of that by now," said Charles.

Garendon followed him.

"Where are you going," asked Bwogi.

"I want to know why he blames me. I've got no lab to play in, so I might as well see how he works."

"Ignore him," said Bwogi. "Your work was brilliant, Garendon."

Garendon shrugged again. "I'm just interested."

After he followed Augustus, Bwogi announced, "That vampire's curiosity could one day break the world."

"It already has," said Caroline. She needed to get word to the outside in a way that wouldn't endanger the one person who meant most to her in the world. Haemo had been the number one priority, but now, it was time to initiate the final stage of the plan. She'd needed Borg in all of this but had no idea he'd be so efficient. The resulting lockdown could destroy everything she'd worked for.

"SEE? HE'S STILL MOVING!"

The congregation of dignitaries were not convinced the mayor's twitching leg was necessarily a positive sign. Even Brian felt a little awkward, and he'd hit pensioners much older—and in wheelchairs. Still, he had to back his mate up. Those were the rules.

"He started it. He went for Sid first."

His ridiculous comments fell on deaf ears. The rest of the tour was desperate to get away from the maniacs. It was better chancing the streets and the possibility of a vampire attack than hang around these violent men. They grabbed the arms and legs of the mayor and his mother and carried them out.

When the brewery tour left, a lot of angry faces turned to Freddy. "Lads, I can explain." Freddy backed away holding his hands up.

"No, you can't, you greedy little bastard," said Brian. "I ain't in the mood for bullshit."

Freddy's eyes tracked the blood trail that led from Sid to the door where the mayor had been taken. "I...I..."

"You were forced into it? Is that right?" asked Arthur. "Didn't have no choice?"

"I...I..." Freddy backed off from the advancing men, before his shoulders slumped and he hung his head. "I couldn't turn down the offer. It was sooo much money. I've gotta get out of this shit. I nearly had my knackers cut off. I'm just an honest brewmaster who likes his knackers the way they are."

"Then why lager?" asked Brian. "Fooking *lager*, mon!"

Freddy waved his hand. "I ain't brewing that shite!"

"But the mayor...," said Sid, a little guiltily.

"Is probably dead."

"He'll be reet."

"I was tied to this place and to the community. To get the money, I had to get the buy-in from the council and the horrible woman who bought the place. She wouldn't let me brew ale. She made sure it was lager."

Brian looked at Sid. "I can't believe you were going to marry that, mon."

"Brian, I don't judge you on your lifestyle choices, so please don't judge me on mine." Dan Shire would've been proud.

"I ain't gay."

Sid clocked the look that the brewmaster gave his alternative friend. "You better change that old-fashioned attitude of yours, son, or you are gonna get it far worse than the mayor did."

Freddy cowered. "I didn't do anything!"

"I saw the way you looked at Brian. You're in enough trouble for giving away our beer, so don't go adding to it by being a homomotoad!"

Freddy held up his hands, not really sure what he'd done wrong.

"Why lager?" asked Brian, getting back to the point.

"Because you won't drink it. That's what Fishman said. I'd never have brewed the foul liquid. I was gonna do a runner with the money. It would have been this afternoon. I'd be on a plane to Spain, but I guess that ain't happening now, is it?"

The three men shook their heads. They meant business.

"What do you want then?"

"Our fucking beer back, man," said Arthur.

Freddy shook his head. "Sheila Fishman bought all the rights to the recipe. No one is allowed to brew it without her express permission. She owns all this now."

"And that's that?" asked Brian.

"That's that."

Tears filled Sid's eyes.

"What are you offering in terms of compensation?" asked Brian.

"What do you mean?"

"You know exactly what I mean you greedy little shit."

"Money? You want money?"

"...Errr...yeah. Right, yeah, of course we want money," said Brian. "But, more importantly, how much beer is left?"

"About a thousand gallons, but it will all be gone by tomorrow."

"No, it fooking won't," said Brian, threateningly. "Not if you don't want to end up in a worse state than the mayor."

"What do you want with it?" asked Freddy.

"You got any nibbles?" asked Sid.

"Nibbles?"

"Crisps, nuts, that sort of shite?" Sid explained.

"I think we have a box of crisps somewhere."

"Good."

"Why?"

"Because we are gonna drink this place dry," said Brian. "This is gonna be the ultimate lock-in, and you're gonna serve us beer until we pass out. When we wake up, you're gonna be there to serve us more beer. If you run before the beer is gone, then we're gonna track you down and mess you up."

Sid winced at the prospect of Brian's alternative messing.

"HARRY, CAN YOU HEAR ME?" Since lockdown, the Coalition had been trying to get hold of their most senior man in the field. Eventually, he answered, but the line was terrible.

"What?"

"Where are you? We can hardly hear you," said Charles.

"Manchester. Like you said, it's a warzone here. You still stuck in the Coalition?"

"Yes," said Caroline. "The Prime Minister has chosen not to send the army to our aid. We've got to deal with this one ourselves."

"Then it sounds like you're pretty fucked, doesn't it?"

The face of every councillor was thunder.

"Dean, what men can you spare?" said Rempstone.

"None," was the curt reply.

"Dean!" shouted Rempstone.

"Listen here, you little shit. You may be trapped, but there's no way anyone can break into your stronghold, so don't waste my time. People are dying by the hundreds on the streets, and we'd lose hundreds of agents taking back the Coalition HQ. It ain't gonna happen. You can demote me, suspend me, or shoot me in the fucking head, but it don't matter, 'cos chances are I'm gonna have my face ripped off before it comes to that."

Rempstone sat shell-shocked and Charles took over.

"You disobeyed a direct order when you left Tillsley alive. Are you going to disobey a second?"

"I'm doing what's best for the human race right now, Charles. You can stick that Agreement up your fat arse. They've started a war, and we're gonna finish it."

"Are you drunk, Dean?" asked Charles condescendingly.

"Hell, yeah, I'm drunk! But that just makes me angrier. We're all fighting for our lives, now. You and your bureaucratic bullshit can get fucked."

The phone went dead and each councillor boiled in their seats.

"At least one of you has a backbone."

The voice cast dread in all the vampires. The room turned to the doorway where Borg Hemsman loomed.

Death was here.

"H...how?" asked Bwogi.

One of Borg's troops strode through the doorway and threw two large objects onto the Great Hall table. Blood splattered across the marble as the heads of Garendon and Augustus bounced, rolled, and came to rest, both of them staring Bwogi in the eye.

"Augustus told us all about the Haemo project a few days ago," said Borg. "He'd hoped I'd spare him for his services. Young Garendon here, he wanted to reach the surface to see if it worked." Borg laughed. "Both of these vampires had no trouble destroying your pathetic guards. We knocked, and they let us in."

Caroline pulled her mobile phone out of her pocket and began inputting a number in what was now a complete and utter gamble. She might only have seconds to call and rehearsed what she would say in her head.

Five huge vampires, headed by Viralli, entered the hall and stood behind Borg. The Coalition members, sitting around the table knew what was about to transpire.

"Viralli, I thought you were dead!" cried Bwogi.

Viralli laughed. "And I once thought you were a good leader. Looks like we were both wrong."

"The Agreement is no more," said Borg. "Between you, you've made a mockery of the vampire race. We are fighting in the streets for the birthright you took away."

Borg circled the table and none of the counsellors dared to look at him. He stopped at Charles and picked him up from his seat by what little hair remained. The fat old man struggled to get to his feet, and his hair ripped out in Borg's hand. Charles fell back to his seat, red, flustered, and petrified. Borg helped him up again by the ear like he was punishing a naughty child, but Charles was too slow and blood poured down his neck from severed flesh. His vampire bodyguards laughed at the noises Charles made, coughing, spluttering, and crying. He was close to a heart attack.

"You let my daughter die." Borg spat in his face. "She followed this nonsensical human ideal and died for it. She died for a *human*. I have longed for this day for three hundred years."

The five vampires ripped into the councillors. Caroline, the only one with her wits about her, dove under the table after hitting the call button on her phone, hoping desperately that Reece would pick up. With the fortress infiltrated, she was left with only one choice.

"WHY DO YOU KEEP PHONING ME?" Reece demanded. He lay on the surgeons table that had recently held Rathbone captive. Even with all his fresh samples, he was no closer to unlocking the answer to Sid's right hand.

"I need you," she shouted down the phone.

Reece barely recognised Caroline's voice. He'd never heard her be anything but calm with a big dollop of arrogance on the side.

"Why should I help you?" he asked.

"Listen to me. I don't have much time."

Her desperation kept him quiet and utterly intrigued.

"This will be traced; I can't afford to give anything away. You must work this out for yourself. Tillsley is linked to Haemo through The Miner's Arms."

"What? How?"

"Go to the source," she said firmly.

His eyes darted to the empty keg of Bolton on the floor that he'd given Rathbone.

"I've been before and checked it out. There's nothing there."

"Look harder. This was meant to be my glory. My glory!" she shouted. "Haemo, Chambers...Haemo..." she sobbed before an agonising scream distorted the line and it went dead.

Reece had no idea what was going on, but he was going to find out.

34

I can categorically state we do not have an army of vampires storming across the country and drinking the blood of our nation. Right now, we need the press to cooperate with us. We are trying to regain order, and inciting blind panic in the general public has contributed to further unrest, further violence, and ultimately more deaths.

We are making progress. We've identified the cause of the illness. Leighton Pharmaceuticals were operating a clinical trial into treating schizophrenia. The drug, PQ1539, was administered to nearly a thousand patients across the UK over the last three months. Fifty per cent of these have been affected. The drug has caused psychosis, with a side effect of aversion to sunlight, which is why the violence has only been observed at night. Now we have pinpointed the cause and the individuals afflicted. We can begin gathering up the patients and work on a cure.

—Government boffin

LIFE IS A FUNNY OLD THING. There're ups and there're downs, and you have to ride the rollercoaster and live through all the other crappy clichés thrown in your general direction. Some could say that Rathbone had been dealt a few bad hands of late, and there weren't many who'd argue. But then, it hadn't been all bad for Rathbone. The vampiring had meant he'd lost his virginity, and being able to wear a cape was pretty mint. Getting buggered by a group of randy pensioners was pretty shit, though.

Ups and downs.

This, however, was definitely an up. This was possibly the highlight of all the vampiring. Rathbone was sat in a Jacuzzi, drinking malt whisky, smoking fine Cuban cigars with his new best friend and three prostitutes.

"This is the life, ain't it, Pete?" asked King, sat beside him.

"S'all right, I guess." He'd never been called Pete before. It made him feel like a young go-getter. The prossies seemed to like it too.

"So you're a vampire are you, Petey?" said an Asian stunner, wearing the skimpiest of bikinis. The bubbles of the hot tub were producing some marvellous effects with the silicon.

"Aye." Rathbone knocked back the whisky and looked over his

shoulder where a tidy little blonde piece stood with a decanter of Scotch. She poured him an extra-large measure.

"And I'm half vampire," said King. He was the reason the third prostitute, a brunette, wasn't in the Jacuzzi with them. There was no room.

"You don't look like a vampire, gorgeous. You haven't got a cape like Petey."

Rathbone looked very smug, indeed. He wore his cape in the pool. The bubbles made it rise to the surface and shimmer and it looked cool. Vampire cool. He farted again, and nobody suspected a thing. This was the best day of his life.

"Looks good on him, don't it girls?" said King.

"He's a cutie," said the brunette. All three of the women giggled like schoolgirls. They were professionals of the highest calibre and had jacked up the price significantly when they saw the horrible, greasy, little bastard walk in with his morbidly obese yet devilishly sexy friend.

"Lying twat." Rathbone wasn't good with women.

The brunette bit her lip and thought of the money. They were drawing straws later to see who had to do the dirty with him. It would be a big heroin dose beforehand for whoever got unlucky. She took a different tact and spoke to King, trying to avoid the horrible, greasy, little bastard. "So, why are you two honeys spending your time with us tonight? You vampires have been all over the news of late."

"We're not like the others," said King. "We're both lovers, not fighters."

"I'm both. Fooking rock, me." Rathbone lifted his arms out of the bath so the girls could get a load of the guns.

"I'm glad to hear it," said the blonde, giggling in a painfully sexy way.

The sexy giggle was special, and Rathbone knew it was well rehearsed. None of the girls believed them, and fair enough. They didn't exactly look like the vampires that had been flashing their fangs across the screen over the last couple of days, all capeless wankers.

"That's disgusting," said the Asian hooker, quickly climbing out the bath.

King looked over his shades. "What are you talking about, baby?" asked the man who'd just taken a huge bite out of his hero sandwich and squeezed a heart-attack-sized dollop of mayonnaise out of the end and into the Jacuzzi.

She pointed, but he couldn't see over his belly to where the oily badness was spreading.

"What's *that*?" she asked, pointing at the equally disgusting foreign substance polluting the pool.

"It looks like grease," said the brunette.

The other oil slick, being jostled by the bubbles, migrated away from the source. Rathbone sucked on his cigar, uncaring of his personal hygiene.

"Let's go freshen up, girls," said the blonde before the other two followed her through.

King took another bite of his sandwich and made sure he caught the mayo out of the bottom before licking it off his hand.

Rathbone's lecherous gaze followed the three arses. "Gagging for it," he said when they weren't quite out of earshot.

"It's good to chill out with you, bro'," said King, taking a swig of Scotch. "My grandpappy and all his vampire buddies are so dull. It's good to finally meet someone I can chew the fat with, share a drink, and bang some whores with."

"I ain't going twos-up," said Rathbone with a threatening finger.

"That ain't a problem with me." King changed the subject. "You were saying earlier that you need beer instead of blood. It certainly sounds a lot more appealing, but I ain't a fan of beer. It's nasty shit."

"Well, don't fooking drink it then," said Rathbone. "I'm gonna need a top-up of Bolton soon, like. I intend to be completely spent after running through the hookers, so I'll need a few pints to recharge me batteries."

"And then, I'll finally meet my daddy." King finished off his whisky with a flick of his wrist.

Rathbone shrugged. He had nothing against Arthur. It was Garforth who left him for dead at the hands and parts of the Allotmenteers. Still, that didn't mean he particularly *liked* Arthur. He didn't particularly like anyone, although there were particular parts of the three hookers he'd taken a shine to.

"What's he like? My granddaddy said he treated my momma like dirt, man. Is it true?"

Rathbone shrugged again. He didn't like all this male-bonding crap. He took another swig of whisky, finishing yet another glass. Looking around for a refill, he was disgusted to see that there were no prostitutes at his beck and call. "You can't get decent high-class hookers these days."

"Really? These chicks seem pretty hot to me. I've never been with a hooker before. Are you used to a better standard?"

Rathbone considered the tenner-a-shot prossies from the Smithson Estate, every single one of whom had turned him down. "Yeah, much better."

"I've got a lot to learn, man." King sunk lower into the water.

"You getting yourself another whisky?" asked Rathbone, hoping King was going to get up so he didn't have to.

"No, man, I'm good with the sandwich."

"Fat twat."

"Sorry, buddy?" said King, not catching the comment, but Rathbone ignored him, getting out of the Jacuzzi so that he could drink some more whisky at Borg Hemsman's expense.

"What the fuck is that?" said King, before slapping a hand over his mouth.

"What the fook is what?" asked Rathbone aggressively.

King looked everywhere but directly at him. "Nothing... err, nothing man."

Rathbone looked down at his naked body and then back at King who looked even more awkward. It twigged.

"It's fooking average for a vampire."

"Don't know what you're talking about." King spent time cleaning his shades.

Rathbone grabbed at his appendage with his thumb and forefinger. "It's this you were looking at, weren't it? It's fooking average for a vampire."

King held his hands up. "Sorry, buddy, I didn't mean to—"

"I thought you'd understand."

"You're right. I'm sorry, man, but I don't think it is average for a vampire."

Rathbone used his cape to regain some dignity. "'Course it fooking is."

King, after a good bit of huffing and puffing, raised himself above the water. His belly covered most, but, as he got up, it swung like a pendulum until he stood with it dipping into the water like a drinking elephant.

Rathbone's eyes widened for a moment, but he played it off. "Well, mine's a grower not a shower."

"I'm glad, man. I'm real glad."

"Let's bang these prossies and then go get some Bolton," said Rathbone sulkily. "But I'm going first!" he quickly added, looking at King's monster.

"Sure thing."

"Oi!" shouted Rathbone through the door where the hookers had left. "I've run out of whisky here! Bring us another bottle!"

King stared longingly at the open door. "The hookers ain't coming back, are they?"

"They never do," said Rathbone with a sigh, relaxing into the bath.

35

A government official said the concept of vampires was laudable, but added it was understandable that the public is in a state of uncertainty at the moment and that both psychologists and scientists are working around the clock to come up with a solution to the madness sweeping across the UK as a result of Leighton Pharmaceuticals' clinical trial.

—Question Time

REECE DROVE SLOWLY through the streets of Bolton on his way to the brewery, not knowing what he was looking for. He pulled around the corner, and the storey-high steel-bar gates of the brewery rolled into view. Reece laughed when he saw Brian Garforth's Capri parked next to the entrance. It was a surprise for sure but of no concern to Reece. They'd be there for nothing more than a piss-up.

Reece put his foot down. It was time to scope out the town. He turned the corner to skirt the premises and something caught his eye, almost causing him to crash his car into a nearby lamppost.

In the centre of the adjacent industrial complex, a massive building came into view. On top of the roof, a winding mass of metal reached high into the sky, gigantic vents designed to carry Haemo into the atmosphere.

He'd been here before to scope out the brewery, but the vents weren't there last time. They must have been the last things to be built. Finding the Haemo plant slap bang next to the brewery was impossible to be a coincidence. It must be linked to the drunks' powers. But why hadn't he discovered the secret?

There were Haemo plants all over the country. Why had Caroline sent him here to this one? His mind raced. Vampire activity had always been low in Bolton, and what few vampires resided here would've left for Manchester ten miles away when the riots started. Putting a Haemo factory in a place like this was a huge waste of money and resources and that summed up the Coalition...but not Caroline. His initial task was to get inside the Haemo plant to see why she'd sent him here.

Driving past the front gate, he tried to piece the information together and wished he had more. The plant was an eyesore. It wouldn't take the vampires long to pin down their target, the vents were visible from miles around. Driving past, he could appreciate the incredible levels of security the building was trying to hide. All the guards patrolling the perimeter were human since the winter sun burned bright.

It took him a considerable length of time to drive around the back of the massive building. Maybe this was the central hub for the entire operation? It would make sense to build it away from the main population, and Bolton had good links to the North. Maybe the plant had the range to affect Manchester? It didn't look operational, and the mass vampire movement attacking Coalition headquarters indicated that Haemo was already in circulation.

There were many questions, but he was only going to answer them by getting into the building and that wouldn't be easy. He continued to case the joint, driving slowly to avoid suspicion. Video cameras meant scaling the fifteen-foot fence was not an option, even though his physical power would make mincemeat of the climb. He drove all the way around the building and there was no let-up in the metal wall, guards, or cameras. It would mean a trip into the sewers and the water systems. If that didn't turn up any opportunities, then he'd knock on the front door. The toys he carried in the boot would ensure they'd hear him.

Soon, he was crawling through the sewers and human excrement. The rats didn't faze him in the slightest. His GPS system told him he was in the confines of the plant, and there'd been no security so far.

The slack security in the sewers, where there was nothing but piss, shit, and vermin, was of no surprise. Haemo was something only a vampire would try to destroy, and to them, it wasn't worth wading through a quarter of a mile of hell for. Their pride and arrogance was always going to be their undoing. And, if Reece found what he was looking for, his fists would finish the job.

He reached a manhole cover directly below the main building. He pulled his backpack over his head, took out a handheld device, and aimed it at the cover. The Radar Flashlight could pick up heartbeats ten feet away, even through walls. It was still a gamble, lifting the manhole, but at least he didn't have to lift it with a guard stood on top of it.

He lifted the cover half an inch, just enough to pop through the camera he controlled from a base unit, another delicious toy stowed away in his rucksack. The camera's range was poor, but fortunately, the room was small. There were no guards, and pipework meandered from floor to ceiling. He popped up the cover and entered the building, not making a sound.

Happy that the room was secure, he quickly stripped off his soiled outer garments and threw them back down the drain. He could move as silently as the best assassin but that wouldn't help if people could smell him coming from the next room.

This was going to be tough. He'd no idea where he was going or what he was looking for. There was only one door out of this maintenance room, and he slipped the camera under the door before opening it to the much larger plant room. No space was wasted. He was confronted with a mass of pipes, valves, and tanks. The roar of pneumatics was deafening, and the smell of chemicals and solvents dizzying. Hiding here would be easy. It was so cramped, it'd be easy for someone with his skills to fight his way out.

He didn't want violence. Chances were high that the humans working here were heroes, part of the human race's fight against the vampire hordes. Any conflict he'd resolve peacefully, if possible.

He moved quickly through the tight walkways, surprised not to find another soul. He scanned the upper parts of the plant room. There were a few gangways passing through the walls allowing quick access to adjoining rooms. There were no windows, although there'd been a few visible from the outside. He reached the next doorway and went through the same routine, slotting the camera under the door. The room was a lot bigger and looked like a laboratory. His mouth dried with anticipation, and then, his heart raced when two figures in white coats popped into the camera's field of vision.

A laboratory and scientists meant answers, not that he knew what questions to ask. The lab was big. There were likely two guards at the very least. He pulled a modified shotgun from his rucksack, unloaded the weapon and reloaded it with non-lethal ammunition. There wasn't going to be any bloodsuckers inside. He had pistols holstered if he needed to kill. Once ready, he opened the door.

To a scientist like Reece, the room was a playground. No expense had been spared setting up this laboratory. Everything he'd ever wanted was in this room. Just a day with this equipment...He snapped his mind back to the task at hand. He'd been right to expect guards, and two was a good guess. A beanbag from Reece's gun hit an unsuspecting guard on the gangway in the back of his head. He was unconscious before falling hard on the metal surface. The second guard reached for their gun, but Reece was faster. He then turned the shotgun to the scientists, cowering from the blasts. "Do exactly what I say and neither of you will get hurt. Get your hands up."

The man and the woman obeyed, and Reece gave the room the once-over again. He was surprised there weren't more guards. He took in the details. Fume cupboards were built into every wall where large reactions were being carried out. Benches ran across the centre of the lab with analytical instrumentation giving these scientists the answers to anything they could possibly think of. There were no signs of other workers, but the walkway above, running through the building, could prove problematic. He wouldn't be able to hear anyone coming.

"Do you know where you are?" asked the woman incredulously. Her nerve was impressive. She was pretty without trying to be. Her hair was tied back and no makeup to be seen on her dark skin. No ring on her slender finger. She'd be married to her work.

Reece reloaded the shotgun, snapped it shut, and held it up. "Yeah, I know where I am. I'm standing in front of you holding a gun to your face."

"How did you get in here?" she demanded.

"I'm asking the questions."

"You haven't so far," she pointed out. She must be something special to be working in a place like this.

Reece circled her and her partner. He was older, receding hair, slight of build. He was more nervy, but then, she was something else. Reece weaved between the fancy chemistry sets.

"What's in there?" he asked, looking at the large volume of green liquid bubbling away in a glass reactor.

She didn't answer. He could see she was itching to call for help. She was one tough lab rat. The man was too scared to talk. Reece circled until he stood in front of the scientists.

"Turn around and put your hands on the bench." The man complied instantly, but the woman didn't until the barrel of the gun was placed against her forehead. She joined her colleague.

"Who are you?" she asked.

"Why aren't you pumping that shit into the atmosphere," he whispered into her ear, ignoring her question.

"I-I don't know what you're talking about," she stuttered. It was the first knock to her confidence.

Time to grab her attention. Reece rammed the butt of the shotgun to the back of the man's head. He collapsed, a dead weight, but he'd be OK...probably. "Fucking answer me. That—" He indicated her fallen colleague, "was a friendly warning."

"He...he was my superior. He knows everything. I am only his assistant."

"Bullshit," he snarled and stamped on the unconscious man's knee, the cracking of bone echoed round the lab.

"I'm telling the truth," she cried.

She was hard as nails. The fearful tone to her voice was a poor act.

He took a different tact. "We're on the same side, but I need answers. Listen to me. I'm a vampire hunter. When are you going to send that shit into the bloodsuckers' lungs?"

She looked back over her shoulder, trying to read him with those pretty dark eyes. "We're ready to go now. All I have to do is press the button." She pointed above at the end of the gangway to where a large computer console sat. "One button and it will all be done."

"Then what are you waiting for?" he asked.

"The order, of course."

Reece took a moment. "From Caroline?"

"You know Caroline?" she said quickly, sounding surprised.

He held in the smile. He'd got to her. "Rather, I knew her..."

Her eyes widened. "What do you mean?"

"I think she's dead."

Tears welled up faster than Reece thought possible for this hard woman.

"Close?" he said, not relinquishing his hold on the shotgun by a whisker.

She turned towards him, staring at him through blood-red eyes. "She was my sister."

Things fell into place.

Caroline wanted him to come here to give her sister the order to activate the plant. She wouldn't have been able to phone her because the call would be traced by Borg, who'd proceeded to give Caroline the send off she deserved. She would've known he'd need little information to get here. But, if Haemo was already being pumped into the vamp's lungs, then why wasn't this plant operational? Maybe it wasn't that simple. He scanned the room once more, and the great glass reactors in the fume cupboards caught his eyes again. "What's the green liquid in the reactors?"

"The carrier of course," she sobbed.

He didn't say a word. He needed to get as much information out of her as possible without letting on that he didn't have a clue what was going on.

Haemo's carrier was supposed to be red.

"Pint of Bolton."

Kev was cleaning some glasses and recognised a voice he hated. However, it was a voice that brought money, and money was the most important thing in a landlord's life. "Evening, Rathbone. Haven't seen you here for a while."

Rathbone and King had cut their losses after the hookers had nicked their wallets and legged it. Beer was needed.

Kev turned away from his glasses to pour a pint and was surprised to see Rathbone had acquired a friend, and a friend twice as fat as Sid. Excess body fat meant outstanding drinking abilities in the land of the 'boro, and that meant yet more money. "Good evening, sir."

"Hey man, I'm King." He offered a sweaty hand that Kev shook warmly after giving Rathbone his drink.

A friendly atmosphere encouraged the drinking of beer. "Can I get you a drink, sir?"

"Pepsi Cola, baby, and make it extra large."

Kev didn't sell many soft drinks, but good money could be made from selling off out-of-date stock from the local Co-Op. "Don't I know you from somewhere?" he asked, opening a bottle too old to fizz.

"I'm Arthur's son." King removed his shades to give Kev a better look.

"Oh, aye. One of them council fellas was flashing your picture about, a week ago. You were a bit, erm...thinner in the picture."

"Well, I have a condition." His tummy rumbled. "You got any bar snacks, man?"

"I'm sure I can dig something out," said Kev, thinking of what crap he could get rid of.

"Bolton!" Rathbone slammed down his glass, and King dug out some notes, which took some effort. His jumpsuit did not allow easy access.

"Is it that good?" asked King when Rathbone demolished another fresh pint. "Get me one of those pint things," King shouted to Kev who was digging out a sixteen-year-old Pepparami from under the fridge.

"Coming up."

A moment later, King was holding the pint up to the light. "It always looks so nasty on the TV, but this looks good. It looks refreshing."

"Best beer in the Northeast, lad," said a proud landlord.

King took a big swig of Bolton Bitter.

"Yep," said Kev, "it's a damn shame that they're gonna shut the brewery down."

Rathbone and King simultaneously spat out their ale, far and wide.

"They can't shut the brewery! I need Bolton to live!"

King's response was a little different. "You actually drink this for *fun*? This is fucking disgusting, man! The taste in my mouth...My god, it tastes like a tramp ate some dog shit...and then shit the shit into my mouth!"

"You sure they're shutting it?" said Rathbone, grabbing Kev's arm, who desperately tried to rid his pink tux from the greasy claw.

"Aye. Remember that bird who tried to get Sid done for benefit fraud? Well, Sid nearly married her, and 'cos he got cold feet, she's royally fooking him over. She won the bloody lottery and bought the lot."

Rathbone played nervously with his cape. "I'm fooked."

"Actually, the second taste ain't quite so bad. I don't want to throw up as much," said King.

"Them wankers are there now," said Kev. "Sid said they're gonna drink the place dry. Bastards owe me a fooking fortune for the amount of booze they put away last night. Sid set up a tab and didn't fooking pay up. They've gone too far this time."

"King, your old man is at Bolton Brewery," said Rathbone. "We need to get there and stop that place closing or I'm fooking dead."

"You know, this ain't bad at all. Hey, barman, get us another one of these bad boys," said King, pointing at an empty glass.

"You got cash?" asked Kev, once bitten, twice shy.

"How much?"

"Three pounds a pint."

"You robbing bastard!" said Rathbone.

"Supply and demand, lad. Supply and demand."

King threw over a note.

"We need to get to that brewery," urged Rathbone.

King finished off his pint. "We'll have a few more here, first."

"At three pounds a pint? He can fook off."

"I'm buying."

"Pint of Bolton, Kev."

36

We're fighting back. People are listening and staying inside. These fuckers ain't crazy. They know exactly what they're doing. I've seen them before. This ain't anything new. Government's known about vampires for years. Some of their suits are fighting with us, tough sons of bitches, and they know how to kill them. Fucking government. This is just another cover-up that went wrong, which means we, the army, have to sort it out, losing our brothers along the way.

—Sergeant S Berkley

AFTER ADMINISTERING a couple of quick injections to ensure the guards wouldn't wake for a few more hours, Reece examined the glass reactors full of green, frothing liquid. Pipes ran from the liquid and up into the roof space, probably to the vents. On the other side of the room were similar reactors full of clear liquids, although on a much smaller scale. If it was Haemo, it would only quell Bolton's vampire population for a matter of days, and there was no point in that. The question was: what was it?

"Why did Caroline send you here?" she asked. She wiped at her cheeks with the sleeve of her coat. Tears were over.

He put the shotgun over the shoulder, just in case she'd forgotten he could kill her whenever he wanted. "How long have you been ready?" Her sister may be dead, but Caroline was just another casualty. Heroes could be hailed later.

Her eyes narrowed. "We've been running off the back of Haemo. We rely on the technology for the carrier and for the pumping system. We were ready yesterday when it was released. You don't know what this place is, do you?"

He shook his head. She was too smart to fool.

"I believe Caroline sent you here. Just tell me what she said."

"She didn't have time to send me a message. She was being attacked. She just told me to come here."

The woman turned and looked up towards the console on the gangway. "It's the signal to begin, or rather, it's the signal to end."

He advanced on her, desperate to know. "End what?"

"What you've fought for your entire life, vampire hunter." She pointed to the smaller reactors containing the clear liquid. "You can put down your gun. Purity is your weapon now. Purity will destroy them all."

FREDDY BUGGLESWAITE wasn't enjoying his last day in charge of Bolton Brewery. He'd hoped it'd be a historic day, meeting local dignitaries and having his back slapped for being a credit to Bolton. Instead, he was serving beer to three drunks holding him hostage in the tasting room, threatening him with gratuitous violence if he didn't continue to serve them until they'd finished drinking the seven thousand pints of beer left in the brewery.

"I've missed this, lads," said Sid to Brian and Arthur.

"Aye, it's good to get back to a bit of normality, like," said Brian, "at least in the short-term."

"What do you mean?" asked Sid.

"Well, once we've finished all the beer, we'll have to go back to the 'boro where there'll be no more Bolton, and no more Miner's."

"Fook," said Sid, lighting up another cigarette, which he'd paid duty on.

"How much beer we got left, baby?" asked Arthur to the brewmaster, who looked at the computer system.

"Six thousand nine hundred and seventy-three pints."

"Shit," said all three at the same time. The lock-in sent from heaven was nearly over.

"What do you think Kev will stock instead of Bolton?" asked Sid.

"That ship's sailed, mate," said Brian.

Sid held up his pint glass, and Freddy reluctantly did his duty. "What do you mean, Brian?"

"We went through hundreds of quid's worth of booze the other night. He was fooking livid when we didn't pay up."

"He's always boiling about summat, like."

"Do you really want to go back there? It ain't the fooking Miner's anymore, it's The First Swallow of Summer. The Miner's died a long time ago."

"But it's got all that chrome and stuff, you lot like," said Sid encouragingly.

"I ain't fooking...ah, forget it."

"It'll be the same once the Bolton starts flowing again," said Sid.

"But it won't, will it, Sid. That's why we're here. That tank in front of you is the last of the Bolton Bitter." Brian pointed a finger at Freddy Buggleswaite. "'Cos that little twat there sold it all."

Freddy feared for his safety for the 532nd time of the day.

"Three more beers, over here," said Arthur. "Boys, this is our last hurrah, and this ain't the place to be moping around. Come on, last time we were here, we had a riot. We should be having fun."

"Aye, it was a riot, all right," mumbled the brewmaster.

"What happened last time?" asked Sid.

"You're joking." Freddy popped down three glasses. "It was only a couple of years ago. You don't remember?"

REECE WAS CONVINCED there wasn't a soul alive who hated vampires more than he did, and now, a weapon—Purity—had been developed that would end the lives of every last one of them.

"Why not release it sooner?" he asked.

"I was waiting for Caroline's signal." She'd followed her sister without question.

"You needed to wait for Haemo? Why?"

"Gas pipes connect every Haemo installation together making a single, massive network. The drug can be pumped to where it's needed most. It's an extremely clever system, so we thought we'd steal it. The pumps in this huge building have more power than all the other Haemo plants combined. From this plant, we can send Purity anywhere in the UK. By the time they realise, it will all be too late."

"How does it work?"

"Well..."

Reece saw the look on her face. "I'm a scientist too. Don't hold back. I've studied Haemo and its carrier, extensively."

She nodded. "The carrier works exactly the same way as in Haemo. Without it, the virus can't enter the body."

"Virus?"

"Yes. Purity is a virus."

Reece's pulse raced. "And that means it's contagious?"

"Yes. Once the carrier takes the virus past the vampire's autoimmune system, Purity will mutate and be passed on to another. A vampire can pass it on without the need for a carrier. It's incredibly potent."

"So why do you need the pumping system?"

"To hit the entire population in one fell swoop. There'll be no chance for the vampire to build immunity to the virus. They will all be infected at the same time. We owe our thanks to Borg Hemsman. He's drawn virtually every single vampire in Europe out into the streets of the UK's major cities."

Reece couldn't believe what a genius Caroline was. "Once exposed to the virus, how long do they last?"

"Oh, that's the fun part," she said, with a glint in her eye. "I've never seen one last more than a minute."

He couldn't help but grin. "What do you have to do to set the system running?"

"The console at the end of the gangway up above is the master control to the pumps and the reactors. All I have to do is input the correct code, and that's that."

"Who else knows the code?" he said quickly.

"Cara..." She shook her head. "Only me, now."

"Shall we start the sequence?"

She nodded. "I've been waiting for this for a long time."

They climbed the metal staircase to the gangway and approached the console that was simplicity itself. A keypad, a screen, and a few buttons was all that stood between Reece and the genocide of the vampire race.

"Seems straightforward," he commented. "I'm surprised someone hasn't tried to crack the code in order to gain the glory, so to speak."

"It may look simple, but no one can crack the code. I doubt anyone on this site has the expertise, and without use of this console, there'd be no Purity."

"That's good to hear."

Reece changed the ammunition in his shotgun to the lethal variety.

"What are you doing?" she screamed.

Without hesitation, Reece fired the gun at the computer.

"YOU CAN'T REMEMBER THE BREWERY TOUR?" asked Freddy. Not sure how anyone could forget a chain of events so memorable, but then, he didn't understand the mechanisms of Sid Tillsley's memory functionality.

Sid scratched his head. "Was Rathbone wearing a snazzy T-shirt?"

"Don't be daft, mon," said Brian. "Although I ain't surprised you can't remember. You were absolutely battered."

Sid put his hand on his chest. "Me?"

"You all bloody were," said Freddy. "It took ages to get over the bad publicity surrounding it all. You keep going on about saving my life, but you nearly ruined it back then."

Sid shrugged.

Brian laughed.

"It weren't funny!" said Freddy. "Knocking out the mayor was nothing compared to that."

"Get the beers in, and tell us what happened," said Brian. "You need a good story or two when you're on a session."

"Pissing hell," said Freddy and three empty pint glasses hit the table leaving only 6,967 pints of Bolton Bitter left to be savoured.

Once the beers were pulled, Freddy took a seat opposite the men on the other side of the tasting table. "If truth be told, it wasn't all Sid's fault. There was another fella causing most of the trouble, but it was Sid who finished it."

Sid nodded. "Never started a fight in me life."

Brian and Arthur didn't say anything.

"Well, you certainly retaliated," said Freddy before continuing the story. "It was a standard tour I used to run after regular working hours. It put a few quid in my pocket the taxman couldn't get hold of. You three, and that horrible, little bastard who used to follow you around were here along with a dozen or so locals from a boozer in Manchester, and then there was a big fella who Sid didn't take too kindly to."

Freddy pulled himself a pint of beer, practising the philosophy *if you can't beat them, join them.* "You lot were pretty hammered when you got here and quickly upset the lads from Manchester. They were really into their ale."

"So are we," said Brian.

"Yeah, but you like *drinking* it. They were them twats that just like talking about it. You know, never got pissed in their lives but look down at a man who can't smell an elderberry from three miles away in a pint of piss."

"I thought a brewmaster would be in with that sort of clique," said Brian.

"Not me. Been brewing the same shite for years, not that I ain't proud of it. Glorious beer it is, but I can't be bothered with all the poncy crap, ya know?"

"Oi!" said Sid. "Don't use that sort of language in front of Brian. He's a homomo-sexual, don't you know?"

"That's not what our Maude on the front desk said, like." Freddy eyed Brian. "Although, it does explain why he was so keen to knock her back doors..."

"Get back to the story, Freddy," said Brian.

REECE'S CAR SKIDDED all the way up to the entrance of his lab. He threw open the car door, jumped out, and hastily unlocked and decoded the security systems. He dropped the keys and cursed himself again before regaining composure.

"Cool it. Time is on your side. They can't activate it, not yet, not without the code, and not without her," he said to himself.

Once he'd opened his lab, he fetched Caroline's sister from the boot of his car. Happy that no one was watching, he unceremoniously dragged her out by the hair. She didn't scream. She really was tough. At least he'd had the decency to knock her out before dragging her through Bolton's sewers, the way he'd entered. He didn't want to hurt her, but she had to know who was boss.

After entering, he locked all the doors and set all the security systems running. This was a time to keep the utmost vigilance. He dragged her into the lab and dumped her on a chair.

"I don't know what you expect to find," she said. "It kills them, and it kills them quick. I didn't have time to work on a formula that would ensure they'd suffer in agonising torment, forcing them to throw their own rotting bodies into the sunlight, but at least we'll be rid of them. They could be dead right now. You've put the entire project at risk. People are dying out there."

He smiled. He liked her a lot more than Caroline, even though he had a suspicion they shared the same dangerous traits. This one, however, didn't cover it with a façade of coolness. "What's your name?"

"Elizabeth." She didn't ask him his.

"I share your hate for them, and I want them to die, but I want them to *know* they're going to die. I want to stalk them, hunt them and ensure every single one of them fears me like the daylight."

"You're a fool to jeopardise the project over some ridiculous schoolboy fantasy!"

"It will soon be reality." He took some rope from out of a desk drawer before binding her to the chair.

"What do you possibly hope to achieve?"

"Do you know who Sid Tillsley is?"

She shook her head.

"He can kill vampires with a punch."

"Impossible," she said. Caroline obviously told her nothing.

He shrugged. "He and his friends all exhibit remarkable powers that they have used to fight the vampire. One of them even impregnated a lamia. Can you believe that? You would've seen the child, the hybrid, on the news."

It was her turn to shrug. "I don't have much time for television."

"Sid and his friends all have one thing in common and that is the town of Bolton."

He enjoyed her look of puzzlement.

"They're all alcoholics and consume gallons of the disgusting beverage, Bolton Bitter, on a nightly basis."

"The brewery is next door."

"I know, and there's nothing untoward about the beer, either. What I do know is that beer has been impregnated into their DNA, and each has developed a skill linked to their own attributes that affects the vampire." He began preparing his instrumentation for the analysis of Purity. "Haemo and the carrier are marvellous inventions."

"Yes, the carrier is something we stole from the Haemo project. Can you believe a vampire scientist came up with it? Purity relies on the same ingestion mechanisms, but obviously, the effects of Purity are more lethal."

Reece laughed. If she wasn't bound to the chair, it would have been like two scientists discussing their latest work over a coffee break.

"I have altered my own DNA with the use of Haemo and its carrier. I have developed Sid Tillsley's strength and some more unfortunate attributes from one of his friends." Reece thought about his recent shrinkage. "Yet, none of the changes linked me to the vampire. The carrier was of use, and I wrongly thought Haemo could be used as a fuel source for the process, but it wasn't Haemo I needed. I believe Purity is what I've been looking for. I believe Sid Tillsley has ingested Purity and gained the power to kill vampires."

She shook her head. "Impossible. We have tested Purity on humans and there are absolutely no side effects whatsoever. There is no way he could have A—ingested it and B—altered his DNA."

"Nevertheless, something did, and I'm going to replicate it in my own body," he said proudly.

"And if you manage it?"

"Then, I'm going to destroy the plant and wipe out every vampire with my bare hands."

She closed her eyes. "You selfish, egotistical fool."

"If you'd lived my life, you wouldn't be so quick to judge," he spat.

A tear found its way onto her cheek once more. "My life has been one of nightmares. That is why I want them all dead, right now. We can wipe them out!" she screamed.

"I deserve this. I've *earned* it." He slapped her with the back of his hand.

Taking the sample of Purity out of his pocket, he carefully took an aliquot and placed it on the slide of the microscope before slotting it into position. He looked into the eyepiece, added a drop of vampire DNA, and laughed manically as he watched the battle.

The Purity latched onto vampire DNA like a vampire onto a helpless human being. It clung to it, consumed it, breaking it down into its basic building blocks until there was nothing left but residue. It would explain why they crumpled into dust when Sid punched them or when exposed to Brian's semen. Purity was sunlight leashed into a molecule, and the men from Middlesbrough expressed its functionality in their own despicable ways.

"DID I HIT ANYONE?" asked Sid innocently.

Freddy snorted. "Something like that. The big fella was on his own, asking a lot of weird questions about the plant next door for some reason. He didn't give a shit about the beer and didn't even drink any. He just kept asking the strangest questions, like where the water pipes ran and where the waste streams were. I think he was a spy or a burglar, trying to case the joint."

"What's next door, baby?" asked Arthur.

"Dunno. Some chemical plant or summat. Something dodgy, like. It's like a fortress over there. Anyway, this bloke started to get a bit pushy when he weren't getting the answers he wanted, and that's when Sid got involved."

"I can't remember any of this, man," said Arthur.

"Yeah, well you were banging my niece in the packaging room so you won't remember a thing, will ya?" said a bitter uncle.

"Send my regards, baby!"

Freddy ignored him.

"Actually, I can remember," said Brian. "He was a reet tall fella, big-built too, if I remember rightly. Weird chap. A looonng way up his own arse. Sid was right to smack him." Brian scratched his head. "He was a bit of a hard case too. Sid caught him with a massive headbutt but didn't put him down. You know what? I reckon he was one of them vampire fellas, now I think about it."

"Too many of them bastards involved in the brewery trade, I can tell you," said Freddy. "That's half the reason I'm getting out. I can't afford to have me nuts cut off, not at my age."

"I don't think it would be good to have your nuts cut off at any age," said Arthur. "If he was a vampire, then surely Sid would've punched him into dust."

"Aye," said Brian. "Good point that, like."

"Well, he certainly punched him. Put him down on a knee with the nut before catching him with a horrible uppercut. Made me feel queasy it did. We were in the brewing room, on the gangway where we add the hops. The lad stumbled backwards into one of the vessels we were adding to."

Sid laughed as if Freddy were describing a Laurel and Hardy film. "A big headbutt, a right hand, and a drenching. All's well that ends well!"

37

Cure? I'd laugh if I was still able to. Nothing's changed. Nothing. Clinical trial? You're having a laugh, mate. It ain't just the freaks drinking human blood that you've got to worry about. Looting, murder, rape is what we have to look forward to if we can't get to our houses before nightfall when the army put bullets in us for fun. The gangs are causing as much trouble as the freaks. London is burning twenty-fours a day. I'll tell you this: it's only going to get worse.

—Pub bore, The Coopers' Tavern, London

CONSCIOUSNESS MERCILESSLY TOOK CAROLINE and brought her back into a hopeless world. When the vampires had attacked, Caroline had begged the Maker for death, and it hadn't come. Being strong wasn't always a good thing. The only reason she was still breathing had to be the Haemo project. Borg was extending her punishment because of the drug being pumped into the atmosphere of Britain's cities. They'd known everything about the Coalition's movements, but Purity had nothing to do with the Coalition.

Her hands were bound with rope, and she hung suspended to the light above the great table. Her arms were dead. She could feel nothing above the shoulders, and her feet felt heavy as the blood pooled in them. She swung slowly, every oscillation bringing excruciating pain. Her feet dangled agonisingly close to the table; she was only an inch away from relieving the crippling tension in her arms. Last night, or day, whenever it was, she'd been half a foot from the table. Something, either the rope, the light, maybe her arms were giving way. With no vampires around, this was a chance for freedom.

Freedom? A foolish thought.

Below her, heaped in a pile, and shown the same respect as road kill, were the councillors who'd suffered degrading, agonising deaths so she could have a shot at releasing Purity. Sadly, she looked into the dead eyes of Garendon's decapitated head. She'd hated him for what he was, but he was a genius. She'd needed Haemo, and Purity needed the technology behind its carrier. Her sister hadn't been able to develop one suitable for Purity, and Garendon had stepped in. She couldn't believe the Coalition had actually believed Haemo would stop the war.

Bwogi was her puppet throughout. She never would have made it this far without his stupidity. Borg's vampires had ensured he suffered the worst fate of all for his traitorous ways. But, Bwogi died sooner than they had hoped; his body giving up after such a cruel and degrading attack. He had screamed for hours during the ordeal of being skinned alive and then given blood to regenerate before being skinned again.

Out of everyone who sat on the Coalition, Sanderson was the only one she'd ever liked. It was a mistake choosing Chambers over him, but Sanderson had always been a loose cannon, and she'd needed discreteness. Hindsight was 20/20. Chambers should've met with Elizabeth by now, and the vampires should be dying. Chambers had either failed at deciphering her clues or turned against the plan. The latter was almost certainly true. The Purity installation, with the exception of water and power, was completely isolated from the outside world. There was no way she could've got word to Elizabeth without outside help. She should've told her to release Purity when it was ready, but she'd wanted to be with her sister when the moment came. They'd suffered together and they deserved to find vengeance together.

Yes, hindsight was 20/20.

Not knowing what was happening and not being able to affect the outcome was sickening. It was a far worse sensation than the feeling in her arms or the many cuts, bruises, and breaks that littered her body from top to toe.

She had to get in contact with Harry Dean. He would pull the trigger in a second and end the vampire race, she was sure of it. She should have called Harry before, but the vampires would've traced his phone through GPS, but not Reece's. But, there was the risk that Harry was drunk.

All of her thoughts were with her sister. If she could get through to Harry, he'd have a chance to save her. There was a phone built into the great table. She'd only have the opportunity for a quick call and her sister was the only person she truly cared for. If the vampires got wind of her conversation, it would bring the entire population down on Bolton...It was an inevitability and that's why the Purity plant had the capability of pumping out the drug from its roof. She had to do it. She had no choice.

She kicked with her legs, alerting her to many injuries she didn't know she'd sustained. Her momentum brought with it movement and creaking from the light fitting above. It was that which had given, not her shoulder joints dislocating. She continued to build on momentum, swinging farther and farther. She lifted her legs so the bodies scattered across the table didn't slow her down.

The snap from above indicated her short-lived freedom. The pain that the short fall brought reminded her that she'd no chance of ever leaving this room alive. Hoping no one heard her fall or the cry that escaped her lips with the impact, she slowly pushed herself off the table, sticking to the blood that was drying on the marble.

She popped herself off the table, and slowly, pins and needles prickled her arms. Her nerves were still working. She limped, hunched over from the pain of broken ribs, to where Charles lay, spread-eagled with his head hanging off the side of table, rigor mortis freezing his silent scream and destined to bring nightmares to the coroners. He had not died a dignified death. The vampires had played a game, seeing how much flesh they could cut from his body without killing him. He had a lot of worthless blubber to lose, and the vampires were well practised. It had taken an age for him to die in such a disgusting way.

Charles' body covered the console housing the phone. She heaved his corpse to one side and tapped away at the keyboard. Soon, Harry's phone was ringing.

REECE PREPARED HIMSELF before mixing Purity with Bolton Bitter and human DNA. There had to be something linking them together. On a microscopic level, he let the two liquids mix. He expected an exotherm, a release of heat, but there was none. In fact, there was nothing.

He bit his lip and waited. The taste of blood brought him out of his trance. "No. No, this can't be right. This is meant to be the answer."

"I told you," said Elizabeth.

"Fuck you!" he snapped at his hostage and turned back to his experiment. He knew Purity wouldn't react with human DNA, but he was convinced that adding the Bolton Bitter would cause...something. "Think, Reece, think."

"We need to end this," she said. "We need to go back to the plant and set off the pumps and end the massacre. People are dying."

"And I said, 'Fuck you!'" he roared, before leaving his microscope and thrashing her across the face again, knocking her unconscious.

He returned to his microscope, without a care for his victim or the people dying in the streets. He looked at the stable mix. There was one thing missing. "Vampire DNA!"

He jumped up from his stool, reenergised, and grabbed a fresh bottle of vampire blood from a fridge and dispensed a tiny amount of vampire blood onto the slide.

Reece watched the miracle of chemistry play out on the microscope slide in front of him. Purity attacked the vampire blood and destroyed it. But, the blood regenerated by grabbing on to that of the human. This dramatically slowed the entire process until all molecular activity ground to a standstill. So what did Bolton Bitter have to do with it? Reece grabbed the slide and started warming up his analytical instrumentation. This could be the greatest-ever scientific discovery, one that would never be published, for it was his and his alone.

"HARRY!" CAROLINE CRIED when the phone was answered.

"Caroline?" came the gruff reply.

She was thankful he'd dispensed with the usual awkwardness he saved for the council. "Harry, the Coalition has been destroyed."

"I thought as much. Why did you ever employ Rempstone in the first place? How could he ever put together a—"

"Harry, listen. I hired Rempstone *because* he was incompetent and cared more for statistics and budgets than he did halting the onslaught of the vampire nation. He was the reason I got away with what I'm about to tell you." Rempstone's head lay not a yard from where she stood. "Harry, where are you?"

"Manchester. I'm winning this bat—"

"Thank God," she cried. "Harry, you need to get to Bolton, right now, with as many men and firepower you can gather." She reeled off the coordinates to him, before looking up, scared of an intruder.

"Why?" he asked desperately.

"Harry, Haemo is a bluff. The Bolton plant is a button press away from firing a drug into the atmosphere that will wipe out the vampire race."

Silence came from the other end of the phone.

"Harry, my sister Elizabeth is the chief scientist. You must get there, unleash the drug, and get her to safety."

"Are you bullshitting me?"

"Harry, I beg you. We can end this today, but the vampires are going to come down on you. They can trace this call. Hurry, Harry. Kill the bastards. Kill the fucking bastards!" she screamed.

BORG LISTENED to the phone call and, for once, was impressed with the human's strength and cunning. She'd been through an ordeal that would've destroyed the most hardened warrior, but she was a rock. He knew she'd been hiding something but never thought it could've been anything quite so catastrophic and total like Purity. She'd given no useful information to Chambers that they could glean anything from, and he hadn't realised how important the secret information was. If he hadn't attacked the Coalition, they would all be dead by now.

"Viralli. Get word to every vampire within a hundred miles of Bolton."

REECE WAS AMAZED by the results printing out in front of him. He believed his hypotheses to be accurate, and, more importantly, the answer he'd sought since first witnessing Sid Tillsley dispatch a vampire with a punch.

During his experiment, the vampire DNA had been completely destroyed, but as Purity attacked it, it tried to consume the building blocks from the human DNA that it needed to repair itself. That reaction allowed the chemicals, the alpha acids of the hops in the beer, to bind to the human DNA helix. It should be impossible, but Purity was remarkable. Bolton Bitter acted as a fuel source with its high levels of carbohydrates and iron being used by the vampire blood while it devoured the human blood.

Reece was convinced that any beer would've been suitable. The beer's building blocks being inserted into the human DNA had stopped the DNA double helix collapsing, preventing a genetic breakdown like an accelerated cancer that would consume the victim in seconds. This was how Purity destroyed the vampire.

Purity attacked and destroyed the weakest part of the vampire's DNA and pulled out the equivalent building block in the human's. What it had essentially done is construct a mirror image, a human key to the vampire's lock. And, who had been blessed with this gift?

Four drunks from Middlesbrough.

FREDDY BUGGLESWAITE gave Sid a filthy look. He'd just described a man's death and Sid found it quite hilarious. "'All's well that ends well?' You sent a man to his death and it's 'All's well that ends well?'"

"He got a drenchin' in a vat of beer, though, reet?" asked Sid.

"Oh that he did."

Sid burst into hysterics again.

"Oh aye, it's funny for you, but the screams that came from the tank when the big lad fell in scared the shit out of the twats from the Manchester boozer."

"Fannies," said Brian with a snort.

"And when we couldn't find the body in the vat, they called the police."

"We legged it in the Montego Estate." Brian laughed. "You were pissed as a fart. It was a little bit hairy on the motorway, like. Remember?"

"Nope, but I can remember the Montego Estate." Sid sighed.

"What did the cops do?" asked Arthur.

"All shit came down on us. An eyewitness saw the fella fall into the beer. They tried testing it, but they found nowt. Bizarre it was. Because they couldn't find anything, they ended up investigating the arse off me, health and safety-wise." Freddy poured himself another beer. "They hammered me for everything, they did. Cost me thousands to put right. They even shut us down for a month."

"Didn't know you got shut down, like?" said Brian.

"Aye, well Ackroyd always kept a good stock of the Bolton with you lads being regulars. He had enough to keep him going," said Freddy, looking shifty.

"Still, a bit harsh shutting you down, man," said Arthur.

Freddy laughed. "Well, that's what I thought—until the health and safety bastards started poking into our water supply and found next door's waste stream leaking into our fresh water supply. They found levels of some unknown chemical, but then, it all went quiet, and we didn't hear another word. So, we started brewing again."

"What did you do with all that beer that the fella disappeared in?" asked Brian suspiciously.

Freddy looked awkward and Brian cottoned on, advancing on the brewmaster. "What did you do with that beer, Freddy?"

The brewmaster quickly went about pouring the lads fresh beers to distract them. It worked on Sid and Arthur.

"What did you do with it?" asked Brian threateningly, and Freddy succumbed.

"I sold it to Ackroyd."

"You sold Ackroyd beer, which he sold to us, which had the remains of a dead vampire and fooking unknown chemicals floating in it?"

"I...erm...I—"

"Bastard!" said Brian through gritted teeth.

Freddy ducked and covered. "But I can expl—"

"Not you! Fooking Ackroyd."

Freddy stood up. "You're not angry with me?"

"We're angry with you for selling the brewery, but fooking Ackroyd..."

Brian cracked his knuckles.

"He shouldn't have sold you contaminated beer."

"It ain't that," said Brian. "He charged us full fooking price."

IT WOULD TAKE YEARS of research to optimise the dose Reece would need to recreate Sid's power, but there was no time. If he was to be a hero, the moment was now, and he was willing to die trying. This was what he wanted. This was what was owed him. He went about gathering everything he needed.

He'd already altered his DNA to take on some of the attributes of Sid and Rathbone, and hopefully the potion he was about to concoct would align itself to him the same way it had done for the Middlesbrough lads. He took a huge beaker and added the rest of the Purity he'd taken from the plant. He opened a keg of Bolton that he'd kept for analysis and poured it on top of the Purity, rapidly mixing it. Out of the fridge, he took every sample of vampire blood he could carry, opened them all, and set them by the beaker.

Once he added the vampire's blood, it would be attacked immediately by the Purity. He needed to consume as much of the mixture as he could, as fast as he could. This was it. Live or die. Death or glory.

He poured in the blood and the mixture bubbled, heating from the chemical reaction. Without pausing, he lifted the massive beaker and poured the concoction down his throat. It grew hotter with every gulp and burned his mouth, his face, and his chest. The pain was unbearable, but he had to drink it. He had to make sure it worked. Suddenly, he dropped the beaker with a crash, the noise bringing Elizabeth back to consciousness.

"What have you done?" she screamed, once she'd regained her senses.

His stomach burned like the centre of a star. He felt it pass through him like a river of molten lava. It spewed from his mouth and from his anus, but it also entered his bloodstream and coursed through his veins. His blood literally boiled, the liquid ripping his body apart.

"What have you done?" she screamed, again.

He couldn't hear her. The liquid forced itself out of every orifice and brought with it the agony of heat and extreme pressure. His heart felt like it was going to explode pumping his blood, carrying the destructive mixture around his body and into his brain. Slowly, and with no lapse in the suffering, Reece began to lose consciousness. Lying on his back, he didn't try to stay awake. He just wanted it to be over. He didn't deserve it, but all he wanted to do was die.

"JEFFREY!" CRIED CAROLINE when her husband stumbled through into the Great Hall. He was unscathed, but she knew what was going to happen. It was a trap. She broke down in front of her husband, who rushed to her aid. She'd never done that before.

He held her close and tears that couldn't be held back fell from her bloodied cheeks. She snuggled into his bony chest, and he squeezed her with his sinewy arms. He took in their surroundings, looking through the jam jar glasses she'd always hated so much. Until the vampires had announced the end of the Agreement, he'd no idea they existed. He'd no idea why he'd been kidnapped, and he'd no idea why his wife was a bloody mess in a room full of butchered corpses. He was simply terrified.

Caroline knew what was coming to her husband. The vampires would now know all about Purity. Harry had to win one battle and unleash the virus. The human race still had a chance, and she hoped the drunk she'd called was sober enough to save the day.

The human race had a chance, but she didn't, and neither did Jeffrey. Slowly, she got to her feet, and Jeffrey helped her up. She took off his glasses and looked into her husband's eyes. He was a kind, caring soul, who would break down if he knew the things his wife had done. He wouldn't understand the necessity of ordering the death of thousands of people. He was soft, gentle. He helped her forget about the day because of how different he was. He couldn't wash a spider down the sink.

He took her in his arms once more, and she savoured the moment. This was something she would keep with her for the brief remainder of her life: his scent, the softness of the jumpers she'd always detested, his tender embrace. She did love him, in her own way.

She leaned back against the table and her hand reached back under the body of Charles, finding the handle of the knife used to cut the flesh from his bones. She didn't hesitate. She pulled the knife out and drove it into her husband's back. Her arm was tired, bruised and battered, but she didn't stop driving it into his bony, loving, caring body. Compared to what Borg would do, this was mercy. He screamed, but only for a second. She had found his heart, causing him to collapse with her falling on top of him.

There she lay, panting for breath between the sobs. She did this brutal act of love out of compassion. It was an act of kindness. Borg wouldn't be so kind to her. She would pay for what she'd done.

"Time to go." Viralli stood at the door. He'd watched the entire display.

She got to her feet and followed.

38

Manchester may be fighting back, but we've been hit harder. There isn't a man alive within ten miles of the Houses of Parliament. The army's evacuated everyone. Whatever's going down there is big. I heard the vampires have kidnapped the Prime Minister himself. For all the propaganda Parliament is spouting, they've not come up with a plan at all. Only thing they've done is lose the city. What's a country without a capital?
        —The pub bore's mate. The Coopers' Tavern, London

A GASPED BREATH brought back life with a surge of adrenaline unlike anything he'd ever experienced. Reece lay motionless and savoured the feeling of raw power. His heart raced like it had just before the pain had consumed him. He closed his eyes and tried to regulate his heartbeat with deep breathing and meditation, but there was no let-up in the intensity.

"How do you feel?"

Elizabeth, he thought. She'd stayed. He hadn't bound her that tightly. It must have been her scientific mind, curious about the results of his experiment, not unlike something seen in the laboratory of Dr Jekyll. He weighed up her question.

"Fantastic."

"What did you do?"

He sat up. Her wide-eyed look said she was unnerved by his physical appearance. "I discovered a way to unlock the power of Purity."

Her eyes fervently scanned his frame. "Did you...did you take all of it?"

He nodded with a wry grin.

"That was a huge dose. What else did you take?"

"Vampire blood."

"I...I don't know what's happened to you."

He got to his feet. He felt lighter, stronger. He caught a glimpse of his hand and fell back down again, grabbing at his wrist.

The muscles in his forearm looked like they'd been sculpted with a razorblade. They were so sharp, so powerful, and so beautiful. Veins pulsed through and around his arm. There was not a sign of any subcutaneous fat. He'd been lean before, but now, his skin was paper-thin and took on the colour of the flesh beneath.

"What the..."

The transformation of his arm was nothing compared to that of his hand. He squeezed his hand into a fist and heard the satisfying crack of dense bone. His joints were thicker, his knuckles appeared calloused, and his hand looked armoured. His nails were black and long. They looked sharp, dangerous, lethal.

"Looks like it worked." He laughed, deep and long, and sprung to his feet with the minimum of effort.

He looked down. His torso had exploded through his clothing. He'd grown in size, stature, and power. His legs had ripped through his black jeans too, and his quadriceps had the same attributes as the muscles in his arm. His knees looked stronger, just like his hands; the bone was dense, unbreakable.

He stretched his chest in a display of power to the scientist, who thought him a madman. It was time to check out the full package. He ran through to his living quarters, desperate to see what he looked like in the full-length mirror.

He grabbed at his face when he saw his reflection. His eyes were bloodshot to the point of being completely red. The veins stood out in his face like they did his limbs. He was hideous. A freak. A nightmare.

He was everything he'd ever wanted to be.

He laughed out loud and noticed in the mirror that even his teeth had changed. They looked razor sharp, every single one of them. He ran a finger across them and lacerated the tip of his finger with only the faintest touch. Blood dripped off his finger and onto the floor. Marvellous weapons had been bestowed upon him, for fortune favoured the bold. He went to suck on his finger, but there was no need, the wound had disappeared.

All his dreams had come true. It was time to test himself once more. When he'd faced Farouq, he'd come close to defeating the vampire in unarmed combat. Now, there would be no "close." He would obliterate the undead without mercy. He looked in the mirror once more. Only the grey hair remained of the old Reece Chambers. He would keep it so the vampires would know who it was breaking them.

"ARE YOU SURE MY PAPA IS GONNA BE THERE?" asked King.

Rathbone floored the limousine's accelerator. King was no longer able to drive. His hybrid disease of gaining weight made it impossible for him to get his belly past the steering wheel.

"If we have to stop for any more fooking burgers, then there's a chance the greedy bastards will drink all the beer and fook off. If that happens, then he'll be gone, along with the beer, and my fooking life!" shouted Rathbone into the rear-view mirror.

It was the longest sentence of Rathbone's speaking career, but he was in desperate need of Bolton, and the fat oaf sat behind him was getting on his tits.

"I can't wait to see my daddy," said King excitedly.

Rathbone rolled his eyes and pulled into the car park of Bolton Brewery. Garforth's Capri was parked up across two disabled parking spaces. Rathbone took immense satisfaction driving into the side of it.

"Watch it, man!" shouted King.

"Accident," said Rathbone, getting out of the car and heading for the brewery entrance.

"Hey, Peter, baby, a little help?" called King, who'd managed to swing his legs out of the car but struggled to get his arse out of the door.

"Fooking hell," said Rathbone, turning back. He was an evil little bastard, but King was his only true friend. King had rescued him, and he'd never forget what he'd done. Rathbone struggled to pull the monstrous half human, half vampire out of the car and used most of his vampire strength to finish the task.

King mopped his brow. "Thanks, man. I owe you one."

"I'm gonna get a beer."

"Me too. I'm dying for more of that shit. It's really grown on me."

Rathbone made his way into the brewery's reception where the secretary sat watching the clock. He recognised her from last time. Miserable bitch. "I'm here to get pissed," he stated.

"So?"

"Fancy some hot vampire lovin'?"

"Get fucked."

Rathbone rolled his eyes. "Lesbian. Come on, King, it's this w—" Rathbone should've known King wasn't there; he couldn't feel the gravitational pull. Rathbone pushed the front door of the brewery open to see King, only ten feet from where he'd left him. "What are you doing?"

"Walkin', man."

Five minutes later, both stood in front of the receptionist. "You seen my daddy?" asked King.

"All your friends are in there, somewhere," said the receptionist. "I'm off in five minutes—for good—so I ain't messing around with tour tickets. Go through."

"WHERE ARE YOU GOING? The turn to Bolton was miles back," asked a desperate Elizabeth from beside the speeding hunter.

"We're not going to Bolton, yet." Reece was crammed into his car. It would've looked comical if his demeanour wasn't terrifying.

"What? You heard the news! The attacks are getting worse! We have to release Purity! Hundreds of civilians were killed last night in Manchester, alone!"

"I know," he said excitedly. "That's why we're going there."

"Are you insane?"

He grinned. "A little."

"There's a curfew. They'll shoot us on sight. It's suicide."

"Not when they see what I can do."

"Leave your ego behind. We can end this now. This is not about you."

The grin faded. "Yes, it is."

They drew near the city centre. The glow from the many burning buildings grew brighter and the sound of gunfire and explosions grew louder. Bullets rattled into Reece's car. Elizabeth screamed when they ricocheted off the windshield.

"Don't worry, it's bulletproof."

It didn't calm her nerves as the rate of fire increased. There was a blockade up ahead, and several soldiers were sustaining fire on the speeding car. Reece flashed his lights, trying to convey a message to the soldiers. The gunfire ceased. They weren't stupid like he'd anticipated. He slowed down and pulled next to the blockade. All rifles pointed at him when he got out the car.

"Get your fucking hands up! GET YOUR FUCKING HANDS UP!" screamed the commanding officer.

Reece obliged. He was wearing shades so not to inspire fear with his eyes and a big coat to try and hide the nature of his size and shape. "I can help."

"Give me one reason I shouldn't shoot you in the face," shouted the soldier.

Reece looked past him to where ten vampires approached down the middle of the street, and smiled. "Let me show you."

FREDDY BUGGLESWAITE weighed up whether to do a runner. His three hostage takers were pissed out of their brains, but it was probably best to keep serving them until they passed out before legging it.

"You got any kids, Freddy?" asked Arthur.

Freddy didn't mind Arthur, even though he'd banged his niece. "Aye, a couple. They've left the nest now, though. Never phone... the ungrateful bastards."

"Beautiful, man. Beautiful," said Arthur, not really listening. "I've got a boy."

Freddy imagined that Arthur had a lot of children. "Oh, aye?"

"Never met him, man!" he banged his fist on the table.

"That's a terrible shame," said Freddy, trying not to get punched.

"I just want to hold him in my arms." Arthur took out a picture from his pocket and showed Freddy.

Freddy didn't say anything when he looked at the grainy picture of a fat Elvis impersonator. He concluded that even though Arthur was his favourite of the three, he was stark raving bonkers.

"He's out there! On his own, man," raved Arthur as the booze brought forth emotion.

"Daddy?"

All heads turned towards the entrance of the tasting room.

REECE LEAPT OVER THE BLOCKADE cracking the tarmac with the immense power of his legs and broke into a sprint. The vampires ahead of him looked amongst themselves, unsure of what was bearing down on them at superhuman pace. They spread out, a wise move, but it wouldn't help them. He was unstoppable. He jumped and their eyes followed him, but he wasn't leaping at them, he landed on a 4x4 parked on the side of the road. The big car absorbed the energy Reece generated and, with the creaking of suspension and the breaking of windows, he fired himself like a missile through the nearest vampire.

The feeling was close to orgasmic when he felt the vampire's body crumble under the weight of his driving shoulder. Landing on top of the broken body, the vampire didn't have a chance. Reece drove his fist down into his face, caving it into the pavement with an explosion of dust. He looked to the heavens, threw back his arms, and roared.

The vampires backed off and the soldiers cheered from afar.

Reece bathed in their worship.

"I have hunted you for twenty years and many of you have fallen to my sword," he said theatrically. "Now, I have the power to destroy you with my bare hands! I will win this war, single-handedly! And you all have the honour of being my first victims!"

A vampire jumped on his back and tried to wrap his arm around Reece's throat while biting into the back of his neck. Seeing the hunter momentarily incapacitated, the rest attacked as one.

Reece drove his foot into the chest of the first vampire that approached, firing her across the road and through the window of a shop front with a mighty crash. He swung around trying to rid himself of his attacker by loosening the vampire's grip. He reached over, grabbed the vampire by his long hair, and pulled him over his head and into another.

"Your attacks are futile! I'm going to do to you what you've seen as your birthright for thousands of years! All of you will fall!" He turned, landing a whipping hook at a foe who'd advanced during his gloating. He didn't feel the contact as the vampire's face turned to dust. It didn't stop his attack. He grabbed the nearest face in a vise-like grip, squeezing with all his strength, feeling the satisfying ooze of ocular juices while his thumb delved deeper into the vampire's brain. The screams ceased when he reached the frontal lobes.

Deciding to test his strength, he pulled his thumb back through the brain tissue until he took grip of the skull, and, like a hammer thrower, swung the vampire around in a circle. His laughter echoed around the built-up area and brought fear to every vampire in earshot. Suddenly, he fell backwards over the pavement's curb, his counterweight released. He hadn't meant to let go, and he hadn't. A gore-filled shard of skull remained in his hand. Again, he bellowed with laughter. The remaining vampires took their chances and pounced on him.

Knives entered his stomach and his chest. Nails ripped at his face and into his flesh. Teeth bit down hard all over his body, yet there was no pain. The wounds healed, and the power never waned.

"Now you will know what it's like to be bitten!"

He sunk his razor sharp teeth into the nearest piece of flesh and euphoria flooded over him. The vampire's blood filled him with a high he didn't think possible.

His muscles bulged and he couldn't believe he could grow in strength. The vampires sensed it too, and all jumped up and away, except the one who was being drained. Reece discarded the body when he'd drunk his fill.

"Those who live by the sword, die by the sword."

He grabbed the nearest lamppost and ripped it in half, electricity sparking. He threw the lamppost like a javelin, taking the head clean off the vampire resurfacing from the shop window she'd been kicked through.

The rest had seen enough. They turned and fled in all directions. The soldiers cheered. Reece would give them a trophy. He would give them some payback. He picked his target: a vampire climbing a high-rise building like a spider. He was quick, but it wouldn't save him. Reece leapt after him, and unlike the vampire who delicately grabbed nooks and crannies, Reece drove his fingers into the stonework and scrambled after him.

He soon reached him, and grabbing his foot, pulled him down, accelerating his fifty-foot fall to the concrete below. The vampire landed with a sickening thud and another cheer from the soldiers.

However, that wasn't the end. The hulking frame of the demented hunter whistled through the air and both feet came crashing down into the prone vampire's stomach, causing a geyser of blood to erupt from his mouth.

Reece dragged the body to the soldiers. "Have your fun. Make an example of him. You've earned it."

None of them dared speak. They looked on in silent disbelief as he got back into the car and sped off.

Elizabeth said nothing. Reece broke the silence.

"Now, we go to Bolton."

"We must destroy the vampires," she pressed.

"Oh, we will." He paused. "Or rather, I will."

She banged her fists on the dashboard. "I must start the Purity project."

"That won't be possible. I have to destroy it."

"But so many will die!" she begged.

"Don't worry. I'm going to save the world."

39

Vampires? Yeah, I've had the displeasure of meeting one. The most horriblist, greasiest, littlest bastard I've ever set eyes on turned up in the massage parlour where I...where my friend...Jill, yeah, Jill works. Whatever they say in the news, they're much worser in real life. Never seen a cock smaller, either.

—A hooker up North

ARTHUR TURNED ON HIS CHAIR and fell off it. "Son!" With the aid of the chair, he got up and couldn't help notice that his boy had some issues. "Son?" he questioned.

Rathbone walked in behind King and made his way towards the beer before taking a seat next to Sid. "Bolton." He demanded of Freddy, who looked disgustedly at the grease being applied to his table top, but complied.

"Eh'up, Rathbone," said Sid. "What you been up to?"

"Shaggin'," was the curt reply.

"Good lad."

Brian simply ignored the horrible, greasy, little bastard. Not because he held a grudge, but because he always ignored him.

Arthur drunkenly stumbled over to where his son was attempting to rush over to him. They embraced and tears streamed down the faces of both.

"I thought I'd lost you. I thought the vampires had turned you against me," said Arthur.

King squeezed tightly. "Oh, Daddy, I'm so hungry. Is there any food in this joint?"

Arthur was hoping for something a little more thoughtful, but his boy needed food, and it was his job to provide. "Hey, Freddy! Where's that box of crisps you said was floating around?"

The brewmaster mumbled some abuse and went off to look for more out-of-date crisps.

"Get my boy a beer first!"

Freddy muttered some more, poured a beer, and went to find food for the fat kid.

Father and son faced each other, supping beer on bar stools. The rest of the lads gave them space, letting them get on with the family bollocks before they'd pick up the drinking pace again. Seven thousand pints of Bolton Bitter wasn't going to drink itself.

"I've missed you, Daddy. I've missed you every day. I've been lonely with them bloodsuckers. I ain't like them." King's stomach rumbled.

"You don't need blood to live?" asked Arthur hopefully.

"No way. That's freaky shit if you ask me." King raised an eyebrow over his shades. "I think I need burgers to live. I feel it inside. Something says that if I don't gorge myself on cheeseburgers, like they do blood, I'll wither and die."

Arthur prodded one of King's folds. "I think you need to cut down on the burgers, son."

"Why?"

"You're a little overweight."

"That's 'cos I'm a hybrid, Daddy."

"No, son, it's 'cos you eat a lot of burgers." Arthur changed the subject. "Have you killed anyone?"

"I'm a lover, not a fighter. I'm an entertainer. I can sing. I can sing better than anyone, and that's what I wanna do."

"Then that's what you'll do."

King smiled, but then, his smile faded. He squirmed awkwardly in his seat.

"What's up, son?" asked Arthur.

"Grandpappy said that you treated my momma like dirt."

Arthur was hoping the question wouldn't come up. He missed Lucia. He missed her every single day. He hadn't been the best partner in the world. He'd shouted at her when she cooked a bad meal; he'd made her wash his karate slacks after some deep-squat training; he'd stopped taking her out; he'd nailed Three-Tits Tracey too. He felt pretty guilty at the recollection. His son would be devastated if he knew the truth. Arthur felt a podgy hand on his knee.

"Daddy?"

Arthur had to bring up his child and teach him right from wrong—and shift some pounds from the chubby little bastard. Arthur bit the bullet, and, like every parent when confronted with a difficult question from their children, he lied out of his arse.

"That's fucking bullshit, man! I can't wait to roundhouse kick that no-good son of a bitch grandpappy of yours in the face!"

A tear trickled down King's face, and he pulled Arthur into a bone-crunching hug.

"Whoa there!" said Arthur. "Easy on the old man!"

"I'm so glad I found you, Daddy."

Arthur smiled. He didn't feel guilty. He did what was right. Plus, lying was a piece of piss when you had twelve pints inside you.

HARRY DEAN slammed his foot on the brakes at almost exactly the same place Reece Chambers had the day before. From a mile away, he'd seen the giant vents on top of the plant that dominated the Bolton skyline. However, it was the black Capri belonging to Brian Garforth that'd caused the emergency stop.

Time was of the essence, but if Sid was in the brewery along with Garforth, then the extra firepower would help. There would be an army of vampires on the way, and Sid would bring panic and death.

Harry whipped the car around in a 180 at the nearest junction and ignored the words of the residents and drivers as he mounted the pavement. He booted the accelerator, pulled into the brewery, and jumped out of the car before it'd come to a complete stop.

He rushed through the empty reception, calling the names of the lads from Middlesbrough. Finally, he heard voices and eventually found Sid and the gang—and the hybrid vampire—all sitting together, drunk as lords.

"Look, who it ish, ladssh!" said Sid pointing in the wrong direction. "It's him who saved The Miner's!"

"Hi, Sid. Long time, no see," said Harry, joining them.

"All in vain, though, mate. All in vain!" lamented Sid. "The Miner's ish doomed without the Bolton. The Bolton was itsh life force! Bolton made that pub grand!"

"No idea what you're talking about," said Harry.

A drunk Brian Garforth filled him in, "That horrible old bitch Sid was going to marry has bought this place out and is ssshutting it down. We're drinking it fooking—*hic*—dry."

"That sounds like a lot of fun, boys, but I'm afraid I'm gonna need your help," said Harry, looking at his watch.

"Not vampire sshit," groaned Sid.

"Vampire shit," confirmed Harry.

"I thought the army was involved," said Brian. "Sshurely tanks and rocket launchers are more useful than a pisshed-up Tillsley?"

"You'd think, but it's gonna be close-quarter fighting. We've got the Coalition and the Special Forces on the way, but it would be good to have Sid there, inspiring fear and doing what he does best: smacking vampires."

"Ain't gonna happen, lad. I'm drinking that tank of beer until it'sh all gone."

"How much is left?"

"Six thousand, nine hundred and forty-four pints," said Freddy, reading off the computer screen.

"And that's gonna take you more than a couple of hours?" asked Harry sarcastically.

Sid rubbed his chin. "Not sshure."

"Send one in this direction," said Harry to the brewmaster. "So, Sid, what happens when it's gone?"

"The end! The end of the Bolton, forever!" he said dramatically, making cutting motions with his hands.

"You come with me, and I promise you this brewery will stay open."

"Eh?" said all drinkers.

"You can't do that," said Freddy. "It's been bought. Money is going to change hands tomorrow."

"Then we fucking cancel it," spat Harry.

"You can't. It's a done deal," protested Freddy.

Harry pulled his gun. "If it's a done deal, then it won't matter if I shoot you in the face, will it?"

"I guess late bids are acceptable," said Freddy before mumbling under his breath, "Brewmaster: the most dangerous profession in the world."

"Sid, what do you say?" asked Harry.

"One more for the road?" ventured the drunk.

HARRY DIDN'T UNDERSTAND Sid's need to drive the fifty yards from the brewery car park to that of the Purity plant, but he didn't question it. They were about to undertake a dangerous skirmish fought in the hazardous setting of a chemical factory. He could pander to simple requests, but he did question Brian's driving. Brian was so drunk, he didn't notice the massive dent in the side of his car, obviously caused by the limo parked next to it.

Harry was a lot happier now he had extra backup, and what backup: A karate master, a man armed with vampire-killing (though disgusting) weaponry, a vampire, a vampire-human hybrid, and last, but certainly not least, the greatest vampire hunter in history: Sid Tillsley. Harry got out the car, surprised the gate to the brewery was open. He took a slug of vodka from his hip flask before Sid grabbed it off him and downed it. *No choice but to go teetotal, now,* Harry thought. *About time.*

"I need a pissh," called the vampire hunter.

Sid was best led, not pushed. In fact, this man had never been pushed anywhere. If the unstoppable force met the unmovable object, it would have been knocked out with a big right hook. If he needed a piss, it was best to let him piss, even if it was outside the plant and even if...*shit!*—ten cars full of vampires were pulling up behind them.

"Sid!" screamed Harry. "There're vampires behind you!"

Sid unzipped his fly and drunkenly took position in front of the wall. "S'all right, there's plenty of room for everyone to have a pissh."

"Sid, mon, hurry up! They've got guns and ssshit!" slurred Brian.

The vampires recognised the bald head of Sid Tillsley and stopped well short inside the main grounds. Sid inspired fear wherever he went, and the vamps found it especially uncomfortable that he'd pulled his pants all the way down to his ankles to urinate.

"Ahhh, fook," said the big man, turning around to see the danger. "I canna go if some bastard is looking at me."

Harry pulled out his handgun and tried to give Sid some covering fire.

Brian pulled out the freshly stocked Cumapult and looked down the sights. "Fook, it's too windy. They're outta range." He turned to Sid. "Come and have a pissh inside, mate, in a cubicle!" said Brian, dodging a bullet.

"Only fannies or people with little ones use the cubicle, Brian."

A bullet buried itself in the brickwork by Sid's ear.

"We're being sshhot at, mate! It has nothing to do with having a little one."

The vampires weren't advancing, not wanting to venture into range of Sid's massive fists. They were happy to put a bullet in his massive, white arse flashing at them. These vampires weren't soldiers, and most vampires weren't used to guns. Harry, however, was a crack shot, and the few vampires carrying firearms earned bullets that made them think twice before firing again.

"Aaaaaaaarrrrggghhhhhh!"

"You alright, Sid?" asked Brian.

"Aye, broke the sseal, mate."

"Now fooking hurry up!"

"Aaaaaaaarrrrggghhhhhh!"

"You alright, Sid?" said Harry, noting Sid's different tone.

"Nah, I've pissed down me jeans, mon."

"You dirty bastard!" scolded Brian. "Come on, get inside!"

Sid zipped up and followed Brian inside while Harry covered.

No security or guards inside the small reception made Harry uncomfortable. A surprise had to be waiting farther inside, and vampires piling up outside behind them was going to push them farther into the building. Rock and a hard place sprung to mind.

The reception looked the same as any other corporate building, basic but sleek.

King was going through the biscuits by the coffee machine while Arthur tried to get him to slow down his munching.

Rathbone looked through the desk drawers for things to steal.

Brian and Sid discussed going back to the brewery because they were bored.

"Sid, Brian, can you hold this door?" asked Harry.

"Eh?" said both of them.

It would be so much easier to send them out for a punch-up rather than get them to fight tactically. "I want you to stop anyone coming through that door."

"I getchya," said Brian. "Sure thing."

Sid shook his head. "If Roger Moore comes through, then I ain't gonna stop him. I fooking love Roger Moore."

"Roger Moore ain't coming, Sid," said Harry.

"Well, I won't know unless I open the door."

"OK, just don't let anyone in *except* Roger Moore, got it?"

Sid beamed before drunkenly stumbling backwards. He caught his feet again and gave a thumbs up.

"King, Arthur, Rathbone," said Harry. "We'll take the other door through to the plant. I don't know what's going to be on the other side, so Rathbone, you go in first."

"That's fooking right, send in the black man."

Harry screwed up his face. "You're not black."

"I'll go in with you, buddy," said King.

King was so big now that every breath brought the wobbling of excess fat. Biscuit crumbs spilled from his mouth and stuck in his chins.

Rathbone looked up at him, his voice wavered with emotion, "Let's do it...buddy." He struggled with the last word. He'd never said it before.

King smiled back and went to go through the door to the brewery, but Rathbone intervened. "No. Me first. I can absorb the bullets. You run in behind and smack people."

"Sure thing, baby," said King, who went to put his hands up in a karate guard but dropped them due to the effort it took.

"You can't go, son, it's too dangerous," said Arthur, walking in front of him, barring his path.

"Daddy, I'm a vampire hybrid. If there's danger, then I've got the tools to deal with it. Let me do this. If momma is looking down, she'll see her baby boy being brave. I want to make her proud."

Tears welled up in Arthur's eyes as King took position in front of the brewery door. Arthur whispered to Harry standing next to him, "First thing I'm gonna do when we got home is get the tub of lard on a treadmill."

There was an almighty crash at the door where Sid and Brian stood, followed by another that shook the entire wall of the reception.

Sid put his weight against the door before shouting, "Ish that Roger Moore?"

"NO!" came the retort.

"Then fook off!" he nodded back to Harry. "All under control, boss."

Harry nodded. If the vampires got through the door, it would be more trouble for them. "Are you ready, Peter?" he said to the bizarre vampire.

"Aye, let's get it over with, like. Ahhhhhh, fook." Rathbone screamed suddenly, hitting the deck with a hole in his cape. "Bastards shot me in the back!" he cried as more bullets burst through the door Sid was guarding.

"Ish that Roger Moore?" cried the big man.

"Errr...yes." came the muffled cry from behind the door.

"SID, NO!" screamed Harry.

"I've been wanting to meet you for fooking ages, mon," said Sid, swinging the door wide open to a group of thirty vampires.

"Sid, shut the door!" cried Harry.

Sid blinked bringing a moment of clarity.

"You lying twat! You ain't Roger Moore!"

REECE SPED TOWARDS BOLTON with Elizabeth in tow, his mind racing. He'd spent his years undercover, years hiding from them, from animals like Ivansey. If Reece had been blessed with these powers before, Ivansey would never have harmed the only person Reece had ever loved. If Reece's father could see him now, he'd be so proud, but he was dead, and there was nothing Reece could do about it. If he'd gained the power sooner...If he could spend five minutes in Hell with Ivansey...

"I'D RIP YOUR FACE OFF! I'D FUCKING RIP YOUR FACE OFF!" he screamed in between fits of laughter and tears. He bit into his knuckle so hard that blood splattered across Elizabeth's face.

She said nothing.

"I'd rip your face...I'd rip your face off, you...you...fuck," he muttered as tears streamed down his face and mucus poured from his nose and into his mouth.

ELIZABETH HAD NO IDEA HOW TO STOP THIS MAN. Purity couldn't cause psychosis, but by the sounds of his mutterings, this was something he'd harboured for a long while. He could snap at any minute and rip her to shreds, like he did the vampires back in Manchester. Once they got into the Purity plant, she had to think of a way of releasing the viral drug without him knowing. It wasn't going to be easy, and she wouldn't survive, no matter what.

REECE STOPPED CRYING LIKE IT NEVER HAPPENED. Having everything he'd ever wanted bestowed upon him was an emotional experience, and he took immense pleasure expressing it in the form of extreme violence. He had to stop Purity. Mankind needed *him*. He was the strongest, most dangerous vampire hunter in the world. He was their champion. They'd love him. They'd worship him. Tears spilled down his face.

SID CHARGED OUT OF THE RECEPTION and into the thirty vampires waiting outside. This caught them by surprise, which was bad for the vampires, because Sid was swinging for the fences. The vampire who impersonated Roger Moore had no chance. Sid threw three punches at the vampire who'd exploded after the first. Sid was really, really angry.

"Sid, get back here!" screamed Harry, but it was too late. Sid waded into more of the armed vampires. Harry charged in behind with his weapon drawn and Brian with his. Harry couldn't fire because he couldn't risk hitting Sid, and Brian couldn't fire the Cumapult because hitting Sid with a loaded rubber jonny would lead to far more catastrophic consequences than hitting him with a bullet.

These vampires, called in by Borg, were first on the scene, but they weren't soldiers like Viralli. Their natural instincts didn't allow them to use their weaponry effectively, and the panic caused by a raging Tillsley sealed their fates. They retreated to safer ground, not far away, but Sid didn't like moving.

"Where the fuck is backup?" called Harry into his mobile phone to Peterson while picking off vampires with his automatic.

"On its way, but the agents and soldiers are fighting vamps *en route*. It's a fucking mess!" cried the young agent.

"This is it, Peterson. Everything happens here. Hurry up!" Harry hung up and put a bullet in a vampire about to attack Sid from behind.

"Sid!" screamed Brian. "For fook's sake, get back in here and save the Bolton!"

The magic word brought Sid almost running back into the reception. The slam of the door brought a resounding silence from outside. None of the vamps were going to try that route again, and no vampire would pretend to be Roger Moore, ever, ever again.

"Rathbone, King, it's time to enter the plant," said Harry, as calmly as he could muster, offering a hand towards the door.

Rathbone had fully healed from the bullet in the back and stood by the door opposite the reception entrance. "Ready?" he said to King.

King nodded. "Let's roll, baby."

Rathbone kicked open the door to the sound and the pain of automatic fire. He hit the deck, courtesy of a firing squad that had been lined up ready for them. With Rathbone out of the way, the clips of the automatic weapons unloaded into the mass standing behind him. King took the brunt of the attack.

From the floor, Rathbone kicked the door shut.

King, whiter than his whiter-than-white jump suit, clutched at his belly. "Oh, momma."

40

The Prime Minister was quick to quash all rumours of a government cover-up today. This is part of the statement he made outside Number 10.

"If vampires walked the earth, don't you think we'd all know? The ridiculous Colin Fitzpatrick show and the influx of vampire films has offered a fantasy that people have bought into. In some ways, it's easier to believe in fantasy rather than believe that we have done this to ourselves with a drug we created. This, perhaps, is the greatest tragedy of all."

—*BBC Breakfast News*

BORG TRIED NOT TO APPEAR NERVOUS. The limousine was travelling over a hundred miles an hour on the motorway taking them from London to Manchester. Viralli sat in the back with him and his hostage, Caroline.

Borg had never spent so long with a human. Everything about her made him nauseous. She was unwashed, and every breath he took was filled with her vileness. Worse still, every breath could contain the drug Purity that would end his immortal life.

This human had concocted the plan while being in the midst of vampires sat on a council whose purpose was to protect their own species. None of them saw it coming. He bit his lip. He couldn't let her know he was frightened for his life. She just sat, looking out of the window, trying to look dignified. It made him sick. He couldn't help himself. He leant forward and punched her in the face, shattering her nose and sending her to sleep.

"I thought of doing the same thing," said Viralli.

Borg spat on her prone body. "I want to kill her so badly. If I only have a day left to live, I'll gladly spend it ending hers."

"We may need her, sir. We need to put an end to this disaster, and then, you can spend a day, a week, a lifetime, giving this bitch what she deserves."

"They never saw it. A vampire elder sat on that council…and he never saw it."

"Bwogi was weak. With the death of Vitrago and Ricard, I left to seek you out."

"Vitrago." Borg shook his head. "We'd never be in this situation if it wasn't for that idiot. He so desperately wanted to be a politician...He should have stayed doing what he was good at—not thinking, just killing."

"Yes, in hindsight, you're right."

"Hindsight? Any fool could see it. Now look at us. We're divided. Pitiful attacks from weak lamia taking place all over the country. We're nothing more than pests, and they have their rat poison ready."

"Purity will not come into fruition. They would have fired it by now if they could."

"We better reach Bolton, fast, and shut the place down. I'm starting to regret ripping Garendon's head off."

Viralli shook his head. "No, he had it coming. I'd prefer to die than watch a lamia like that live."

"I've always liked you, Viralli. If my beautiful Lucia had never blessed me with her presence, then the world would've been a very different place with you and I in charge."

Viralli nodded. "I don't doubt you, sir, but what of your grandson?"

"What of him?" said Borg, playing idly with the switch of the electric window.

"You know what I mean."

Borg sighed. "He's dead to me. There's no vampire in him. He's his father's son, Viralli. Do what you must."

"I will." Viralli barely suppressed a grin.

Borg closed his eyes. If Purity is thwarted, a new epoch will begin. There'll be no room for the bureaucrats anymore, only blood and violence. They were the two things he understood, and two things the human race understood too. It would be a good way of getting reacquainted.

"SON!" SCREAMED ARTHUR. "I've only just found you, I can't lose you!"

"I...I think I'm alright," said King, clutching his stomach, searching for the bullet holes.

"You've been hit," said Harry, feeling at the wounds. Miraculously, there was no blood. "I don't think the bullets reached your organs."

"Hey man," said King, "I've been wondering what my vampire skills were. I think I'm impervious to bullets."

Harry shook his head. "I think you're just really, really fat."

"That's because I'm a hybrid. It's a strange trait, you know," King pulled out a cheeseburger. He put it in his mouth and savoured the cheesy healing before screaming and grabbing at his jaw. "Frruckkinggghhh brrras..." He spat the bullet on the floor. "They fucked with my cheeseburger, man!"

"I'm sure you've got another one in there. Don't worry about it," said Harry.

"No one fucks with the burgers, man." Against all the odds, King was ready for action.

"Look, calm down," said Harry. "If you get shot in the face, then it might well be game over."

"No one, and I mean, NO ONE! FUCKS WITH THE BURGERS!"

King charged, albeit slowly, at the door. Force equals mass times acceleration. The door could easily cope with the acceleration, but the mass was where the money was. The door disintegrated in an explosion of splinters.

The guards were forced to cover their eyes but were quite safe from the hybrid who was twenty feet away, meaning he was still minutes away from getting his chubby hands on them. Ten rifles pointed at his heart, but he didn't care, he was hungry.

"DON'T SHOOT!" screamed Harry from behind King, who blocked the doorway.

"Give me one reason why not?" shouted back a guard.

"I'm here because of Caroline," yelled Harry. "I know about Purity. So do the vampires camping outside. We can help!"

"Then call off your...thing, and get through here."

King was still advancing on the guards but wheezing heavily. The anger had subsided. He was just trying to prove he could jump into action if he wanted to. His hands dropped to his knees, but he couldn't reach round his belly to grab them. "I'm done." He felt a rumbling in his stomach, and not from hunger. It didn't feel right making King worry about the location of the bullets.

Harry pushed himself past King and introduced himself to the chief security guard Captain Brook. He was ex-army, a tough-looking, stocky man. Harry gave him a rundown of his unorthodox team, who were all relaxing in the reception.

Brook had seen King on TV before, but in a fitter state. He'd heard of Sid Tillsley and his group of friends but never thought he'd meet them.

"So that's him." Brook said, following Harry's pointing finger through to reception. Distantly, both men heard Brian say: "I don't give a fook if you can hear an ice-cream truck, there're fifty fooking vampires out there!"

"Yeah," laughed Harry. "That's history's most prolific vampire killer."

"Until Purity is released," said Brook confidently.

Harry nodded. "How secure is this place?"

"The only entrance is through the reception, or so I thought until Reece Chambers infiltrated us through the sewer system and kidnapped our chief scientist. He was in and out before we had a chance to stop him."

Harry raised an eyebrow. "And what does that mean?"

"It would mean nothing if he hadn't destroyed our activation console and took away the only person with the code. We're rebuilding it, but we ain't ready."

Harry breathed a huge sigh of disappointment.

"But we're nearly ready. Possibly within the hour. We've just got to hold this place from the vamps outside."

"And then you've got to crack the code?"

Brook grimaced and nodded. "We're working on that independently and making good progress. Don't worry. We're safe here. They'd need a tank to get through the front doors. We can lock down in a minute, and we've blocked off the sewer entrance."

"Well the doors better be up to the task and there are more vamps on the way."

"How many?"

"Borg Hemsman is going to be here any minute with some major muscle and some real gunman, not like the jokers outside just taking a fag break from kicking the shit out of Manchester."

"You got any backup?" Brook asked hopefully.

"These boys will do a good job, but we have Coalition and army *en route*, and we're gonna need them." Harry took in his surroundings. "What do we have to defend?"

"If the outside defences hold up: nothing. If they get through, we have to defend a computer, nothing more. They won't be able to touch the pumping systems. Purity has already been charged to the holding tanks underground. It's all ready to go."

Harry reached in his pocket for his reserve hip flask. Maybe not the time to go completely teetotal. "A computer?"

"I'll take you to it."

Brook barked some orders for a couple of guards to stand by the front door, and Harry called the lads through. The vampires wouldn't build up the courage to attack for a while after witnessing the wrath of their most feared hunter.

The unlikely mix of individuals made their way to the central laboratory, followed by the remainder of the guards. The boys, who liked a drink, hung back with the fat hybrid who wasn't making great pace. It suited Harry, because he could talk to Brook without any interruptions.

"Why didn't you blow the system when you had the chance?" Harry noticed the look of frustration in Brook's eyes.

"I wanted to. God, I wanted to. Every one of us who works in this building eats, sleeps, and shits here. We've given our lives to wiping out the vampire race." Luckily, Rathbone and King weren't within earshot.

"Why?"

"Every one of us lost our lives, years ago. All of us were happy, until the vampire came into our lives and destroyed them. I lost my wife just after she gave birth to my daughter, and then, a vampire took my daughter from me, leaving me with this." He pulled up his sleeve to show a map of scars. "She was kind enough to ensure my entire body matches. Everybody who works here has a similar story to tell."

Harry didn't say anything. He had his own demons but none compared to the vile acts that he had been forced to commit on his fellow man.

"When Purity was ready, we raised the pumping system to the roof. Until then, the building would've looked like any other. The windows are fake; they only open to the inside shell, a giant concrete bunker. We had a few issues with our waste stream contaminating the local water supply, but we've got some high-powered friends who've been subjected to a life of pain brought on by those bastards."

"Caroline sent me with the order to release Purity."

"Yes." Brook rubbed the stubble of his chin. "Her sister wouldn't let us start Purity without it."

Harry's head snapped to look at Brook. "Sister?"

Brook laughed. "Caroline never tells us anything, either. She hardly speaks to us, and we've never even seen her. She hides her personal life well, doesn't she?"

Harry could only nod.

"Caroline and Elizabeth are the only ones who know the code, and then, Chambers kidnapped Elizabeth." He punched a wall.

"Why didn't Caroline give the order beforehand? Why wait?"

"Those two were put through far worse than any of us. They endured all the pain and suffering together as children. Some sick vampire made her and her sister watch the rape, torture, and finally the murder of her parents. Coalition thought they'd be too young to remember. Thought they were doing the kids a favour by 'allowing them' to live. That sort of thing sticks in a kid's mind, you know? The sisters' names got lost in the bureaucracy and they disappeared. You can forgive Caroline for wanting to be at her sister's side when they finally had their revenge."

"Jesus." Harry took his cap off and mopped his sweaty scalp. "How come no one knew? She sat on the council for years."

"She's one of thousands of children." Brook continued relaying the master plan. "Caroline had to ensure the Haemo system was initiated. We're tapping into the pumping systems. All the plants are connected. We'll be able to send Purity far and wide. We'll take out as many of the fuckers we can in a single hit. It's a shame that neither sister will see the final chapter." His voice wavered.

"Let's make their dying wishes come true," said Harry.

They entered the large laboratory where scientists hurried around, checking various machines and computers. All the reactors were empty, their contents ready to be sucked into vampire's lungs. The guards patrolling the labs looked jumpy. Brook pointed to the gangway above. "The console is at the end, there. They'll need to destroy that to stop the Purity, short-term. Long-term, they'll have to dismantle the whole plant."

"Why phone me? She knew the vampires would trace me. Why not contact you?"

"There're no communication devices in the building. None of us can be contacted. Putting together something this big and this secret in the UK, we could take no chances."

A scientist limped over to the group. He held onto a crutch and looked in a bad way. Harry put two and two together and concluded he was a victim of Chambers. "W-what's it looking like outside, Brook?" stammered the scientist.

"We have it under control," said Brook honestly. "Harry, this is Dr Rise. He and Elizabeth are the brilliant minds behind Purity."

"Pleased to meet you, Doctor." Harry offered his hand to a saviour of mankind.

Dr Rise nodded but didn't offer his hand. Instead, he pulled at his receding hair in an irritable manner. "Any sign of Elizabeth?"

"None," said Brook. "What's wrong?"

The doctor looked everywhere but at Brook. "We're struggling to break the code."

"Is the console working?"

He nodded.

"Then crack it," he said sternly.

"We need Elizabeth."

"Do your job, man!" said Brook aggressively before his radio buzzed. He picked it up. "Yep?"

"Elizabeth's back," said the voice through the radio.

"Thank God!" he said, shaking his head. "We need to fight off the vampires outside and—"

"But she's brought company," said the voice.

REECE PULLED INTO THE PURITY PLANT. Not a word had been spoken between him and Elizabeth for a while now. She was terrified, and it invigorated him. As long as she did what he said, she would stay alive.

The welcoming party put a smile to his face. A group of vampires waited outside the building while others scaled it, looking for openings. None of the vain bastards would consider the sewer system route he'd taken.

The smile disappeared when he saw what was in the car park.

A black Capri.

Garforth.

Some of the vampires advanced towards him. They'd recognised him, but he paid no heed to their taunts and threats and got out of the car. They circled him, but Reece had one target: the weasley bastard's pride and joy.

The vampires stopped advancing when he leapt twenty feet onto the bonnet of the black Capri. Reece felt the satisfying crumpling of metal and the hissing of steam from the engine. Destroying Garforth's car made this experience a thousand times more pleasurable.

Some of the vampires turned their attention to Elizabeth, sitting in Reece's custom-built car. She looked petrified of the animals stalking her. A face appeared at her window and she screamed.

A vampire pointed at her and then slid his finger across his neck before trying to punch the window through.

She ducked with the impact, but the window was solid. The vampire screamed with frustration and punched it again but disappeared in a flash of black.

Reece laughed as the vampire who dared attack his beloved car cartwheeled away with Garforth's passenger door embedded in the side of his head. His accuracy had always been good, but now, he had limitless power to match. He was happy he'd done enough damage to Garforth's car, but it would pale in comparison to the damage he'd do to Garforth when he finally got his hands on him.

He danced into the sea of vampires, struggling to control his excitement. Everywhere he turned, a vampire was ready to absorb his strength, crumbling under the weight of his fists. Soon, they fled. These were just waifs and strays. There was no power here. These were the sort he'd spent his life hunting. Until Tillsley came along, he'd never been able to hunt big game, but now, there was no one he couldn't destroy, and he wouldn't rest until he brought down the last.

He grabbed at the vampire who made the mistake fleeing last. He caught her easily by the scruff of the neck and threw her to the ground before grabbing her leg and dragging her round to speak to Elizabeth. A sensation filled his hand that he'd once associated with pain. He laughed when he looked down to see the vampire desperately gnawing at his hands, like a rat caught in a trap.

He let her go and stamped down hard on her ankle. She now used her mouth to scream rather than bite. He liked the change. Lifting his foot, he surveyed the damage. Her leg was nothing but gore and broken bones. He gave her a matching set by stamping on her other ankle. Her attempts at escaping would be comical now, if nothing else.

Once word spread of his power, he would have to stalk his prey. Not one of them would have the guts to stand up to him.

"Come with me," he said to Elizabeth, who got out of the car. "No need to be scared. Nothing can harm you, not when you're with me." Once he worked out how to shut Purity down for good, the only thing to harm her would be him. He'd make it painless. He didn't want to do it, but he was Purity now. He was mankind's saviour and nothing could get in the way of that.

She followed apprehensively, but he noticed the glimmer of a smile when she surveyed the violence he'd caused.

The vampire he'd left on the ground cried out, and Reece picked her up by the remains of her ankle and squeezed. All air in the vampire's lungs escaped with an explosion of pain.

Elizabeth covered her ears.

"Have you ever enjoyed a sound so terrible?" he asked before turning his attention to the vampire. "Why are you here?"

There was no pretence of bravado. Brutal pain brought with it brutal truth. "They're going to wipe us all out. They're gonna spray a...a virus into the air that..." She burst into tears.

Reece hadn't often seen a vampire cry. He looked forward to getting used to it. "And you are all there is to stop it?"

"No." She sobbed. "We were in Manchester. There're warriors coming. They'll destroy it. They'll destroy you."

"Really?" He lifted her up and held her at arm's length before kicking her in the face, dislocating her jaw so that it hung limp from her mouth. "You think they'll be able to take me?"

She didn't—couldn't—answer. She grabbed at her mangled face and despaired.

Reece had a fight coming, and he couldn't wait to take on the legions, single-handedly. He dropped her and headed to the main entrance. Killing her would've been easy, but he wanted to see her again. He wanted to see the look on her face when she saw her worst nightmare return. Just like he'd felt when he'd seen Ivansey again, outside The Miner's Arms at Ladies' Night. He wanted every one of the bastards to experience the same terror and helplessness.

41

This is the closest we've been to normality for over a week now. Many places in the UK have reported fewer violent outbreaks, especially in the South. However, riots and skirmishes continue to rage in the Northwest. The curfew is still in place in the South, where a significant army presence will remain, although many forces will be redeployed to the Northwest if the trend continues.

—London Today

SID WAS REALLY BORED, even though he was drunk. It was a combination that didn't compute. Everything was normally great when you were drunk. But, there'd been a lot of sitting around and not much boozing since he'd agreed to his latest mission. He'd even climbed a flight of stairs to a gangway where the stupid computer they had to defend sat. He'd been good and hardly complained. In fact, he'd only needed one rest, whereas Arthur's son had needed six. It dawned on Sid that he was sobering up.

This mission was shit.

But, it was possibly the most important mission he'd been on since becoming a vampire hunter. He was here to save Bolton Brewery. He wasn't really sure what he had to do. He knew it would involve smacking people, eventually, and hoped it would happen sooner rather than later since there were only six and a half thousand pints left in the brewery, along with a tied-up Freddy Buggleswaite. Sid worried that some other bastard would drink them while he was gone.

All his buddies looked bored too, including Arthur's lad, who seemed like a decent kid. He didn't like walking, which was a good thing for Sid, but even he had to admit the lad was a bit on the porky side. Brian looked like he needed a beer too. "'Ere, Brian, what's going on?"

"Dunno, mate. They're all being hush-hush about it," said the swordsman trying to listen in to Harry, Brook, and the scientist's conversation farther down the gangway.

"Canna you use your feminine intuition?" asked Sid hopefully.

Brian raised his eyes. "I ain't a fooking lass!"

"Haven't you got summat similar?"

"Fook off!"

Sid was aware that women were angrier at certain times of the month and assumed Brian was going through a *them homomo-sexuals'* equivalent.

"I need a beer," moaned the big man. "Shall we sack this shit off?"

"Sounds like a plan," said Brian. "Arthur?"

"Yeah, baby. Me and the boy need a beer."

King groaned and rubbed his belly. "I'm not sure if a beer is a good idea, but I still fancy one."

"Harry, mate," Sid called "We're bored of this shit. We're off."

Harry looked over from where he was in discussions with Dr Rise and Captain Brook. "You ain't going anywhere, lads."

Brian laughed. "And who's gonna stop us?"

"Reece Chambers is here."

"Never heard of him," said Brian truthfully.

"The vampire hunter? The guy Sid used to work with?"

"Oh, *Rich*! Well, if that prick is coming, then we're definitely off."

Brook interjected. "We're on lockdown. There's no getting in, and there's no getting out."

"Says who?" asked the swordsman aggressively.

"My automatic rifle." Brook brandished the weapon, but it didn't bother the man from Middlesbrough.

"Your automatic weapon and whose army, pal?"

"Her Majesties'. Army and Special Forces are on their way." His radio buzzed, and he picked it up. "Yep...OK...Right." Brook put the radio back on his belt. "The army is here, but so are the vampires. There's a war raging in Bolton. We've planned for this, don't worry."

"Ah, fook," said Sid. "Things always kick off when I need a piss."

ELIZABETH DIDN'T HAVE A PLAN. She was inside the plant with Reece, and he'd destroy the Purity project the first chance he got. She was running out of time. She was waiting for the *right* time but began to think there wasn't one. The closer she took him to the main console he'd disabled earlier, the closer he came to ruining everything. The guards hadn't attacked him on entry because he was with her, and he'd just massacred the vampires outside. The guards gazed upon him with the awe and respect he desperately craved.

It would be a futile attempt to order the guards to try and kill him. They'd last seconds. Any moment he could charge off and lay waste to years of research. The vampires arrived as they'd entered the building swiftly followed by the army, guns blazing. The vampires were a useful distraction. Reece was desperate to get back outside and lay into them.

If she could get to the main lab, hopefully, the guards would be able to distract him long enough for her to enter the code and initiate the system. She'd be dead soon after, but she didn't care. She'd already given her life to the cause, and without Caroline, she had nothing to live for. Her sister had found a man, but she hadn't. She had science. She hoped the system would be fully operational, because she wouldn't have much time.

Once they'd passed through the reception and into the main building, the grinding of gears indicated lockdown. Now, they were trapped inside along with the biggest threat to the programme. If only Caroline were here, she'd know what to do. She'd come so close to pulling off the perfect plan. Why had she phoned this maniac?

BORG'S LIMOUSINE was the last car to pull outside the plant. Terror was an unusual feeling for the old vampire to experience and was something he'd only felt when considering the safety of his daughter. The giant vents atop the building heightened his fear. He'd always wanted to go out fighting. He hoped he'd have his wish.

The journey had been an eventful one. The armed forces had done their best to stop the influx of vampires, but there was no way they could stop all who'd travelled in haste to Bolton. A convoy of armoured vehicles had protected Borg. Viralli, skilled in all forms of warfare, had trained other vampires where he'd deemed fit. A vampire didn't need to fire an automatic weapon, but armoured personal carriers were a useful piece of kit.

Hundreds of lamia now fought outside the plant, skirmishing with the armed forces and the Coalition agents who outnumbered the lamia by just three to one. It was only a matter of time before the vampires overran the plant, but the Purity vents could announce their doom at any moment.

Vampire blood flooded the gutters all around the vast building. Casualties were low and the gunfire incessant. There were plenty of soldiers to feed on, but breaking their lines was proving impossible. The humans packed a lot of firepower. All of it meant nothing when the vampire's nemesis was only nanometres wide.

Borg got out of the limousine, and Viralli followed, holding the unconscious Caroline under his arm. A guard surrounded them as they approached the front gates of the plant's grounds.

A massive hand came down on Borg's shoulder. "Wait."

"We must get to the plant," snarled Borg.

Viralli scanned the perimeter slowly. "There're no humans on the grounds."

"That's because we're holding them outside."

"Something isn't right," he said. "PULL BACK!"

No one could hear him over the battle, but even that was drowned out when the car park erupted in a fireball that would be seen for miles around. Borg was thrown back with his guard, but Viralli stood strong against the force of the explosion. Borg despaired. Getting in was not going to be easy, even with the largest congregation of vampires ever assembled.

PETERSON KNEW THE ODDS were stacked against the Coalition forces. But, the plan was now a simple one—stop the vampires entering the building at any cost. This was more like a scene out of Hollywood than a military operation as they unloaded magazine upon magazine into the masses.

He hadn't spoken to Harry since the plant lockdown. Harry just got word to him about the rigged car park when the line went dead. No signals went in and nothing came out of the fortress. The explosives in the car park had taken out a great number of vampires, and they were thinking twice before assaulting the building again.

The vamps were probing their defences. They had to destroy the Coalition and the army before attacking the building, because the heavy machine guns the army commanded were merciless. Bigger toys were on the way, but Peterson hoped Harry would start up Purity soon. The vampires were getting desperate and taking more chances.

KING RUBBED HIS STOMACH. Getting shot was painful, hungry work. He wasn't quite sure if the bullets were wreaking havoc on his innards or if it was because he was all out of cheeseburgers. Being out of cheeseburgers caused him the most distress. His belly made a rumbling sound, loud enough to interrupt the heated discussion of the group he was following. Even the guards twenty yards away turned to look at him.

"Sorry. Having a little tummy troubles," he said, holding up an apologetic hand.

"You OK, son?" asked his wonderful, caring papa.

"I'm fine," lied King, a trooper, scanning the lab for crisps. He hoped this would all be over soon. By the sounds of the explosions outside, the fight was vicious. King wasn't surprised. His grandpappy was a nasty piece of work and would burn this place to the ground without a moment's thought for those inside. King didn't have a clue why his grandpappy was attacking this place, but the thought was quickly discarded when King remembered that he'd hidden spare burgers in all of his grandpappy's limos, in case of emergency.

The thought of burgers evaporated when the bastard who'd captured his best buddy Petey stormed into the lab. He looked angry and big. Really big.

"YOU!" roared the giant, pointing at Rathbone with a talon, his eyes burning with hatred.

"Whooooa, he's pissed," said King and called to Rathbone, "Man, you shouldn't have taken that dump on his face."

Rathbone hid behind his cape.

VIRALLI HELPED UP BORG, who shooed him away and brushed down his suit, his pride hurting more than the shrapnel wounds. "It will take a lot more than that to bring me down," snarled the old vampire.

"I know, sir,"

"In my prime, I'd have torn down the walls with my bare hands," he cried.

Viralli said nothing. He felt sorry for his master who was a shadow of his former self and had given up his power, both political and physical, for a daughter who'd stabbed him in the back by cavorting with a human. No wonder he wanted to tear the world apart. Viralli was more than happy to help.

Borg pointed at the unconscious, singed figure of Caroline under Viralli's arm. "Did it survive the blast?"

"Yes, sir."

"Good. It may be needed for bargaining, later."

"The army and the Coalition are advancing, sir. We lost a lot of brothers and sisters in the explosion. We have to break into the building."

Vampires scaled the building like ants over a nest. The army had split into two sections; some fired on the masses outside the grounds while the others picked off the scurrying vampires on the building. Lamia prised open windows and tested the integrity of the roof. Many would suddenly fall from the building with a flash of red, cut down by a streak of bullets. Some attacked the vents at the top of the plant, and they received the majority of the fire. The vents were vast, and the alloy was impervious to the vampire's strength.

"We've made it through the windows!" cried Borg.

Viralli's radio buzzed and he picked it up. "Drejen?"

"The whole building is a cocoon!" the vampire reported.

"What're you talking about?"

"I've made it through the window. The exterior is just a shell surrounding a concrete bunker. I have no idea how thick it is, but there's no way we're getting through."

"Check for weaknesses and get back to me." Viralli put the radio back on his belt. There would only be one weakness, the same one as in every castle. "Sir, we've got to go through the front door. It's the only way in."

"FUCK!" screamed Borg before grabbing Caroline by the throat. "I might as well enjoy this before I die."

Viralli grabbed his arm. "No. There's still hope. We can knock on the front door. The army has brought a toy that will ensure we'll be heard."

RATHBONE SLOWLY EDGED his way to the back of the group. He wasn't one to shy away from a fight, especially if the other guy was a lot smaller and weaker than him, but his odds of a flawless victory were not good. He'd never beaten Rich in a scrap and had only got one over him by taking a dump on him when he was unconscious. Rich wasn't the forgiving type, and he looked pretty angry right now.

This wouldn't have been too bad if the vampire hunter hadn't grown three feet in width and height. Rathbone could feel the platform give as Rich climbed the metal stairs and onto the walkway followed by Elizabeth. The lads, Harry, and a few armed guards stood in his way, but he wasn't bothered about them.

"You!" Spittle flew from Reece's mouth and hung off his pointed teeth.

"Me?" asked Sid, still drunk.

"Not you..." Reece paused. "Well, you too. All of you, in fact. I hate every single fucking one of you."

"What's happened to you?" asked Harry.

The look of hatred gradually dispersed. Reece raised his arms aloft and the lads from the 'boro all raised their eyebrows. They'd seen enough of his bollocks to last a lifetime.

"Look at me. Look at the power coursing through my body. I am what you've been looking for. I am mankind's answer. I am Purity in human form. I can punish the vampire. I can stalk the earth and bring every last one down."

"The drug will do that for us," said Harry.

"I won't allow it."

Harry's hand slowly went for his piece. "Are you insane?"

"No. I am a—"

"Wanker," suggested a sniggering Brian Garfoth.

"Garforth!" snarled Reece. "You will die today. I am fed up with you putting your foot in your mouth at every opportunity and that will, literally, be the cause of your death."

Brian rolled his eyes.

"What's Purity?" asked Rathbone.

Reece was happy to answer. "Purity is what this facility was going to pump into the air. Purity is the reason you're a vampire."

"Not the cape?" said Rathbone with a flourish.

Reece ignored it. "You all must have drunk some beer that had been contaminated with Purity. I'm not sure how you managed to consume vampire blood at the same time, though."

"Sid smacked one into a vat of beer," said Brian, "and that bastard Buggleswaite sold Kev the lot."

Reece nodded. The puzzle was complete. The beer would've diluted the Purity, and these four alcoholics would have drunk it quickly enough to prevent it from consuming all the vampire DNA. His own acute reaction was due to the ridiculously large dose. It was wondrous. "Purity gave all four of you your powers and was also the reason that your blob was born, Arthur."

"Hey, man, don't talk to my son like that!"

"You got any burgers on ya, buddy?" asked King, holding his guts.

"I was born to kill vampires," said Reece. "I will hunt them down until the end of my days. I cannot allow Purity to take the pleasure away from me."

"Set it loose. Fook 'em, is what I say," said Rathbone. "All the ones I met were a bunch of twats."

"You're a vampire, Rathbone," said Brian.

Rathbone scratched his head. "Shit."

THE ARMY HAD BROUGHT the key to the front door. Viralli laughed and sprinted towards the tank whose purpose was to hold back the vampire hordes. His peers had often scoffed at his interest in the human military, but a 120-millimetre cannon was going to save the entire species. The Challenger 2 was an awesome beast.

Three hundred yards would usually take a handful of seconds to cover, but the terrain was harsh. The tank could blow him to pieces, but before he got to that, he had automatic weapons, grenades, and the melee of vampires testing the human soldiers to negotiate. The vampires ascending the plant would help draw the army's attention, and hopefully the tank wouldn't see him...

He felt his eardrum knit back together as he flew through the air. The tank not seeing him was pure optimism. He rolled after hitting the ground, all wounds healed. He was strong. He was surrounded by soldiers as startled by the explosion as he was. There was no time to kill them.

He charged again on his path towards the tank. It would only have time to fire one more shell, and then it was curtains for everyone inside. He leapt onto a nearby police car to avoid the mess below where vampires gorged on human flesh. Apparently, Haemo didn't quell the feeding instincts if a lamia's body was injured. Bloodlust had taken his brothers and sisters. They were sitting ducks. He felt a pang of guilt leaving them, using the cars like stepping stones to close the distance to the tank.

This time, he was prepared and watched the shell pass him. He was too fast for the explosion to catch him. Bullets entered his body, but they were of no concern. Within moments, he stood on top of his prize. The tank's hatch was ripped asunder...and death came to its occupants.

42

Violence has come to a head in Bolton where a battle is taking place on a scale not seen on British soil since the Battle of Culloden in 1746. The affected are massing in the town, and the army has intercepted. At this time, we do not know why they have been drawn to Bolton, but the death toll is rising.

With many hours to go until dawn, we can only pray that our troops can put an end to this week of terror that will go down as one of our nation's darkest.
—Prime Minister, emergency broadcast

"YOU'RE NOT GOING TO RELEASE PURITY." Reece's words carried weight. His imposing figure was terrifying standing on the gangway. The only thing between him and the Purity console was four lads from Middlesbrough, a fat hybrid vampire, and what little firepower the Purity guards and Harry Dean brandished.

"Yeah," backed up Rathbone, not enjoying the sound of this Purity lark.

Brook, however, had not come this far to simply give up, even though his bladder demanded relief at the sight of Chambers. "We can end the war now. Our men are dying."

"I can end the war. I can hunt them all," said Reece grandly. "You won't take that from me."

Reece advanced down the narrow gangway with Elizabeth behind him. Brook and another guard pushed in front of Sid and, eventually, around King. They raised their rifles. "Don't take another step."

Reece didn't hesitate.

"Drop him!" screamed Brook.

Two bullets to the brain slowed him, but it also enraged him. "You are going to regret th—"

The building shook to the foundations, stopping Reece and the guards in their tracks.

"What was that?" snapped Brook into his radio.

"The vampires have stolen a tank!" reported a fuzzy voice. "They're firing on the front doors!"

"Will it stand?"

"I...I...don't know," came the reply.

"Fuck!" shouted Brook.

"Can we go down the boozer, yet?" asked Brian.

"Chambers!" cried Harry, "Get out there and stop that tank! They'll bring the whole place down!" Another rattling explosion, this one greater than the last, made Harry's point.

"I will, but first, I must destroy the console."

Another shell hit the front doors and dust fell from the ceiling. The designers of the building hadn't planned on vampires commandeering armour and attacking the building with sustained fire.

"Well get on with it then," said Brian. "I'm dying for a pint!"

"No!" cried Harry. "We can wipe out every vampire on the planet! Don't be a fool!"

"Try and stop me." Reece advanced down the gangway.

Elizabeth followed close behind, ready to sneak past if the chance presented itself. It would take no more than a few seconds to input the code.

Harry pulled out his revolver. "Stay where you are." His gun didn't waver.

"How can you stop—" the bullet to the brain took away Reece's train of thought, but only for a moment, "—me?"

"Sid, do something," called Harry, not taking his eyes off the advancing psychopath.

"Go for a pint?"

"Stop Chambers!"

"Ahhhh, fook!" Sid looked at a clock on the wall. "It's only nine o'clock, and mourning the Bolton doesn't end till kicking out time. That's the time for scrapping." Sid sighed and trudged in front of the group to oppose Chambers who now towered over him. "You had a haircut or summat?"

"Tillsley, you are the reason for all of this," Reece said, looking down and admiring his own body. "Without you, I'd never have discovered the secret to limitless power. I have a lot to thank you for."

"A few pints will be sufficient, Rich."

"IT'S *REECE*! IT'S FUCKING *REECE*!" the screams echoed round the cavernous lab.

Sid gave him a strange look. "You changed your name too? What's all that about?"

"It's always been Reece, you fucking idiot!"

"Don't call Sid an idiot!" shouted Brian from behind the big man.

"Keep quiet, weasel," spat Reece.

"You've turned into an even bigger wanker since we saved you from that bumming, Rich," said Sid.

"IT'S FUCKING REECE!"

"Eh?"

Reece shook his head. "Fuck this. I've wasted too much time on you losers. I don't need you any longer."

"Hit him, Sid!" cried Brian.

Sid rolled up his sleeves. "I haven't smacked anyone properly for ages, but, Rich, you need to learn some manners." Sid cracked his knuckles.

Reece, too, rolled up his sleeves and cracked his knuckles, imitating his opponent, although everyone in the lab could hear the sound Reece's knuckles made. "I am so much more than you, now."

Sid shrugged his big shoulders. "I couldn't give a shit, lad."

The atmosphere was tense as the two squared off. The guards and Harry hoped the famous Sid Tillsley would knock out the huge hunter.

Elizabeth looked for a chance to get to the console.

The boys from the 'boro wanted Sid to get this over with quickly so they could get down the boozer, and King was really starting to feel unwell.

Sid closed the gap.

Rich didn't have a guard up.

"Cocky twat," mumbled Sid. Last time Sid had smacked him, he'd gone out like a light. Saying that, he'd definitely put a bit of size on since then. "You been doing some press-ups before bed or summat?"

Sid was in range. He'd never been one to shy away from punching first, so he threw the right. He couldn't miss. And he didn't.

BORG WATCHED WITH PRIDE as Viralli rained fire on the front of the Purity complex. The vampire was the son he never had. The humans concentrated on destroying the tank, and the vampires swept through them before the army was forced to split its forces and try its best to stave off the vampire masses while dealing with the tank.

Even though gunfire and the screams of the dying filled the air, it was as if silence descended when the tank ceased its tremendous barrage.

Viralli appeared from the top of the tank, waving his hands. He was out of shells.

Borg could see the front of the building had been destroyed, exposing the metal doors of the bunker. Their integrity was seriously compromised.

"MY LAMIA! BREACH THE DOORS!"

Vampires left the battle with the humans and poured through the front gates of the plant's grounds.

CAROLINE WAS AWAKE and had watched helplessly as shell after shell powered into the front doors of the plant. She was in desperate need of medical assistance, but she cared not for her pain or her own life. She was praying she'd see a haze appear from the vents, indicating the death of the vampire, but she had a sickening feeling that it wasn't coming and that the vampires would break into the factory any minute.

REECE FELT EACH KNUCKLE of Sid's hand drive into his jaw. His teeth were clamped together tight, but he felt them part, and a few left his mouth, slicing through his lips as they went. His jawbone slipped across his face, and the resulting force whipped his head round at a speed that could only bring sleep. The lights flickered. He felt his body crash into the railings of the gangway, and then, the gangway itself. The lights grew dimmer. This wasn't right.

Must fight. Can't lose. Not now.

"THEY CAN'T GET THROUGH!" The message from one of the vampires sunk Borg's heart while bringing hope to Caroline.

Borg tore at his hair. "We need another tank. We're so close. We can't lose. Not now!"

"WELL, THAT TOLD THAT TWAT!" said Brian.

Elizabeth couldn't believe the monster dropped when Sid punched him. But, this was not a time to admire Sid's work, it was time to finish hers. "Quick! I must punch in the code."

"What is it?" asked Brook, rushing to the console.

"Hold on a sec," said Rathbone. "Are you saying that thing will kill all vampires?"

The atmosphere turned frosty.

"Well, get on with it so we can get back to the boozer!" shouted Brian.

"You can't kill all vampires, man," said Arthur. "Say if it kills my son?"

"It might help him lose a little weight, like," said Sid, licking his lips at the prospect of a pint.

Elizabeth was having none of it. She set off for the console, but soon the wind was driven from her lungs when she crashed onto the gangway. Reece had swept her legs away with his huge arm.

He got to his feet slowly and wiggled his jaw a couple of times before putting up his guard. A grin spread across the demented vampire hunter's face. The teeth that had been knocked out had regenerated, and light glinted off their razor edge. "Is that all you got?"

Sid nodded his approval. "You must've been taking a few of them protein shakes those *them homomo-sexual* bodybuilders drink."

VIRALLI REACHED BORG'S side at the same time the vampires assaulted the doors, clawing, biting, desperate to get to whomever and whatever was inside.

"How can we get in?" asked Borg, pacing.

Viralli knew the vampire's rudimentary attempts would be futile. "We need more shells."

NO MORE GAMES. Reece wouldn't risk taking another punch from Sid, whose powers were more impressive than he'd originally thought. Reece would be quick, efficient, and ruthless.

"Should have stayed down, lad. I've got another one of these waiting for ya." Sid wafted the right in the air as a warning. It was a mistake.

Reece threw a left hook, and there was no way Sid could dodge or parry it with his face exposed. Reece's fist crashed into its target with the compassion of a wrecking ball.

"WE NEED TO CHASE DOWN MORE TANKS. Can we get more shells?"

"They'll not send more tanks in, not now they know we can use them," said Viralli. The army were peppering the vampires at the plant's doors with slugs and explosives. "They're sitting ducks, sir."

"DO SOMETHING!"

SID HAD NEVER been knocked down with a punch to the face before, but not even a bull elephant could stand its ground when exposed to a force so destructive. Sid bounced off the railing and his legs wobbled. He bounced off the other railing before swaying, eyes rolling, and then, just when he was about to fall, he shook the cobwebs and managed to stand. It wasn't even a standing eight.

A cheer went up from the boys from the 'boro, but Reece didn't care. He was in control now and dominated his opponent further by driving his foot into Sid's private area. *That* took the big man down. That took him down like a sack of shit.

The cheers stopped. It was like having a goal disallowed.

THE LIFE OF EVERY vampire on the planet was in Viralli's hands. "We need to find a vehicle, something big, something fast. We ram the doors. It's the only thing we can do."

"Then do it!" screamed Borg.

"I'm on—" He stopped, cocking an ear. "What's that noise?"

Borg got down on a knee and put his ear to the ground. "Something's coming. Something big."

"WHAT DO YOU THINK OF YOUR CHAMPION, NOW?" said Reece, gesturing to the floor where Sid was rolled up in a ball, eyes tight shut, massaging his parts.

For once, Brian was speechless, and Reece never felt so happy. He strode towards the group from Middlesbrough and both Rathbone and Garforth stepped back. He walked past them without saying a word. He could've killed them, but he wanted to savour the moment later. For now, he was revelling in the glory of defeating their totem. He leapt over King and Arthur in an impressive display of power.

Guards stood in front of the console, but the weapons pointing at him didn't bother him. He wanted everyone to see his victory. Slowing down, he again resorted to theatrics. He had transcended into a living god.

"I will end their existence. Have no fear. I will—"

He was interrupted by something landing on his shoulder. It was wet, slimy, and the unpleasant feeling could only be attributed to one thing. Turning his head slowly, he could smell the condom filled with Brian's toxic fluid before he saw it. It sat on his shoulder and Reece did his best not to heave. He brushed it off. "You'll regret that," he said coolly before turning back to the guards.

"Fook!" Brian holstered his Cumapult. "Rathbone, do something."

"Why? If they set that bastard thing off, it will kill me."

"Yeah, but..." Brian didn't have a good argument, so he turned to King instead. "You got any magic powers, mon?"

"I don't feel well," said the fat kid, rubbing his belly.

"It's up to you, Rathbone. Don't you want to really piss him off?"

"Well, yeah. He's a reet wanker."

"Didn't he get piss on your cape?"

Rathbone's face transformed into that of dark, greasy thunder. "He's fooking in for it now."

For the first time ever, no one tried to stop Rathbone talking complete and utter bollocks. No one even tried to stop him pulling down his pants.

"What are you doing, man?" asked Arthur.

"Don't, man!" said King, looking green. "I feel bad enough as it is. I nearly barfed last time."

"A vampire's gotta do...what a vampire's gotta do."

Everyone turned away in disgust.

REECE FELT SOMETHING HIT HIM in the back of the head. Like the condom, he could smell the offending missile before he could see it. He reached into his hair and felt the warm, sticky substance that had desecrated him once before. Rage built up inside him that could not be contained. He hated that horrible, greasy, little bastard more than anything.

"I think I got his attention," said Rathbone.

"FOOKING RUN!" screamed Brian.

43

We've been here as long as you have. Man and vampire have lived, side by side, for thousands of years. This is not every vampire's war. Most stay hidden, lamenting our species' fall from grace. This war didn't have to happen.

We've guided you. We've guided you through every major scientific breakthrough in the last thousand years. Some of us love you like our children. The end of the vampire will lead to the stagnation of the human race. No one can win this war.

—Unknown

THE MINISTRY OF TRANSPORT TEST, the MOT, is issued for a reason. Cars are dangerous things, and it's important that they're roadworthy, since people's lives are on the line when half a tonne of speeding metal careers down the road. The Smithson Estate had never considered MOTs a necessity. An MOT was something poncy for posh Southerners, like vitamins.

If a car hasn't got an MOT certificate, there's a good chance that it's dangerous to drive. A coach without an MOT, however, has got "death trap" written all over it. After all, it's ten times heavier and carries fifty people at a time.

Kevin Ackroyd regretted borrowing the bus from an acquaintance of one of the lads who drinks down The Miner's. The hire only cost him a crate of knocked off gin, but it now dawned on him that it might cost him a lot more, possibly his life.

Karma? Aye, Kev was owed it big-time for performing such a selfless act. He'd seen the Bolton Brewery on the news. Vampire shit was going down. His customers were in trouble, and he was going to help them. If his customers died, there'd be no one to buy beer off him later. This was going to be a dangerous mission and he'd needed backup, so the bus was teeming with some of the oldest and most dangerous individuals in all of Middlesbrough: the Allotmenteers.

Kev had once lived amongst them until one cold winter's night, when they'd banged the shit out of his elaborate collection of sex dolls. The bastards owed him, but they answered to no man. Kev, however, knew they'd succumb to the power of his dolls with wigs and merkins of real human hair.

"YOU'RE NOT GONNA STEAL MY BEETROOT, YOU TWATCOCK!"

Shit, thought Kev. He had to get to Bolton, fast. He'd sacrificed his harem to entice these degenerates of society onto the bus. The subsequent noises that'd haunted the bus were unholy and shouldn't have been made on the earth realm. They'd had their way with the plastic fantastic and, one-by-one, had drifted into a post-coital snooze. The shout from the beetroot maniac meant they were waking up.

His dolls were ruined, but they'd already been sullied after their last encounter, and he'd never been able to rekindle the spark. He'd sacrificed what was most precious to him. Once he put the price of the beer up, he'd buy some more dolls. Kev put his foot down.

It probably wasn't a good idea.

RATHBONE RAN FOR HIS LIFE. Shit flinging always pissed people off, and today's antics had been no exception. It was damned handy being a vampire when legging it. It meant you could jump for miles. Unfortunately, Rich seemed to be pretty good at it too. They were causing a hell of a racket, leaping over tables, smashing fancy equipment, running up walls, and all the guards were trying to shoot Rich too. Who could blame them? He was an utter twat.

"I'LL RIP YOU LIMB FROM LIMB!" screamed Reece, bearing down on Rathbone's dirty bum.

AN INTERMITTENT, HIGH-PITCHED SQUEALING caught Viralli and Borg's attention as the rumbling sound got ever closer. "What is that noise?" asked Borg.

"It sounds like a fan belt slipping."

"What's that?" asked Borg.

"It's...it's caused by that." Viralli pointed at the clapped-out bus hurtling towards the plant. He could see the fat bus driver with a ginger moustache making desperate signals for people to get out of the way while hammering the horn. The vampires and the army scattered from its destructive path.

"What's going on?" demanded Borg.

Viralli shook his head. "I've no idea."

BRIAN TRIED TO REVIVE SID, who was sporting the most pained expression that a man could make. Sid was in the foetal position, a hand on each nut, eyes tight shut, with a grimace that said, "I've been kicked in the bollocks."

"Sid, you reet?"

"Oooohh...Brian...that...was a...big hit," he said between deep breaths.

"Can you stand?"

"Fook that."

"Come on, mate. We can get to the brewery while Rathbone is taking a shoeing."

Sid mustered the strength of Geoff Capes to get to his feet and seek out more beer.

Brook was by Elizabeth's side. She was wheezing, still not able to talk after the fall caused by Chambers. "Give me the code." He said desperately.

She gulped in breath but wasn't able to utter any words. She clutched at her ribs.

"We've gotta be quick," said Brook. He grabbed her and lifted her up to the railings. She let out a silent scream. There was no breath to exhale, and the agony was paralysing. He dragged her along towards the console. Nothing else mattered.

KEV WAS REGRETTING HIS DECISION to rescue his best customers. He was heading for a building about to drive into a big-arsed set of steel doors. The brakes had failed a long time ago, and again, more regrets. This time for racing the twat in the Audi off the last roundabout.

Kev's best course of action was to take his chances with the Allotmenteers at the back of the bus. Kev jumped out of the seat, and ran to the back as the metal doors drew ever closer.

REECE STOOD ON RATHBONE'S THROAT. This was going to be the most satisfying experience since becoming immortal. Unfortunately for Reece, yet fortunately for Rathbone, a 30,000 pound bus travelling at sixty m.p.h. tore through the front gates of the building allowing vampires to pile into the plant.

THROUGH THE DUST, a portly figure appeared from the bus, wobbling a little after the impact. Kev saw the lads on the walkway. "You're all clear kid! Now let's blow this thing and go home!"

"What are you talking about, ya fat twat?" shouted Brian from the gangway above.

"Dunno. Just wanted to say it. I've come to rescue you."

"Fucking RESCUE!" screamed Brook. "You've let an army of vampires through the front door!"

The gap between the twisted wreckage of the bus and the metal door was small, creating a bottleneck, but still, vampires piled in behind Kev.

He held up his hands. "Ahh, shit. Sorry, lads!"

A CHEER WENT UP, music to Borg's ears, and his vampires infiltrated the plant.

"RIP IT DOWN! RIP IT ALL DOWN!"

REECE HAD JUMPED out of the way when the bus had punched a hole in the fortress. It'd helped him regain his senses and concentrate on the most important thing: destroying Purity. He threw a fist at the odd vampire running past; it was rude not to. The vampires had no idea what they were doing. They were simply trashing everything in sight with no method to their madness. They were lucky that Purity was charged to the holding tanks because they showed no respect for the chemicals contained within.

The grinding and screeching of metal on metal assaulted the ears as the coach began to move. The vampires were trying to make space. If more got through, he'd be swamped by sheer weight of numbers. He had to destroy the console before they made it through. With a single bound, he made it to the gangway where Elizabeth had limped to the console.

THE BUS HAD TAKEN Peterson completely by surprise. The troops fighting next to the plant had received no warning, and luckily, there weren't too many casualties. The bus had torn through the warring parties and ploughed into the doors. The tank had done enough damage to allow the bus to power through, and now, the vampires were desperately trying to move it aside to give them enough room to attack *en masse*. The bus was providing cover for the vampires, and it was impossible to track round and attack from the rear where a legion of vamps still stood strong. It had taken all the army's strength just to hold the line.

His radio buzzed. Now the doors were breached, radio contact was possible. "Peterson, pick up!"

"Harry!"

"They're getting in. We need more time." His desperation scared Peterson.

"We can't stop them. The bus is covering them, and we can't get through from the other side. How long before Purity is released?"

"We're nearly ready, but a few vamps can stop us, and we need gunmen."

Peterson scanned the catastrophe again before nodding. "Open the doors!"

"Are you crazy?"

"The vamps are being covered by the bus. Open the doors and we can get in the other side."

Harry laughed drily. "Shit or bust."

"GET TO THE BUS!" screamed Peterson to his men.

ELIZABETH COULDN'T pull any air into her lungs. She'd never been the most active of people, and the fall had taken its toll. But, she was determined. The console wasn't far away.

With Brook's aid, she passed the Northern men who paid her no attention and was quickly surrounded by the remainder of Brook's personal guard.

"Quick, Elizabeth," said the fearless Brook, "let's end this."

The groaning of metal on metal grew louder. She turned to see what was making her ears want to bleed. Chambers was back on the gangway, but the doors, too, distracted him. The hydraulics were powerful and, even with the restriction of the bus, they opened up. One side immediately filled with the vampire and the other with the green uniforms of the army. It was utter chaos, but she just needed a moment.

THE ONLY SOUND more plentiful than the screams of the dying was the sound of ricocheting bullets. Kev had joined the lads on the gangway once he realised he'd royally fucked up by letting all the vampires in.

"Nice one, dickhead," said Brian.

Kev rubbed his hands. "These fookers will all be thirsty after this scrap. I can take 'em back in the bus for a piss-up."

Brian shook his head, disgusted. "It's all you think about!"

Kev shrugged. "There's a recession on, you know."

"I think the bus has taken its last journey to the scrapyard in the sky," said Arthur.

"It'll be reet," said Kev confidently.

"We'll be lucky to get out of this alive, thanks to you," said Brian.

Kev waved a hand. "We'll be reet."

"Really? Look behind you."

Chambers was advancing towards them. Sid was up but still rubbing his nuts from the last encounter. King looked like he was going to be sick, and Arthur was too busy worrying about his son to throw any karate shapes. The lab was manic and packed to breaking point with guards, soldiers, and vampires. Brook or Harry shot down vampires making it to the gangway, or had their lives ended instantly by Chambers.

"He's gonna tear us all a new one," said Brian.

Kev laughed, for he had an ace up his sleeve. "Don't worry. I've brought backup."

"Where?"

"You'll see," said Kev looking at his watch. "They'll be awake soon."

"Who?" pressed Brian.

The groans coming from the bus were the definition of eerie. Hearing them, Rathbone legged it from under the bus, where he'd been hiding from Reece. He clambered up the walls and the vessels to get to the gangway with the lads. The guards defending Elizabeth didn't shoot him down because they recognised the cape.

"Ackroyd! You haven't brought them fookers from up your allotment, have ya?" said Rathbone, terrified.

"YOU'RE NOT GONNA STEAL MY BEETROOT, YOU TWATCOCK!"

"Ah, fook!"

The Allotmenteers made their way slowly from the bus. No one knew who was fighting whom anymore. The Allotmenteers weren't on any side; they just got in the way—a lot. They were devastatingly annoying, like pensioners chatting in the middle of a supermarket aisle. They'd all just sowed their wild oats so none of them were in the mood for scrapping.

"Sid!" shouted Harry. "We have to protect Elizabeth!"

"Who?"

"The woman at the console." Harry pointed behind Sid.

Sid shook his head. "I'm going for a beer, mon. I've had enough of this bollocks."

"There's no way out of here unless we stop the vampires. The sooner you do, the sooner you can have a beer."

"Alreet," said the big man reluctantly before turning back to protect Elizabeth, who was tapping away at the keypad. Dr Rise stood at her shoulder, shouting advice into her ear. The guards protecting them were desperate, shooting anything that moved.

"Howay, love," called Sid, "get that code typed in and we'll be on our way."

"If she types in that code, I might die," said Rathbone.

"Aye, but you might not, and Harry said we can go to the boozer when we're done.

Rathbone rubbed his hands together. "Champion."

ELIZABETH TRIED to drown out the sound of the anarchy around her. She only had seconds and could feel Reece thundering down the gangway. None of the men behind her would be able to stop the monster's charge. Her life was over, but she had to ensure she gave birth to her life's work. She tapped in the code and waited for access to Purity's release mechanism to be granted.

REECE RAN THROUGH THE BULLETS. He focused on his target and nothing else. Elizabeth was close and he had but moments. The lads from Middlesbrough and Harry Dean were cast aside as he drove his weight through them. King's mass was questionable and Reece jumped onto the handrail and over the fat blob.

Elizabeth turned to look at him, checking how much time she had left. She was waiting for the system to grant her clearance.

Tillsley moved in front of her. There was no time to give him the send-off Reece had hoped. Left with one option, Reece drew a handgun. He absorbed the bullets of the guards while unleashing a barrage of his own.

BLOOD SPLATTERED across the console screen, and Elizabeth suddenly felt alone and exposed. Dr Rise collapsed on her shoulder and then onto the console, before sliding to the floor, leaving a trail of red across the keypad. Brook and the guards were no longer in her peripheral vision. Tiredness swept over her and a strange pain in her back was growing. She felt at her stomach and despaired when her hand came away slick with blood. She stumbled backwards. The code was entered. She was only a button press away. She'd been so close...So close...

SID'S KNACKERS WERE SORE AS FOOK. He'd only walked twenty yards but doubled over again when he reached the black lass at the computer thing. A shot to the stones had a horrible way of going right up inside the stomach. He stood up again, slowly, tentatively.

Strange...He was sure everyone wasn't dead a second ago.

He scratched his head and rubbed his balls at the same time; it was the most intellectual thing he'd ever done. "What the fook?"

"Get away from that console!" someone screamed behind him.

"Eh?" said Sid, not into techno-speak.

"From the computer!" clarified Reece.

"Release Purity," said a pained cry from the floor.

"Eh?" Sid looked down at the black lass. Poor lass had been shot!

"The computer...release Purity." Her eyes closed as life left her.

Looking at the computer screen, Sid realised he had a choice to make...

And he didn't have a clue what it was or why he had to make it.

VIRALLI MADE IT THROUGH TO THE LAB, followed by Borg, carrying the unconscious body of Caroline. Like all the vampires, they were being held up by the elderly who were making the war between the vampire and the army extremely confusing.

"STOP HIM!" Viralli screamed when he saw what was materialising on the gangway above. The vampires, fighting without clear purpose on the lab floor, listened to their leader and tried to mount the gangway, but Peterson and his troops kept them at bay with the expert use of assault rifles.

REECE POINTED HIS GUN directly at Sid, but he was out of bullets. He was only a stone's throw away, but it was too far. Reece could see the question on the screen that confronted Sid: "Release Purity?" The choice was a simple one: "Yes" or "No."

VIRALLI TOOK AIM. He was an impeccable shot, and Tillsley's fat, gross head was a target the most inept of marksman could hit with their eyes closed. He pulled the trigger, but his gun flew from his grasp. He snarled and looked up at a grinning Harry Dean who stood, looking down his rifle at him.

"STOP! STOP FIGHTING!" screamed Borg, and his vampires obeyed. The bullets ceased, and both sides regrouped with the Allotmenteers generally getting in the way of things and complaining about the price of ham.

SID'S FINGER WAS ABOVE THE "YES" BUTTON, but he didn't know what he was pressing. He was only doing what he was told. He just wanted a beer.

"Don't press YES, Sid," said Rich, a twat.

"Fucking press YES, Sid," urged Harry, provider of beer.

"You can't do it!" screamed an old vampire fella with greying hair.

"What the fook happens if I press it," asked the big man, his words echoing in the lab.

"If you press that, then every one of us will be wiped out!" said the old vampire. "Every single one of us will be wiped from the face of the planet."

"Do it!" shouted Harry. "You can end it, right here."

"No, Sid," said Rich. "I can hunt them. I can bring them down."

"Things have changed, Rich," said Sid.

"It's fucking Reece!"

"Things have changed," lectured the big man, finger still poised above the console. "All those months ago, when I was out dogging, I was approached and I didn't react well. I struck out. I attacked without asking questions. I ain't the same Sid Tillsley that I was then."

"Sid," said Harry, "they've ruined the lives of millions of people, and they'll continue to ruin the lives of millions more."

"We give more than we take!" shouted a vampire. "You wouldn't be where you are without us! You'd still be drawing on the walls of caves without our influence! There would be no art, no music; we are the culture that binds you together!"

"Aye, *you lot* are all into that shit," agreed the big man.

"Not just that," shouted another. "Look at this technology. This is all built on *our* knowledge and our foundations. You won't be able to march into the future, pushing the boundaries of science and discovering new miracles. You can't move forward without us!"

"We built this without you!"

Sid recognised the woman who, to him, looked a little like Trevor McDonald. She was shouting at the vampire bloke with grey hair. She'd taken a pasting, poor lass. "The power to destroy you was cultivated by human hands, and human hands alone!"

"You're beneath us," said the old vampire, before slapping her back down to the floor.

"Listen to him, Sid. 'Beneath us.' They'll enslave mankind," said Harry. "Press the button. Don't let it happen."

"They canna enslave mankind, mon. I know they've tried. Fook me, they've been all over the telly with their ice dancing shit, but they canna take over. They just want to live their lives in peace. They're no different to us...except they prefer bums."

"What are you talking about, Sid?" said Brian. "They're a bunch of bastards who've given you nowt but grief since you met them."

"Now, now, Brian, just because we're in a room full of people, don't think you have to pretend you're summat you're not. It's time someone stood up for you."

"What are you talking about?" asked Reece, still staring at Sid's finger.

"*Them homomo-sexuals* have just as much a right to do stuff and things as the rest of us. I was once scared of 'em, but I've seen the error of me ways. These fine people are right. They bring music that us red-blooded men would never dream of. Do you know the bloke out of Queen was a vampire?"

"Freddy Mercury wasn't a vampire," said Harry.

"Aye, he was. He was was one of *them homomo-sexuals*, and he's one of the greatest!"

A lot of confused faces stared up at Sid.

Brian tried to explain matters. "He thinks that he's gonna release a gas that will wipe out homosexuals."

"And I ain't gonna do it," said Sid with conviction.

"Sid," said Harry, "releasing Purity will wipe out the vampires."

"I know. Every fooking vampire I've met has been one of *them homomo-sexuals*, but that doesn't matter. I'm fooking liberal me. How dare you suggest I release a gas that will kill my best friend just because he bummed a vampire to death in the bogs? All of you fookers with guns should be ashamed of yourselves."

"Sid, you've got it all wrong!" screamed Harry. "Release the—"

"No! I won't hear anymore said about it! There's nowt wrong with *them homomo-sexuals*, and I ain't releasing this Purity bollocks! I CHOOSE NO!"

Sid Tillsley slammed his fist down on the button. Sid Tillsley chose life, and he was proud of it. Dan Shire's student had passed with flying colours. Sid Tillsley had beaten the Northern man's greatest adversary: homophobia.

With the exception of the groaning of the Alltomenteers, everyone was silent, listening intently for the grinding of machinery or the hissing of gas. The vampires held their breath, not quite believing how anyone could be quite so stupid.

"You twat," said Brian, shaking his head.

Suddenly, Reece darted past Sid and drove his foot through the console, disabling the system and putting an end to the machine.

"Purity won't bring justice," he announced. "Reece Chambers will. You're dead! All of you are fucking dead!" he screamed before jumping into the nearest group of vampires.

"Come on, lads," said Sid. "Let's go get a drink."

"You twat," repeated Brian.

"What's that, Brian?" said Sid, aghast. "I stood up for you. I just saved your life, mon!"

"You could've—ah never mind. Let's get a beer." Brian put an arm around the big fella.

"Sid, what have you done?" Harry's head was in his hands. "You could've ended it all. You could've destroyed the vampires forever."

"You homotoadic bastard!"

"It doesn't kill gays, for fuck's sake!" shouted Harry "It kills vampires! Just vampires!"

"Oh, reet." Sid scratched his head. "Fancy a pint?"

"A pint? A fucking p—" Harry stopped mid-sentence. "Yeah, I would, actually, but we're all going to die instead."

THE ARMY WERE LOSING THE BATTLE. More vampires joined the fray, and, apart from those getting caught up in the pensioners milling around, they were pushing the soldiers back through the plant. The soldiers had regrouped, but with the loss of Purity, their morale was shot. Reece destroyed vampires within his reach, but he was putting on too much of a show and not taking them out quick enough. For every one he killed, two would fill their place. He didn't care. He had all the time in the world now.

Up ahead, Viralli walked towards the lads along with Borg and some other old, powerful vampires. The gangway ran all the way to the end of the building where the boys could escape. The boys were going to have to fight their ways out. That was going to be tough since these vamps were armed to the teeth.

Borg grinned from ear to ear. "It looks like I owe you our lives, Sid Tillsley."

"Can you save the Bolton Brewery?" asked Sid hopefully.

Borg looked at Viralli for a clue, but Sid was there to help.

"The brewery next door makes me favourite beer. Can you get it back for us?"

Borg and Viralli both burst into laughter. "No. I can kill you, though."

"You son of a bitch!" screamed Arthur.

"And you. I've been waiting to kill you for so long. I can't believe I am going to get my chance."

"Leave...leave...him alone," said a wheezy voice.

"King!" Borg smiled. "And don't you look well? You are your father's son. Your mother—" The smile disappeared. "I can't believe I lost her for you."

"Fuck you, man!" screamed Arthur. "Lucia would've loved him. Just because he ain't an animal like you and a bit fat—"

"Hey!" objected King

"—You pushed him away. He's your grandson, man!"

"And that's why I'll be the one to end his life," announced Borg.

Arthur unleashed some blistering karate shapes. "Just try it."

The vampires and Viralli all unholstered and lifted weapons.

Borg smiled. His moment of triumph was here. "We will take this country. We will enslave your women."

"Yeah, yeah, yeah," said Brian, who'd heard it all before from Geordies.

Borg laughed loudly until he started to cough and then splutter. Suddenly, he spewed forth a torrent of blood, grabbing at his throat. The rest of the vampires on the gangway were repeating the performance.

"What's up with ya, ya daft twat?" asked Brian again.

Blood streamed from the vampire's eyes and ears.

"Ah, shit," said the big man as if he'd thrown a 26 at darts.

"What is it, Sid?" asked Brian.

"I've never been good with them computer things."

"Eh?"

"I've got a funny feeling I pressed the wrong button back there."

Brian laughed and shook his head. "Let's get the fook out of here and get a fooking beer in. Rathbone, hold your breath."

BORG WAS POWERLESS to do anything as his nemesis, Sid Tillsley, passed by. Lying on the gangway, Borg knew death was seconds away. He'd promised his followers the end of an era, but he never thought it would bring the extinction of his entire race. There was no time for remorse. There was nothing in Borg's future apart from a brutal demise.

PETERSON HAD MANAGED to make it into the plant in one piece, but most of his agents hadn't been so lucky. Once inside, he was greeted by a wondrous sight of vampires vomiting blood and haemorrhaging from their eyes, noses, and ears before exploding into dust as if being hit by a ray of light from the midday sun.

He picked out his radio before calling a subordinate outside the building. "The vampires—"

"They're all dying!" interrupted the excited soldier. "All of them! We've done it!"

Peterson's elation was quickly brought plummeting back down to earth. "We may have a bigger problem."

Reece ran from vampire to vampire, desperately trying to engage them in combat, but as soon as he approached, they exploded. He was manic. He batted a few old age pensioners away with the swing of his hand before he sunk to his knees and screamed to the heavens. The hellish bellow driven from lungs fuelled by frustration silenced the celebrating troops with a primeval fear, causing them to cower.

"Everybody out!" yelled Peterson.

44

They're dying. Everywhere. All over Bolton. All over Manchester. They're dying.
—Frontline soldier, Bolton Brewery

"DADDY, I AIN'T FEELING TOO GOOD."

The lads from the 'boro had snuck out the building without anyone noticing. There were no vampires outside, and the army were too busy celebrating and avoiding contact with the Allotmenteers to worry about them. Harry had entered the fray on the ground in order to find Caroline and tell her the tragic news of her sister's death. He said he'd meet the lads in the brewery later.

Arthur and Sid had helped King out of the plant and into the car park. "You're OK, buddy," said Arthur. "We'll get you a doctor. Let's get you sat down."

"He looks on death's door," Brian whispered to Kev. "It's where he got shot. He keeps grabbing at his stomach."

"There's enough of it, like," said the uncaring landlord.

"Aye, he's a porker all right, but we need to be compassionate because—WHAT THE FOOK HAS HAPPENED TO MY CAR?"

There wasn't much left of the Capri. After Rathbone had driven into it, Reece had ripped bits off it, and it had been blown up by the bombs in the car park. It was not looking its best.

Brian didn't cry, but his bottom lip resonated at a very sad frequency.

"Come on, Brian, let's go get a beer," said Sid, putting an arm around him, leading him towards the brewery. Nothing was going right for the boys from 'boro of late.

"I think I need the bathroom, man," said King weakly.

"Are you sure, son?" Arthur held the door of the brewery reception open for his son to squeeze through.

"Yeah, man. I think I'll feel better after laying a log."

"OK," said Arthur, watching his son waddle into the disabled toilets, a necessity for the extra space. "But don't strain yourself."

"I love you, Daddy," said King with a tear in his eye.

"I love you too, son," said Arthur with a tear on his cheek mirroring King's.

"I SMELL BOLTON!" bellowed Sid.

"Come on then, big man," said Brian. Drowning sorrows was the only option now. "Let's go drink what's left."

The four lads and their loyal landlord made their way to the brewing room where they'd got battered previously. They'd built up a hell of a thirst.

"You all right, Rathbone?" asked Brian.

"Yeah. What's it to you?"

"Oh," said Brian, slightly miffed that Rathbone hadn't been killed by Purity.

Sid rubbed his hands together. "We need to drink as much as we can, as quickly as we can. Them vampire bastards might be back at any minute!"

"I think you killed them all, mate," said Brian.

"Well, we'll drink it all, just in case."

"Hopefully Freddy'll sell me a few more barrels," said Kev.

Brian asked the million-dollar question: "You putting the prices up?"

"You lot owe me £300!" Landlords never forget a debt.

"You sold us beer with fooking chemicals in it!" protested Brian.

"Aye, but I just saved your lives."

Brian shook his head in disbelief. "You let all the vampires in."

Kev put up his hands. "Alright, we call it quits, but beer goes up 5p a pint."

"Done, but when the Bolton goes..."

"I'll sort it." Kev's determined face was a believable one.

"Good. Now, let's get on it."

They pushed open the double doors to the brewing room, not to find a bound and gagged Freddy Buggleswaite, but a Freddy Buggleswaite shaking hands with something far worse than a vampire: Sheila Fishman.

They were signing papers, and that was never a good sign. A slimy-looking bloke in a suit sat with them too. That would mean it was official. Slimy blokes wearing suits always made things official.

"Look what the cat dragged in," spat Sid's ex-fiancée.

"You not worried about all the vampires?" asked Kev.

"Bollocks no!" She cackled. "They're a bunch of fannies. Nothing is going to stop me taking this brewery away from Tillsley or stop Buggleswaite, the greedy bastard, from getting his money. You will never—ever—drink Bolton Bitter again."

"Well, there're six and a half thousand pints that I'm gonna drink," said Brian.

"Are you shite! Buggleswaite, send it to waste!" she ordered.

"I can't do that," said Freddy, looking at the fearsome sight of Sheila, to the even scarier sight of Sid, and back again.

"Yes, you can! It's mine! Now, send it to waste."

Sid's face was reminiscent of a *Pink Alert* from yesteryear. Freddy went to press the button on the brewing room computer that would send it down the drains.

"Freddy," warned Brian, "I'd seriously consider your next action. If you press that button, Sid will repeatedly punch you in the face."

"Then I'll do it for him," said Sheila, marching towards Freddy's computer.

"NNNNNOOOOOOOOOOOOOOO!"

Sheila pressed the big red button that sent the beer flowing back to Mother Nature and, to the disdain of the 'boro boys, not via their bladders.

"YOU FOOKING BITCH!" shouted Brian. "Sid! Sort her out!"

Sid shuffled towards his ex, unsure of his course of action. He hadn't been able to sort her out while living with her...not in any kind of way, which was quite a relief now, considering she had a cock.

"Fuck off, Tillsley!"

"Yes, dear," he said, retreating back to Brian's side.

"Sid, mon, you ain't married now. She canna tell ya what to do!"

He waved a hand. "It ain't worth the hassle!"

"Well, I'll sort her out then," said Brian, rolling up his sleeves.

"You touch me, Garforth, and my lawyer here will have you up for assault. They'll throw the book at low-life scum like you."

"Say I punch him in the face too?"

The lawyer went pale.

Arthur was stuck in two minds. He wanted to save the beer but was worried. His son should've been back by now. "I'm gonna check on my boy."

"You do it, mate," said Brian, "and when you come back, you can help me carry this fooker into the car park." Brian pointed threateningly at the suit.

"You can't waste all that beer, Freddy! Let me buy it off ya," begged Kev.

"It's my beer, Ackroyd, you thieving bastard!" screeched Sheila. "Do you really think I'd give you—or him—the satisfaction of enjoying it?"

"What is wrong with you?" asked Brian. "Haven't you done enough damage to our lives, already? Sid just wiped out the entire vampire nation. He deserves a pint."

"He ruined my life! He doesn't deserve anything!"

"Oh, I think he does."

All turned to Caroline, who was leaning on Harry's shoulder.

"Trevor McDonald woman!" cried Sid happily.

"Good evening, Sid." Caroline was a mass of bruises; her nose was spread across her face with dried blood covering her cheeks and mouth.

"You all right, lass? You look like you've been crying."

"I'm fine, Sid, thank you. A tough day, that's all. I lost someone very close to me."

Harry interrupted with more pressing matters. "You need to get out of here, and fast!"

"Why?" asked Brian.

"The troops aren't going to be able to hold Reece back for long."

"Who?" asked Brian.

"Reece Chambers."

"Never heard of him."

"The vampire hunter who kicked Sid in the nuts," clarified Harry.

"You mean *Rich*!" said Brian. "Oh, Sid can handle him now he's recovered from that shot to the knackers. Ain't that right, buddy?"

"Aye, but what does it matter now the Bolton's gone? What's the point of smacking someone if you can't celebrate with a beer afterwards?"

"What's he talking about?" Caroline asked Harry, who explained.

"Someone's bought this place. It brews Sid's favourite beer. The new owner is going to shut it down."

"That's right, ya posh cow," said the blonde bombshell. "This is my place, and there's nothing you, or anyone else, can do about it."

A mighty crash echoed round the brewery and the walls shook.

"What's that?" asked Freddy, suspecting vampires.

The crash came again, and a fist drove through the external wall, only feet from where Freddy stood.

Caroline scowled at the woman opposite her. "I don't think your investment was a wise one."

"KING?" CALLED ARTHUR, who made his way into the extremely smelly toilet in the brewery reception.

There was no reply, but Arthur could've found the disabled toilet with his eyes shut just by following the foul vapour trail that was diffusing through the building. He knocked on the toilet door, but there was no response, not even the sound of wiping or grunting. Maybe his son was a shy one and hadn't built up the man-confidence—the manfidence—to let rip in any situation. He knocked on the door again. "Son, you in there?"

Still no answer.

"Don't be shy."

Arthur started to worry. He put his foot through the cubicle lock with an impressive sidekick and fell to his knees.

"Oh, God...not like this..."

King's jumpsuit had been pulled down around his ankles. Dead eyes stared back at him. The cheeseburger in his hand dripped onto his massive belly. He'd gone in the most undignified way possible.

He'd died on the throne.

A SECOND FIST drove through the wall like it was made of paper. Reece ripped a massive section of brickwork down with a heave and emerged through the hole, covered in plaster and dust. There was no mistaking what he was here for. The look of murder on his face said it all.

"That's my fucking wall! You're gonna pay for that!" screamed Sheila.

"I HATE YOU, TILLSLEY!" he roared.

Meeting a fellow-Tillsley hater changed Sheila's tune. "Kick his head in!"

The hole in the wall brought the sound of gunfire, and the bullets missing Reece pinged around the brewery, ricocheting off the various tanks and pipes. He hadn't finished battling the army because of his desperation to get at these men from Middlesbrough.

Reece moved to the side of the opening to avoid the annoying bullets riddling his body. "You had to take it from me, didn't you?"

"I pressed the wrong button, like," said Sid, "but anyroad, what have you got against the gays, anyway?"

"It was vampires! FUCKING VAMPIRES! I deserve—" Reece noticed Rathbone gazing at the beer vats, longingly. "Why the fuck are you still alive?"

Rathbone stuck his middle finger up.

"Now all the vampires are dead, you haven't got to go round being such a twat." suggested Brian. "Can't you take up a hobby? Darts or summat?"

A wail took the attention away from Reece.

Everyone turned to see Arthur stumbling in, tears streaming down his face. "He's dead!"

"Who? Rathbone?" asked Sid.

"He's there, ya daft bastard," said Brian. "Arthur, what ya talking about?"

"My son...he's dead!"

"Ahhhh, shit," said the boys from the 'boro in unison.

Rathbone shed an actual tear. "We'd gone see hookers together and everything."

"The hybrid died? Was it because of Purity?" asked Reece, his inquisitive, scientific mind momentarily calming him.

"No. He was OK coming out of the plant. He wasn't the healthiest of cats," said Arthur. "I don't think getting shot in the stomach helped."

Reece laughed. "What a disappointment he turned out to be. But don't worry, you will only have moments to mourn, for soon, you will be dead."

"Fuck you, man!" said Arthur with fire in his eyes.

"What? Will you use your karate on me?"

Arthur threw out some blistering punches. "Fuck yeah!" He charged at the giant and jumped, turning his flying mass into a flying kick that seared the air with unquestionable ferocity.

Reece stepped to one side. "Pathetic!" he spat and threw an arm out that plucked Arthur out of the air and brought him down to the floor. Arthur had never been troublesome, rude, or problematic. He wouldn't suffer like the others. Reece raised his foot and brought it crashing down. It whistled through the air—but missed its target. The bullet to his chest had knocked Reece off balance.

"When will you learn, Dean? You were never as good as Sanderson.

You're a drunken bum with a good aim." Reece fingered the bullet hole that closed up after his body spat out the slug.

Harry let fly with a few more rounds, knocking Reece back into the side of a great vat.

"It's nothing but a scratch to me, you weak fool."

More bullets penetrated the former hunter, but these carried more weight, and the damage was far greater. Army personnel, led by Peterson, piled through the hole in the wall that Reece had created. Reece ripped out one of the empty, enormous vats and launched it at the soldiers. Most dodged out of the way.

Harry closed his eyes.

Peterson was dead a millisecond after impact. His body was not shown an ounce of respect as it was crushed into the side of the hole. His bloody remains smeared across the wall like road kill.

"You're paying for that!" yelled Sheila.

Another vat flew into the doorway of the only other entrance to the brewing room.

"At least, now, we won't be disturbed," said Reece, eying his prey.

Harry and the soldiers unleashed a huge barrage, and soon, the only thing filling the air was smoke drifting up into the rafters. They waited for the oncoming onslaught, but it didn't come. The smoke cleared, and Reece hadn't moved, but he was bleeding.

A horrible realisation dawned on the vampire hunter whose prey was extinct. No vampire blood...meant no regeneration...which meant death. His wounds weren't closing as fast. The damage his body had taken and the strength he'd used to throw the vats meant he needed to feed, and there was only one vampire left alive.

Peter Rathbone.

A used condom hit Reece in the face and reminded him of something he had to do before feeding. "I should have done this months ago," he said, bearing down on Garforth.

"Bring it on, ya twat!" retorted a raging swordsman.

Reece was only yards away from committing murder when a massive fist filled his vision, stopping his charge. The fist was replaced by lots and lots of stars.

"No more silly buggers," growled the familiar voice, and Reece hit the cold brewery floor.

He got to his feet groggily and, after pushing his jaw back into place, said, "There's no saving you, Tillsley."

"Rich, you've sorted me out with loads of tabs, and you've got the beers in, I canna deny that, but—reet now—you're being a reet wanker."

"I hate you," he said, half laughing, half crying. "I hate you so much."

Sid rolled up the sleeves of his leather jacket. "That wasn't very nice."

Reece didn't rush. Since his wounds weren't healing properly, he still wasn't one hundred per cent.

"Rip Tillsley's fucking head off!" shouted Sheila. It was the only support he'd got since his transformation.

Reece went straight for the groin with a lightning kick, but his foot landed on something hard, and Sid didn't budge an inch.

"Didn't have me cricket box in earlier, you dirty bastard. You won't get me that way again," said the exponent of the Rules of Queensbury. "You're getting the special, lad! You're getting the fooking special!"

45

The army has contained the affected. The curfew remains in place, but it is unlikely they'll be another outbreak. The Prime Minister will release a statement shortly.
                                                                 —*A government scientist*

REECE HADN'T SEEN Sid angry often, but he was now. Reece threw a jab and Sid dodged it easily. He was a good fighter—no—a great fighter. Reece threw a combination, and Sid dodged the first couple of punches and took the hook on his guard, shaking it off. Reece was losing power, but he was showing his opponent too much respect.

He darted low to take Tillsley's legs away but, instead, met an uppercut that almost took him from his feet. The next hook turned his jaw, and the next punch, aimed low, brought pain he hadn't experienced since he'd fused with Purity.

"If you kick a man in his nuts, expect some fooking payback!"

Reece fell to his knees, clutching his genitals. The unbearable agony amplified another feeling, a thirst. Bloodlust. He had to feed. Feeding would make the pain go away. Rathbone was his only hope. He got to his feet even though he wanted to pass out. He had to catch the horrible, greasy, little bastard.

"Finish him off, Sid!" shouted Brian.

"He's had enough," said Sid, happy that Reece had learned his lesson.

"KILL HIM!" shouted every conscious person in the room.

RATHBONE SAW HIS CHANCE FOR REVENGE. Sure, he'd laid a cable on the guy's face, but killing him would be more satisfying.

Rathbone had never killed anyone before, but that didn't mean he didn't have the heart of a murderer. He'd certainly tried a few times. Rich stumbled towards him, covered in blood, grabbing onto anything for stability. This was Rathbone's chance.

Rathbone decided to start with a kick to the shins because Rich would be expecting a kick to the nuts. Rathbone initiated his running toe punt with confidence. Reece dodged to the side, grabbed Rathbone by the hair, and pulled him close, biting deep into his neck. Suddenly, Rathbone wasn't so cocky.

MOMENTS LATER, Reece threw the vampire to one side. He only took what he needed, leaving Rathbone alive. Rathbone, the only living vampire, was now precious to him. Reece's thirst was quenched, but the life-bringing blood made him nauseous. Even Rathbone's blood was greasy. Strength returned to his body and he roared. "Now, what are you going to do, Tillsley!"

"I'm gonna smack you in the face again, ya fooking twat!"

"TRY IT!" screamed Reece, bounding towards Sid.

Reece quickly found his range and threw his arms like clubs. There was no need for precision now his strength had fully returned. Sid got his hands up, but his guard couldn't stop the devastating force driving continuously into the side of the head.

SID KEPT BACKING OFF, biding his time, playing a bit of rope-a-dope while his brain rocked around in his skull. He backed up, momentarily distracted by a sharp sensation in his leg. He looked down to see he'd caught his leg on a pipe to the main system that'd once connected the vat that Rich had thrown. He looked down and felt a foot drive into his stomach.

Wind came out of both ends like a gale. Sid had lost a lot of weight under Sheila's regime, and the layers of fat weren't there to protect him. Sid took a knee, and met Rich's with his chin on the way down.

"Bastards!" said the big man, hitting the deck.

BEFORE REECE could take advantage of Sid's predicament, the Coalition agents opened fire with the last of their ammo.

Brian rushed to Sid's aid in the way only he could: by firing used rubber jonnies.

The condom projectiles were slow, and Reece dodged them all as he advanced. He grabbed Brian around the throat before he could think of running.

Reece lifted Brian off his feet, and the gunfire from the troops stopped. Brian's face was the colour of a plum. Slowly, Reece tightened his grip and smiled when the pressure behind Brian's eyes made them bulge almost to breaking point. Spittle collected on his thin, cracked lips as he desperately tried to draw in breath.

"I always knew I'd be the one to kill you." Reece pulled him close. "Nothing to say? I wouldn't want to hear you speak anyway. I hate your voice. I hate everything about you."

"Put...put...him down," managed Arthur, who'd somehow made it to his feet. His arm hung unnaturally, dislocated from the fall.

"I thought you'd had enough," said Reece.

"Buddies stick together to the end," said Arthur.

"Yeah, ya twat!" Sid was back up. Apart from the quick wiggle he gave his chin, he didn't look like he'd been in a scrap. "And Brian turned *homomo-sexual* to save Arthur."

"I'm...not...fooking...gay," managed Brian.

Meanwhile, Rathbone had ripped off the top of the beer tank that had been drained and was licking the insides, trying to heal after the loss of blood. He wouldn't get involved, but if they put Reece down, he had something baking...

"You can't stop me," said Reece. "You can't save Garforth. He's dying in front of you, and there's nothing you can do about it. NO ONE CAN STOP ME!" Reece screamed. Garforth's pulse slowed.

A tonne of metal flew past Reece at a speed defying physics.

"I can stop you, baby!"

The blockade to the reception was gone, and in its place stood a masterpiece. Blistering karate punches whirred and the static friction brought forth lightning that danced around the room, jumping from vat to vat.

"Son!" cried Arthur and then paused. "Son?"

Reece let go of Brian, who breathed air into his lungs like his life depended on it, which it did.

"What are you?" asked Reece.

King snapped a knee back and forth, causing a sonic boom. "I'm an entertainer, baby, and I know karate."

"Son..." said Arthur, "you look different."

"I told you, Daddy. I had some weird hybrid shit going down. I needed the burgers to fuel this beautiful transformation. Check out my abs."

The white jumpsuit now hung limply from King's muscular frame. The only thing that was familiar was the thick black hair, baby blues, and devilish good looks that had been hidden below mounds and mounds of flab. Now, muscles were the only things that were rippling, and the hybrid was stacked like a condom packed full of walnuts.

Reece didn't see a hybrid. All he could see was DNA and new opportunities to upgrade his genetics. Maybe he could rid himself from the curse of needing vampire blood to live. Reece beckoned King. "Let's see what you've got."

King looked over his shades. "I'm gonna take care of business."

The two slowly approached each other and met in the middle of the brewery floor. They were abnormalities of nature not meant for this earth. The onlookers could see the power radiating from their bodies. This was like the battle that would have taken place between Sparle and the Bellator...if Sid hadn't run the Bellator over in his Montego Estate while he was pissed.

King danced, but not like a boxer, like an entertainer. Reece was not impressed but perturbed by the newly found confidence the athletically built hybrid exhibited. Still, there was no way he could keep his balance while performing such utterly ridiculous moves. Reece's legs would make quick work of his ridiculous foe.

Reece snapped a sidekick out into the hybrid's midsection. It was powerful enough to bend steel and smash reinforced concrete, but it couldn't stop Reece from reeling back. He hadn't seen the counter. The hybrid was faster than anything he's seen before...

Or rather, he was still a fanny.

As the kick landed, King doubled up on impact, just like he had when he was twenty-five stone heavier. The headbutt that accompanied King's pained, theatrical fall was quicker than before due to his svelte figure, and Reece took the full brunt of it on the nose.

Reece stumbled back and tripped, landing on top of the broken pipe Sid had cut his leg on earlier. With a spurt of blood, the thick pipe protruded from his forehead and Reece's eyes rolled into the back of his head before coming back round to focus. His superpowers couldn't help him now. His arms moved awkwardly, robotically, but with no purpose. His motor functions were in tatters. The three-inch thick pipe had ripped his brain, literally, in half, and there was no way it could knit back together.

The boys from the 'boro all limped round to where their former ally and beer provider lay helpless on the floor. The rest of the Coalition troops and Harry, supporting Caroline, gathered round too.

Sheila Fishman, lawyer in tow, landed a boot in the ribs of the prone vampire hunter when she took her place. Last was Freddy Buggleswaite, who was glad he'd got rid of the place before these nutters kicked the crap out of it.

Caroline broke the silence. "We've done it."

"No more vampires," said Harry.

"What about this poor fooker?" asked Sid.

"Finish him off. He's lost it completely," said Caroline.

Reece pointed at Rathbone, gurgling something inaudible.

"What does he want?" asked Brian.

"He needs Rathbone's blood," said Harry. "It's the only thing that can save him."

"I've got something else for him," said Rathbone, unbuckling his belt.

SLOWLY, THE TROOPS BEGAN to pull out of Bolton, and the extensive clean up began. The place was literally a warzone. Many of the surrounding buildings had been reduced to rubble, and neither the stars nor the moon on this clear, winter's night could be seen for the smoke billowing into the atmosphere.

Harry sent away the agents who'd made it through the ordeal in the brewery, and that left the boys, Caroline, the repulsive Sheila Fishman and her slimy lawyer, and the annoying Freddy Buggleswaite, whom the lads insisted on keeping around. They'd moved away from Reece, who was starting to stink up the joint, and not because he was dead. He was twitching away, dying one of the worst deaths imaginable.

"You owe me for this, Tillsley!" Sheila Fishman had been demanding compensation ever since Rathbone performed his deed on her premises. To be fair, it was pretty nasty.

"Yes, dear," he said dutifully.

"Why the fook are you agreeing to it?" demanded Brian, punching Sid on the arm.

"Habit, I guess."

Brian turned on Sheila. "Sid just rid this country of every bloodsucking vampire. People can walk safe at night because of him. You're still giving him a hard time because he touched your tit once."

"How dare you bring that up! You won't be so fucking smart when you're back in that shithole of a pub without your precious Bolton Bitter," she said smugly.

"Bitch!"

"Harry," said Sid, "You said if I helped you, you'd save the Bolton."

Harry nodded and looked at Caroline. Sheila had newfound enemies, very powerful ones.

"What are you bastards gonna do about it? I'm a fucking millionaire. I own this. This is fucking mine."

Caroline limped over to Harry, pulled his revolver from the holster, turned, and shot Sheila Fishman between the eyes. When Caroline turned the gun on the lawyer, he said a prayer as a wet patch appeared on his trousers.

"That wretched woman turned this brewery over to Mr. Tillsley here. It's now his property. Do you understand?" she said calmly.

"Of-of c-c-course."

Caroline stuck the gun in the waistband of her skirt.

"Eh?" asked Sid.

"You mean...Sid owns the brewery?" Brian asked excitedly.

The lawyer nodded.

"I ain't fooking cleaning the bogs!" cried Sid.

"Sid, you daft bastard! This is yours! You own it! You can get the Bolton flowing again!" Brian explained.

"Freddy! Will you brew us the Bolton?" Sid's smile, powered by hope in his heart, would have lit up the room if he wasn't such an ugly bastard.

Freddy shook his head and waved his hands. "I'm off to Spain. This trade is crazy enough without you lot getting involved."

"You've been paid for this place, once," said Brian. "How about Sid gives you forty-nine per cent share if you keep on brewing?"

"Done," said the tight brewmaster.

"Brian?"

"Yes, Sid?"

Sid looked down at his deceased fiancée, and Brian wondered what was going through his best friend's mind. It must have been tough. He was probably still harbouring feelings deep down.

"Can I touch her tits now?"

CAROLINE HAD REFUSED ALL MEDICAL ATTENTION. She couldn't be doing with it, not now. This was her alone time. After saying goodbye to her sister's body, she drove one of the Coalition's cars into the Peak District National Park and now sat in the car as dawn approached over the hills. She hadn't admired a view for years. Most of her life had been spent underground in the Coalition's headquarters, sending people to their deaths or covering up the murder of children.

No longer.

Years of pressure and mortal danger had taken their toll, yet, somehow, through it all, her plan had come into fruition. The surprise was that she was alive, but that didn't mean it was a pleasant one. The only person she ever truly cared for was dead. Her sister died a hero, helping initiate Purity. She was so proud but felt so empty without Lizzie.

She hadn't time to mourn the death of her sister or the mercy killing she'd performed on her husband. There was no one in her life to turn to. Revenge was not just hers or her sister's; this was revenge for every man, woman, and child whose lives had been touched by the cursed vampire.

She'd paid a price, and not just one that ended up in the deaths of Lizzie and Jeffrey. The dreams that haunted her night's sleep she no longer wished to experience. Sanderson's death had played deeper on her conscience than she thought possible. He was a true hero who would never be acknowledged.

Her life's work was over. A new age was dawning. Maybe mankind would struggle without the vampire to guide them with their wisdom. It would be tough, but what was done, had to be done. What the vampire had put her and her sister through—it couldn't happen to another family.

This was now the Age of Man. She'd done her job, and it was time for someone else to take over. Taking the pistol that had killed Sheila Fishman, Caroline placed it in her mouth.

She couldn't pull the trigger fast enough.

46

Life in the UK is returning back to normal once more. There have been no more outbreaks since the fighting came to a head in Bolton. The Prime Minister made this announcement today:

"Leighton Pharmaceuticals has been shut down, with the M.D. and the scientists involved all facing criminal charges. The drug PQ1539 was the culprit for these terrible events. All details of the drug's manufacture have been destroyed, and an antidote is being distributed in the water supply to counteract any terrorist attack. I can guarantee this to every one of you: nothing like this will ever happen again.

"Rebuilding this great nation will be a slow process, but we will grow back stronger. We acted as a nation, and in the face of adversity, we have grown together. We have lost many, and we will remember them. Now, it's time to look forward, as a United Kingdom."

—CNN

THE PREMIER LADIES' NIGHT at The First Swallow of Summer was well underway, although Kevin Ackroyd didn't book a stripper this time, not after Mr Newcastle had been hospitalised by the hands, and other things, of the 'boro girls. Now every stripper in the Northeast demanded danger money. They knew they had to show the love truncheon, but with these girls, none of the strippers were confident they'd measure up, not even Luke "The Limb" Martin, who'd once, for a bet, beat a badger to death with his appendage.

Nope, this was a run of the mill Ladies' Night, with ten pence off a pint of Bolton, and sparkling wine for ninety-nine pence a plastic glass. Bolton Bitter flowed once more, and it was a damn sight cheaper now Sid co-owned the brewery.

Sid sat at the bar with a smile that split his face from ear to ear. He'd dreamed of retiring, and all he'd had to do to achieve it was commit genocide.

"Champion," he said and took a long draw of the greatest beer in the world—and as the majority shareholder—his beer.

Sid wore his leather jacket and Esso Tiger Token T-shirt. Over the past couple of weeks, since wiping out all the vampires, he'd put the lost weight back on. The tiger on the shirt looked pretty snug and not particularly comfortable. Sid's blue jeans were, as usual, very tight. He struggled to pull a new fag packet out of them, and when he finally managed it, he lit up and savoured the cigarette.

He'd obtained a hundred Tibetan cigarettes (not endorsed by the Dalai Lama) "Tab-etans," for giving Middlesbrough's only resident Sherpa— Sherpa Pasang—a lift home from Hartlepool because he was pissed-up and couldn't be arsed to walk.

Even though Sid was loaded and could buy fags from the corner shop (he wasn't rich enough to buy them from pub vending machines, but then, no one was), he just couldn't bring himself to pay the huge duties that came with them.

Sid lit up another. Things were better than back to normal, because this time, there were no Benefit Bastards on to him, no vampire shit, and a brand new car parked in the drive: a Ford Grenada Scorpio.

Arthur supped ale with him, looking a million dollars, dressed all in white without a hair out of place, and the half smile/half sneer tantalised the ladies. He'd every reason to be happy. His best friends were reunited, he had his son back, and he had his beer back.

"Good night, hey, buddy?" he said.

"Aye, mate, fooking champion!" said Sid. "Heaving with fanny and not all regulars, like."

"Good day for Kev. Look at the greedy bastard. He's loving every minute."

Kev was taking money left, right, and centre and crooning with the lasses. Life was back to normal for him too, even though he was disappointed the vampires wouldn't be in to spend their wedge. He was pleased to be buying in Bolton Bitter at half the price—and selling it to non-regulars at full price. The lads got theirs cheap, but who was he to argue with the owner of the Bolton Brewery. Landlording—no better trade in the world.

"I thought your lad was leaving?" asked the big man.

Arthur nodded. "I'll be sorry to see him go."

"He's a good lad, Arthur. He's done you proud."

"Sure has. I can't believe how well him and Rathbone have been getting on."

"Aye, Rathbone ain't such a horrible bastard when King's about. He's good for him."

"It helps that King's been telling everyone that Rathbone was the one who put an end to Rich."

"Ah, reet." Sid chuckled. "Didn't know that, like."

"Yeah, he's been telling people that Rathbone used his martial arts skills to bring him down."

"Rather than take a dump on his face when he was dying?"

Arthur laughed. "Sort of obvious which version the chicks prefer, ain't it?"

"Yeah," said Sid. "He's been doing well, though. Got fingers and tops the other week, apparently."

"That's good for Rathbone. Brian's been on a hot streak too."

"Speak of the devil. He's just come out of the bogs with another lass."

Brian strode over, pushing his member into a more comfortable position. "Bolton, Kev!" shouted the swordsman before making conversation with his friends. "How do?"

"Another lass?" asked Sid.

Brian rubbed the sweat from his forehead. "She was a goer, like. I'm blue-pilled up till next Christmas too. Tell you what; this gay rumour is paying off. They think they can change ya and see it as a challenge. Fooking mint it is."

Rathbone and King left some ladies to join the boys at the bar. King was a picture of health, covered in muscle, even though he still packed away the cheeseburgers. He didn't need them anymore; they just tasted damn good.

"How did you two get on?" asked Arthur.

"Got some chicks lined up for later," said King.

"Any for me, lads?" said a hopeful ex-vampire hunter.

"Sorry, Sid, there were only two of them. There're still loads of chicks left, though," said King optimistically.

Brian and Arthur quickly surveyed the women left in the pub, "Not unless you want to become custard cousins," they said in unison.

"Ah, shite!" said Sid. "Still no fooking jump and no fooking sign of one, either."

"Things will pick up, mate," said Brian.

"If you stopped doing them all and went back to the fellas, there'd be more left for me."

"I ain't fooking—forget it!" Brian was relieved when Harry Dean came in from the cold, distracting Sid from the gay chat.

"Hey, mate," said Sid, "fancy a pint?"

"Not for me, thanks, I'm off the booze." Harry looked longingly at Sid's pint but then snapped his gaze away.

"You ought to hook up with Brian," suggested Sid.

"Why?" asked Harry.

"He's a *homomo-sexual* too." Sid said seriously.

Harry laughed at Brian who stamped his foot in frustration. "No, I was hitting the sauce a bit hard, and it was time to stop. I'm an alcoholic, Sid."

"Apparently, so am I." Sid sent off a pint.

"Yeah, but you're something else."

"What can we do you for, Harry?" asked Brian. This man had earned the respect of the Smithson Estate for helping reopen the Bolton Brewery.

"Nothing but a social visit. Things are getting back to normal out there. We managed to keep you out of all the major news stories. Just wanted to tell you, you'll never have to deal with any politicians ever again."

"Fooking great!" said Brian.

"And, you won't have to deal with any more 'vampire shit,' as you call it, either. The virus is spreading. There hasn't been a vampire sighting in Europe for the last fortnight...Rathbone not included."

Sid had the decency to look a little guilty. It was an accident, after all.

"So what now for you, Harry?" asked Brian.

"I'm gonna retire. I'm gonna work through some of my problems."

"Counselling?" asked Sid.

"Yep," said Harry. "I ain't thrilled about it, but it's needed if I'm going to live any sort of life. Who knows? Maybe my ex-wife will talk to me again."

"It's alreet, if you ask me, like. If I hadn't had counselling, then I'd never have come to terms with me inner fears, and I'd never forgiven Brian for the years and years of non-stop buggery."

Brian took Sid's pint from the bar and downed it.

"So, what've you lot got planned," asked Harry. "I should imagine that you, King, have been getting a lot of attention for your unusual appearance."

"Yeah, man, I look like my grandpappy on steroids! I'm still stoked I take after the Duke of Rock 'n' Roll. It's got me a lot of action, but I'm leaving Middlesbrough. The papers said my grandpappy died banging a hooker on the back of a donkey on Blackpool Pleasure Beach, but I know he's still alive, I can feel it in my rock 'n' roll bones. I'm going to Blackpool to find him, and when I do, I'm gonna go on tour with him, maybe even go as far as Great Yarmouth. It's my true purpose. Rathbone's coming with me."

This did surprise the rest of the locals.

Rathbone shrugged. "Going for the sluts."

"What about the rest of you?" asked Harry.

Brian leant against the bar and picked up the fresh pint that Kev had served. "This, my friend, is it."

Harry nodded. "I thought as much. You got the money I transferred to your accounts?"

The lads nodded, and Brian continued, "Aye, cheers, Harry. With the brewery safe, it will see us through for a long time to come. You see, lad, this is all we ever wanted. Cheers." Brian toasted a pint.

"You can't say fairer than that," said Harry.

"A fooking shag would have been nice, though," said Sid.

THE END....?

Epilogue

THROUGH THE BUSHES HE PASSED, quiet like the mouse scurrying across the ground before him. Walking in this world, stealth was of the essence.

They thought they'd purged his kind, but they were wrong. He was alive and well, and they'd never catch him. He hid behind a tree and looked into the clearing ahead.

Oh yes, he thought to himself. Fresh victims. Victims? No, that wasn't the right word. They never saw him. They didn't suffer. Some wanted to suffer. Some had even thrown themselves at others like him, but that's not what he wanted. He wanted to be unnoticed. He didn't want them to see him coming.

There were many cars in the car park, but the closest one would get his full attention. He could see movement within. Two human lovers intimately entwined. The windows were steamy, but not enough so he couldn't see in. He pushed aside his Macintosh, and the cold wind whipped around the naked body of Middlesbrough's most prolific pervert.

Here be dogging.

But, staring through the window of the car did not bring the Peeping Tom the arousal he'd hoped for. The monstrous, fat skinhead on top of a lady being crushed into the seats of the Ford Grenada Scorpio was not a pretty sight, nor was his crusty backside, vigorously pumping up and down. There was no stirring in the Tom's nether regions. This wasn't enjoyable viewing, especially when an orgasmic cry echoed around the car park, and possibly all the way to Newcastle.

"HOWWAAYYYY THE LAAAAAADDDDDS!"

THE END...?

YEAH, IT'S THE END. NOW FOOK OFF.

THE GREAT RIGHT HOPE

Book One of The Sid Tillsley Chronicles (2nd Edition)

Even the best vampires need a good smack...

Sid Tillsley, forty-six, is an alcoholic benefit fraudster from Middlesbrough. He's sexist, homophobic, overweight, extremely lazy, and a dogger. However, there is *one* thing setting him apart from the rest of his fellow Northerners.

Sid Tillsley can kill vampires with a single punch.

In Northeast England, a monster has arisen, and one that doesn't subscribe to *Tits* magazine. A vampire beast is stalking the Yorkshire moors, mutilating and destroying everything in its path. The vampire elders fear the Firmamentum has cast its shadow on the world once more–a phenomenon that occurs every few millennia when a human and a vampire are born, ultimately powerful, and destined to oppose each other.

The Coalition, a council of vampires and humans whose purpose is to hide the existence of the creatures of the night, believe Sid to be the Bellator, the chosen one destined to fight the vampire beast. But, Sid is more concerned about drinking down the pub with his mates, and maybe, just maybe, ending his two year drought with the ladies. Besides, Sid has more important things to worry about. The Benefit Office is on to him, and, if they see him scrapping immortal vampire monsters from Hell, they'll take away his disability benefits.

A FISTFUL OF RUBBERS

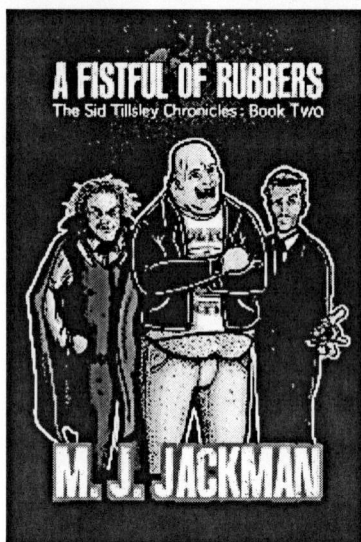

A FISTFUL OF RUBBERS
The Sid Tillsley Chronicles: Book Two

M. J. JACKMAN

Book Two of The Sid Tillsley Chronicles (2nd Edition)

Sid Tillsley, forty-six, is an alcoholic from Middlesbrough. He's sexist, homophobic, overweight, extremely lazy, and a dogger. However, there are now *two* things setting him apart from the rest of his fellow Northerners.
Sid Tillsley can kill vampires with a single punch.

AND, he's no longer claiming benefits.

In the eyes of everyone apart from the taxman, Sid Tillsley is officially a vampire hunter. The old hunter, Reece Chambers, is using Sid to strike fear into the heart of the vampire nation, and Sid is doing so with gusto—for he gets a packet of fags for every vampire he knocks out.

But all is not rosy in Sid's world...

The Coalition, a council of vampires and humans whose purpose is to hide the existence of the creatures of the night, have shut down his local pub in a horrific act of cruelty, separating Sid and his mates from their beloved Bolton Bitter. Sid doesn't realise that he has a fight coming, one that will test him to his very limits. There's something else lurking in the shadows, or rather, the closet. A Northern man will punch anything in the face, but what terrifies him, what saturates him with carnal fear, is a direct attack on his sexuality...and the Campire draws near.

About the Author

"M J Jackman is one of the most talented, exciting, and hilarious writers to explode onto the fiction scene in the twenty-first century," was what Jackman hoped to read in the papers after the release of The Sid Tillsley Chronicles. He hoped his mastery of the written word and his elegant wit would bring celebrity status, which, in turn, would bring fast women, hard drugs and liquor, and then slower, more understanding women.

To date, he has successfully installed a decking area into his garden.

You can follow Jackman's antics on Twitter (@Mark_Jackman) and Sid's antic's on Facebook (search Sid Tillsley Chronicles)

Oh, and he's gone back to university to be a "mature student." And, no, he hasn't gone back to learn how to write (arsewipe!).

He gets an NUS discount.

Even his own characters would hate him.

Lightning Source UK Ltd.
Milton Keynes UK
UKOW04f0243041214

242632UK00002B/174/P